HEART
OF A
HUSKER

TOM OSBORNE'S
NEBRASKA LEGACY

MIKE BABCOCK

SportsPublishingLLC.com

ISBN-10:1-59670-017-3
ISBN-13:978-1-59670-017-8

Publishers: Peter L. Bannon and Joseph J. Bannon Sr.
Senior managing editor: Susan M. Moyer
Acquisitions editor: Mike Pearson
Developmental editor: Erin Linden-Levy
Art director: K. Jeffrey Higgerson
Dust jacket design: Kenneth J. O'Brien
Interior layout: Kenneth J. O'Brien

Sports Publishing L.L.C.
804 North Neil Street
Champaign, IL 61820
Phone: 1-877-424-2665
Fax: 217-363-2073
SportsPublishingLLC.com

Printed in the United States of America

Library of Congress Cataloging-in-Publication Data

Babcock, Mike.
    Heart of a Husker : Tom Osborne's Nebraska legacy / Mike Babcock.
      p. cm.
    Includes index.
    1. University of Nebraska--Lincoln--Football--History. 2. Nebraska
Cornhuskers (Football team)--History. 3. Osborne, Tom, 1937- I. Title.
GV956.N2B33 2006
    796.332'6309782293--dc22
                            2006021932

This book is dedicated to the TeamMates Mentoring Program established by Tom and Nancy Osborne and to all of those who have been and are involved.

Table of Contents

Foreword

I remember the first time I met Tom personally. We were playing Nebraska in 1980, up there in Lincoln. It was the first time we played them, and I'm in my dressing room before the game. We're getting dressed. And somebody knocks on our door. We open it up and there's Tom, with his red shirt, I think red pants, and his red hat. And he says, "Did ya'll get in okay? Is everything okay? Is there anything I can do for you?" I wasn't used to that, you know.

We sneaked out on that one. They were favored, but we pulled the game out. They were down on our goal line, fixing to score. The game was about over. We tackled their quarterback, he fumbled, and one of our linemen recovered it. That's really where we got started. I always felt, and I've said it many times, our win at Nebraska in 1980 was the biggest win I've had since I've been here, because nobody knew who we were until then. Back in those days you didn't go to Nebraska and beat them. You just didn't do it.

Nebraska is one of the perennial names in college football. You take Southern California, you take Notre Dame, you take Alabama and you take Nebraska, you know; they're just one of the big names year after year after year for a hundred years. So that game kind of put us on the map.

That's when I was so impressed with the crowd, so impressed with Nebraska fans, because they were real good to us, you know. I wrote an open letter to Nebraska fans; I sure did, because I hadn't been around a school where it felt that warm to the opposing team. I wouldn't be surprised if that was a reflection of Tom. I would think so. Tom probably let people know, in the community, what he wanted, how he wanted people to act. I imagine he played a pretty big role in that.

I've enjoyed my visits up there. I've hardly ever turned down a chance to visit Nebraska, if somebody invites me. Now if I have something where I can't go, I can't go. But I don't think I've ever turned down an opportunity to speak at Nebraska when I had an open date. A lot of that has to do with Tom and then the charm of the Nebraska people when we were up there. I'm sure Oklahoma isn't going to say that. I'm sure there are some that didn't have the same experience we had. But they were mighty good and fair to us, I'll tell you that. You can't believe how many Nebraska fans write me. They still do. And I've communicated with a lot of them, too. Some come through Tallahassee and call me. I feel good about Nebraska.

Anyway, playing against Tom is where I got to know him, where I was introduced to him, and really got to know him. Then we were together when Nebraska was with Nike. Every year Nike would take all of the coaches that were members on a cruise, a kind of five-day seminar where we'd talk about equipment and stuff like that and then have a lot of fun together. So I got to know Tom even better.

If Tom doesn't know the answer, he'll go get the answer. He was a good listener. I think he's always been that way. That's probably one of his greatest assets. Instead of trying to talk all the time, he's listening. And Tom's one of those guys, when he talks, everybody listens. We would swap information after we didn't play each other. I would send my coaches to Nebraska in the spring to get information, and Tom would send his coaches down here.

Then Tom came down here one time and visited. Remember when we won a national championship in the Orange Bowl against them in '93? There was ol' Tom, he'd never won a national championship, and there was ol' Bobby, he hadn't ever won one either. So one of us was fixin' to win a championship. And the other one was going to catch heck. We were lucky enough to win. Though they outplayed us that day, we won. So Tom called me and said, "Can I come by and visit you, kind of see what ya'll are doing?" So he came down here and stayed with us two or three days. He and I had supper together. I let him sit in our staff meetings and everything. Then he won three national championships the next four years.

I wish I could say I was responsible. But that was just Tom. I think it was a case of him executing his offense. You know, it really doesn't make a lot of difference what offense you run if you block. If you don't block, you can run anything you want to, and it's not going to be any good. Tom was an executioner. He was meticulous. It's like when he played us in the '94 Orange Bowl. We couldn't get the ball away from him. I mean, he ran that option beautifully. We were lucky to win that darn game, very lucky.

We're pretty good friends, which I would think is unusual for coaches. It's not like you've got a bunch of them. I don't know anybody I was more close to in the coaching profession than Tom. As far as agreeing with the way he did things, admiring the way he did things, having the utmost respect for his handling of people and his public relations—that just made him a perfect fit for me. He was the kind of guy I wanted to be associated with, wanted to be around. Then on top of that he was super-successful.

His sincerity was apparent right away. It was something you had heard about and then when you got around him, you could see it first-hand. There's nothing phony about Tom Osborne. What you see is exactly what you've got, and it's better than what you expect. That's the way I size him up as a human being.

Bobby Bowden
Head Coach, Florida State

Preface

Tom Osborne coached 255 victories in 25 seasons at Nebraska. He coached only 49 losses. With three ties, his winning percentage was .836. Equally remarkable, the Cornhuskers won three national championships in his final four seasons and were a combined 60-3 in his final five.

At the risk of focusing on a negative, however, I want to mention one of the few losses, against Alabama at Legion Field in Birmingham to open the 1978 season. The game was my first on the Cornhusker football beat for the *Lincoln Journal and Star* (now just *Journal Star*, following a merger). I had been on the beat about a month, after teaching at a community college in Champaign, Illinois, for seven years. Anyway, even though the record shows that quarterback Jeff Rutledge and linebacker E.J. Junior led legendary Coach Bear Bryant's Crimson Tide to a 20-3 victory that night—and, as it turned out, the national championship that season—I was responsible for the loss. My first time out I did something Kansas, Kansas State, and Oklahoma State never did: defeat an Osborne-coached team.

Let me explain. A week before the game, Nebraska conducted a scrimmage, which was closed to the public but not to reporters. After the scrimmage, Osborne addressed his players in Memorial Stadium's south end zone before sending them to the locker room. Among other things, he told the defense that if it played against Alabama as it had in the scrimmage, the Crimson Tide would be lucky to score more than a touchdown. I quoted him as saying that in my next-day's story about the scrimmage.

On the Monday following the Alabama game, I was sent to cover the Touchdown Club luncheon, a weekly gathering of fans and boosters at which Osborne would speak, a graduate assistant would give a scouting report on the upcoming opponent and a full-time assistant would show film of the previous game. This Monday, however, the assistant coach told the audience he wasn't going to show the film as long as a certain sports writer was present. I won't identify the assistant. But I was the sports writer.

The coach relented, but only with an assurance I wouldn't quote anything he said. My having quoted Osborne after the scrimmage had provided Alabama with bulletin-board material, he explained to the audience, thereby costing Nebraska the game. Barely a month on the beat, and I was 1-0 against Osborne and not in the good graces of many members of the Touchdown Club. At that rate, I figured, I would be back teaching composition and introductory literature in a community college by the Big Eight opener.

After practice that day, or maybe the next, Osborne took me aside and explained practice policy. Reporters could attend but not write about what they saw or heard. They could ask about what they saw and heard, however, and he would respond to their questions. He was casual about it, not condescending and certainly not angry.

Any thought that he held the loss against me was further dispelled three years later, early in the week before the Cornhuskers were to play a Colorado team they were almost certain to beat. The newspaper office was a short walk from Memorial Stadium, where I was headed to interview a player before practice. Times were different then. Locker rooms were open, and players were available at their convenience.

As I was preparing to cross the busy one-way street behind the newspaper office, I heard someone call my name. Osborne was in his Wheel Club station wagon (he could have driven any sporty vehicle he wanted, but he chose a station wagon), waiting at a red light, ready to make a right-hand turn toward the stadium. He wanted to know if I'd like a ride. Just then the light turned green, meaning if I didn't hustle, he would be blocking traffic. So I cut across the intersection diagonally, at a jog.

When I passed in front of his station wagon, I slipped on gravel and went down, disappeared from his sight. Though only an instant, it seemed much longer. My arm was bleeding, my slacks were torn and worst of all, my reporter's credibility, whatever there might have been, was smeared on the pavement.

I managed to pull myself up and into the station wagon, wishing I could decline the ride or even that he had driven over me and ended my misery, making sure I didn't bleed on the upholstery and looking straight ahead. Osborne finally broke the silence as he turned into the parking lot. "You know, Mike, I don't think the fans are taking Colorado seriously, do you?" That's all he said. As soon as the station wagon came to a stop, I thanked him for the ride and hurried away.

The incident, a reminder never to take myself too seriously, illustrated qualities that contributed to Osborne's Hall of Fame success. He knew how to deal with people, a theme repeated throughout this book and possibly the reason he hadn't acknowledged my clumsiness on the way to the stadium. And he treated every opponent the same, regardless of record. So he might have been so focused on preparing for Colorado that he hadn't even seen me disappear in front of his Wheel Club station wagon.

Even though I tried to maintain a reporter's distance in dealing with Osborne for 20 of his 25 years as head coach, he had my respect. And when offered the opportunity to compile these interviews, I talked with him first. If he hadn't been comfortable with my doing it, I would have respectfully declined, just as some of those I interviewed would have done without assurance that "Coach" was OK with the project. His initial reaction was that he wouldn't want a bunch of "disgruntled" ex-players discussing old grievances, but he guessed it would be all right. I told him I wouldn't be looking for disgruntled ex-players, and had no idea where I'd find any even if that were my purpose.

Acknowledgments

Basically, I've been an intermediary in this project, a collector and compiler. So my name goes on the cover, an honor that carries the responsibility of acknowledging everyone who has allowed me to be in this position. I will fall woefully short in trying to meet that responsibility. So I'll only mention a few.

First, thanks to everyone represented in this book as well as to many who agreed to be interviewed but were left out because of time or space constraints. Some probably are waiting still for follow-up calls. To them I owe not only thanks but apologies for not allowing them the opportunity to share and see in print their recollections of what it was like to play for or coach with Tom Osborne.

Second, thanks to all of the folks at Sports Publishing, and in particular, Mike Pearson and Erin Linden-Levy, Mike because he proposed the project and offered it to me, and Erin because without her patience and encouragement the project wouldn't have gone beyond the interview stage. Thanks, also, to Kenny O'Brien for his book design and Andi Hake for her work in marketing.

Thanks to Brian Hill, *Huskers Illustrated* editor, and those at Landmark Communications who have allowed me to write for their publication as a freelancer while dividing my time with such projects.

Thanks to those in the University Athletic Department who have always treated me kindly and with consideration, among them athletic director Steve Pederson and executive associate athletic director Mark Boehm as well as Chris Anderson, Keith Mann, Jeff Griesch, Shamus McKnight, Jerry Trickie, Vicki Johnson, and Don Bryant, people who have made what I've done for nearly 30 years so easy and enjoyable.

And finally, thanks to my wife Barb for her support and toleration in the face of frustration when my projects don't go as smoothly as I'd like. Thanks to son Chad and daughter Heather for never complaining about the demands on a sports writer's time while they were growing up. And thanks to my parents Bab and Dorothy and brother Jim for their love and constant encouragement from so far away.

Hundreds of others deserve mention here. They know who they are, or at least I hope they do and won't think ill of me for copping out. But better to do that than forget someone.

1

Following a Legend

(1973-79)

Looked at through the filter of time, the coaching transition from Bob Devaney to Tom Osborne was seamless. Everyone had time to prepare. Devaney, who served a dual role as athletic director, picked his own successor. And he announced his choice before his final season in 1972. The 35-year-old Osborne, his receivers coach, would replace him. There were no questions about what would happen.

Osborne had been on staff from the beginning, first as a graduate assistant and then dividing his time between coaching and teaching educational psychology before finally picking the former. He hadn't planned to become a coach. He asked Devaney for a job, in effect walking onto the staff, primarily as a way to stay involved with football while he did graduate work. After a multi-sport career at Hastings College in Hastings, Nebraska, he had spent three seasons in the NFL, the last two with the Washington Redskins, and he wasn't ready to give up football completely. He probably wouldn't have retired from the NFL if not for a persistent hamstring problem. He had been the Redskins' second-leading receiver in 1961.

After four years of consideration, Osborne settled on coaching. His goal was to become a head coach by his mid-30s, and he applied for jobs at Texas Tech and South Dakota as well as looking into a job that also would have involved teaching at Augustana College. By 1969, however, it was becoming increasing apparent that Devaney regarded him as a potential successor.

In the wake of 6-4 records in 1967 and 1968, Devaney gave Osborne the responsibility of redesigning the offense. Though he didn't have the title, Osborne coordinated the offense that produced national championships in 1970 and 1971. In addition to working with the receivers, he began meeting daily with the quarterbacks, and he called the plays from the coaches' box on game day.

If not for the back-to-back national championships, Devaney would have stepped aside after the 1971 season. But he was persuaded to coach one more season in an attempt to win an unprecedented third consecutive title. After the 1972 Orange Bowl game victory against Alabama, he announced that he would return and that Osborne would serve as assistant head coach before taking over the program in 1973.

Osborne would have preferred his first head coaching job to be elsewhere. Devaney had a built-in grace period when he arrived from Wyoming in 1962. Nebraska had managed only three winning seasons since its appearance in the 1941 Rose Bowl game. Osborne would have no such grace period. He would be a "caretaker" of a program that was a combined 101-20-2 with two national titles under Devaney. The transition also would involve a dramatic change in personalities. Devaney was a storyteller, much more socially inclined than the stoic Osborne, whose sense of humor was dry, at best.

Nebraska's record in Osborne's first season was the same as it had been in Devaney's last season, 9-2-1, no small accomplishment given the departure of wingback Johnny Rodgers, the Cornhuskers' first Heisman Trophy winner, and middle guard Rich Glover, who won both the Outland Trophy and Lombardi Award. But the back-to-back national championships had raised expectations to an unrealistic level, which would be magnified by an inability to beat Big Eight-rival Oklahoma.

Like Osborne, Barry Switzer had been promoted to head coach at Oklahoma in 1973, and his Sooners extended a winning streak against Nebraska to six games before Osborne got his first victory against them, a 17-14 upset at Memorial Stadium in early November of 1978. Oklahoma was ranked No. 1 nationally at the time, and the victory put the No. 4-ranked Cornhuskers in position to play Penn State in the Orange Bowl game for the national championship.

A week later, however, they were upset at home by a Missouri team coached by former Osborne assistant Warren Powers. So instead of playing Penn State on New Year's Day, they played a rematch with Oklahoma, losing to the Sooners 31-24.

Before the unexpected bowl-game rematch, Osborne considered an offer to replace Bill Mallory as head coach at Colorado, getting far enough along in the interview process that he and wife Nancy traveled to Boulder, Colorado, to talk with athletic director Eddie Crowder. When he met with the Colorado players, however, Osborne realized he couldn't coach them against those he had recruited to Nebraska. So even though he would have tripled his salary by going, he opted to stay at Nebraska.

The Cornhuskers' record was 64-18-2 during Osborne's first seven seasons as head coach. They played in seven bowl games, winning four. And they tied for the Big Eight title twice. His winning percentage was better than Devaney's in the first seven seasons. But the Oklahoma stigma loomed.

Frosty Anderson (1971-73)

Osborne was Frosty Anderson's position coach before succeeding Devaney. An all-state quarterback at Scottsbluff (Nebraska) High School, Anderson played split end at Nebraska and led Osborne's first team in receiving yards (524) and touchdown receptions (eight), despite missing the Colorado game because of a shoulder injury suffered against Missouri, Osborne's first loss as a head coach. His first touchdown catch came in Osborne's debut, a 40-13 victory against UCLA. When Anderson was recruited, his father, Forddy, was the basketball coach at Hiram Scott College in Scottsbluff, Nebraska, also having coached at Michigan State when Devaney was a football assistant there. Anderson earned first-team academic all-conference recognition twice.

Tom was a very concerned boss, if you know what I mean, very complete. As my position coach, and he was more the offensive coordinator then, his thoughts were always, "How can we make this thing go better?" He was a receiver himself. I don't want to say he was demanding, but he expected you to do what you were supposed to do. It was an 18-yard out, not 17 yards, not 20 yards. But he was never ugly about it, ever, always encouraging. It didn't seem to be fun for him when he took over. And that's probably a misconception because it was my impression.

I can vividly remember standing there Tom's first game against UCLA when Randy Borg took that punt return back for a touchdown. I was standing next to Tom, and when it was obvious "Borgo" had broken into the clear, I grabbed Tom by the arm and started jerking up and down. He was shrugging me off, wanted no part in the celebration because he was busy…busy, busy, busy. He was thinking two plays later, two plays down the road, six plays down the road, I don't know.

It just didn't seem like he was having much fun. Then I find out like eight years later he goes to the senior party and shoots a beer with those guys. I'm like, "Wait a minute, where did the fun go when we had him?" I'm being a bit facetious, but he was just awfully focused; let's put it that way. He was serious, but we're all serious. It's a serious business. But he was awfully focused.

It was a little bit of a change from when I had Tom as a position coach, but not much of a change, because he was always kind of somber. He would look at me like, "You've got to be nuts over there, playing the air guitar," or whatever we did.

When Jerry Moore came in to coach the receivers, he basically said the same thing, "I don't know how you guys think you can be ready for a game when you're dancing around like that," just staying loose and ready to get after it. I can see it. I'm not passing judgment because Tom was obviously successful. It could have been pressure. But I didn't want to see it that way. I was 20 years old. We were rocking and rolling. We were doing our thing, and the coaches did their thing. Somehow we meshed in the middle to do good things.

And of course, that first year, I couldn't help but feel like a miserable failure, losing two games and tying one. I walked away from that senior season with my head down. That's just what we learned to expect. Individual kudos aside, they just didn't matter that much. Two losses and a tie? We won national championships at Nebraska. If you didn't win it all, you were a severe disappointment. Tom never said that. But I certainly felt it personally.

It didn't feel the same with Coach Osborne as it did with Coach Devaney. And maybe, again, that was obviously a difference in personalities. It just was. I'm slightly tainted because Coach Devaney was at Michigan State when my dad was there. So there was a different relationship. But my personal relationship had nothing to do with the way Devaney interacted with the squad versus the way Coach Osborne did. Devaney was just different. He was more of a gambler, put it out on the line, and Tom was an Xs-and-Os-type of guy. Tom was the mastermind for the first national championships.

Devaney? It's better to say I knew of him because I was growing up when my dad was the basketball coach at Michigan State and he was one of the assistants in football with Duffy Daugherty. Then he went to Wyoming and I didn't know that, as a kid. We moved out to Scottsbluff. My dad took that job, and Devaney had moved to Lincoln. There were times when we ran into him traveling through the state. So I had some personal meetings, at least, with him. I would see him and know, "Well, that's the football coach at Nebraska." But when I was at Scottsbluff High School, I couldn't think of anything but playing football at Michigan State. That was an unrealistic want. But that was my team. Nebraska? What about them? At that point they hadn't done anything stellar. I didn't know about them, simply because they weren't UCLA. It was Notre Dame and Michigan State as far as I was concerned, growing up.

Tom had the typical first-year, bizarre situations, like the famous I-hit-him-in-the-face-with-a-football. Terry Luck and I are off to the side of practice; they're doing extra points and field goals, and we're not involved in that, so we're playing catch from about 40 yards away. I had a terrible arm. When I'd go long on a pass in practice and have to throw it back, they all had to duck. So I let loose with this one and it's off the mark. Terry starts to move but then he realizes, whoa, Coach Osborne is over there. And he's walking into the picture. The ball's getting closer, and Terry's not saying anything. And wham, right in the face—it decks Coach Osborne. It drops him like a rock. I couldn't believe it.

I run up there and they're just pulling him up as I get there. And they're pulling him up toward me. He gets on his feet right as I get there, so we're standing face to face.

"Dadgummit, who threw that ball?"

Well, I look immediately over my shoulder, back where I had been. And Terry Luck says, "Well, Coach, I think it was some of those freshmen down there."

"Dadgummit, quit screwing around out here. That about knocked me out."

It did. I couldn't believe it. And then a couple of days later he shows up in front of my locker; I'm laying on my back and he comes into my line of view. Of course, my eyes are completely bloodshot. "Did you throw that ball at me the other day?"

"Yeahhhhh."

"Why didn't you say something?"

"You never asked me, and I wasn't about to."

He threatened that he would get me for that. I don't know exactly when that happened. But I'm sure he did at some point in time, get me back, and it was well deserved. But what was he doing over there? How come he wasn't over watching the kickers? Oh, man. I felt bad for him.

But it was Terry Luck's fault, not mine. The guy used to be a defensive back before he was a quarterback. Come on, get over there and knock that thing down. At least warn him.

You've got to admit, the personality change from Coach Devaney to Coach Osborne was stark, so some might not have enjoyed it. I don't know. At that point, everybody was out to win games, so it just didn't matter. The receivers, we got a new coach out of the deal. So it was like, "OK, here we go." In fact, for me it was kind of a lucky break. My junior year Bob Revelle had come in as a juco transfer and kind of bumped me from first position. It was my fault. But I had a fresh start with a new coach and was able to win the position back, and I don't know if that would have happened if Devaney hadn't left and Coach Osborne hadn't moved from the position coach. So personally, for me, it was a thankful thing to get somebody else that had a fresh, non-history look at the position.

Tom was always prepared and complete in his recruiting. He was sincere in what he was doing. He put his life into his work. And the really strong, faith-based approach, if you want to call it that, came later. I think maybe when he started with us, the changeover was so overwhelming, and I wouldn't say he didn't have his faith then, but he just wasn't able to get his arms around everything and include that or at least allow that to be the part of himself that it was at that later stage of his career.

I'm the most foul-mouthed piece of crap there is, and I don't think he ever said it more than once, but he did say it. "You don't need to say that. You don't need to swear when you drop that pass."

He said it because he felt it, not because he was trying to teach somebody something or preach, quite a stark contrast to later in his career. I would have to think it was because later he had everything under control. And he knew exactly what everything was and it gave him a little more time to bring those things into the program. But he never pushed it on anybody. "If I don't go to the church service in the morning, I won't get to play." It was never anything like that. It was literally leading by example.

I wasn't all that surprised when he stepped aside. When you look back at it, it's just typical that he would do that because he had accomplished something, and that's the way he was. He wasn't out for a goal. Everybody knows the story, after we had beaten Alabama in the 1972 Orange Bowl, on the bus, he commented, "That's it. We start again." It was almost an empty feeling. To let that sink in at that early of a stage in his career and then go on and win three more national championships as a head coach and be right on the doorstep a number of other times? No, it wasn't surprising.

Steve Manstedt (1971-73)

If not for Osborne, Steve Manstedt might not have gone to college, and he almost certainly wouldn't have gone to Nebraska. By his own admission, he was an indifferent high school student in Wahoo, Nebraska. As a result, he had to walk on and pay his own way initially. Osborne recruited him after watching him compete in the shot put and discus at the state track and field meet, held at the university, promising he would be put on scholarship if he improved his grades as a Nebraska freshman. Manstedt became a two-year starter at defensive end, earning first-team, All-Big Eight recognition as a senior—he also was a first-team, academic all-conference honoree. His 65-yard fumble return led to the Cornhuskers' first points in the 1974 Cotton Bowl victory against Texas, Osborne's first bowl game.

To try to follow Bob Devaney was really tough because everybody thought the world of him. He walked into a room and everybody just shut up. You didn't talk. We used to call him "the old man." And when he walked in, you didn't really say much because you just respected him so much. Tom was well respected, too. I really liked Tom.

I think one of the things that was different was Tom put more time into it on the field. We went from hour-and-a-half practices to two-and-a-half-hour practices. Everybody was used to what Bob did, and then all of a sudden, some things were a little bit different. Tom was under a tremendous amount of pressure from the fans following Bob and having to try to meet expectations. People said, "Hey, we shouldn't have lost this game. We shouldn't have lost that game." I think we ended up 9-2-1 Tom's first year, and the year before we were about the same. But everybody was down on him, just because it was him.

I can't imagine they'd have been on Devaney. Of course, I'm a little prejudiced because I thought the world of Tom. He recruited me. He was very up front, very honest with me. I would have never gotten to the University of Nebraska if it hadn't been for Tom Osborne. I was actually kind of a Prop 48, where my grade-point average wasn't high enough. And because of that, everybody just kind of backed off. Of course, I was small, too. I wasn't real big. But Tom gave me the chance.

I was throwing the shot put at the state track meet the first time I met him. He called on the phone and said he was going to meet me out there. Nebraska was turned off by my grades. But Tom came up with a deal where, "Hey, you can come, sit out a year, and we'll guarantee you a scholarship if you get your grades up." And that's how I made it.

Tom said, "I go all over California looking for kids like you, and you're 25 miles away from us."

I was pole-vaulting almost 13 feet. I was putting the shot 60 feet. And I was running the 100 in 10.2 seconds. I threw the discus, too. I told him it was my own fault my grades weren't higher. Clete Fischer, the assistant who recruited in the state of Nebraska, came in and talked to me one time, said, "Hey, you need to go to a junior college." But then Tom worked out this deal.

When I got there, everyone wondered, "Who is this kid?" I'd get to the quarterback in practice and Coach Devaney would say, "This guy's from Wahoo, Nebraska. Do you know where that is? You're getting beat by him?" I didn't know what I was doing. They just said to go for the quarterback. So I did.

Ursula Walsh took over for Tom as the academic counselor my senior year. What I had to do was come back to finish a degree, and my first year out, she helped me. I needed 10 hours to get my degree so I could graduate in four and a half years. I had to pay for that. I worked as a graduate assistant for two years in the off-season. But that first year I came back, I graduated.

You know the famous card game that took place in the fieldhouse with Jim Ross, who was the freshman coach then, and all those guys—Paul Schneider and George Sullivan, the trainers? They'd let me play once in a while. Otherwise, I sat and watched. Coach Ross would just rip me to shreds. Devaney told me one time, "Hey, Steve, that means he likes you. If Jim Ross doesn't like you, he won't talk to you. You don't have to worry about that."

I graduated, got my degree. I had to pay $15 to get it, because I had two parking tickets I didn't even realize I had, from the campus police. I told Ross and those guys, "I just wanted to let you know I got my degree." And I'll be damned if they didn't stop the game to shake my hand. They were great to me. I never played for Coach Ross because I couldn't play as a freshman. But he always asked how I was doing. I'd be in the weight room working out and he'd pull me off to the side and ask, "Steve, how's everything going? You've got your grades? You're going to class?"

Anyway, everybody was scrutinizing everything that Tom did. I felt sorry for him. I wouldn't have wanted to be in his situation. Nobody should ever have to deal with that. Devaney was a legend. And then, of course, Tom turned into that. He was just phenomenal. He was always fair, and you knew that at any time if you had anything that bothered you, you could go in and talk to him. He would help you. His door was always open, just like Bob's.

Tom changed the offense to the spread. He designed that whole offense. The reason we were national champs in 1970 and 1971 was because of Tom. Tom was the brains behind the offense. He just needed his time. Time was going to make Tom. He had a tough road because of the guy he had to follow.

Tom Ruud (1972-74)

A co-captain along with quarterback Dave Humm as a senior, Tom Ruud was from Bloomington, Minnesota. He played strong-side linebacker and led the team with 112 tackles in 1974, earning first-team, All-Big Eight honors. He also was the co-conference athlete of the year and a two-time, first-team, academic all-conference selection. Ruud was a first-round NFL draft pick of the Buffalo Bills and played five seasons with the Bills and Cincinnati Bengals. His brother, John, played for Osborne, and his sons Barrett and Bo followed him at Nebraska as well, also playing linebacker. Barrett became the leading tackler in Cornhusker history as a senior in 2004.

There were some rumors that there was going to be a coaching change and there were a few other names besides Tom's thrown around, who might be the head coach. I don't remember. We're talking 30-plus years now. But if my mind serves me correctly, Carl Selmer had his following, people who thought he should have been the head coach.

Tom was younger and didn't have the experience. I remember there were some unhappy people when Tom got the job. But obviously, Bob Devaney had good foresight in seeing a pretty talented person there.

I think part of the difficulty, and I don't think it's a whole lot different with probably any new coach, and especially a younger coach, was following a Bob Devaney. Bob was very successful and personality-wise, what's the best way to put it? He really had everybody's attention because of his Irish temper. He was either real happy or real mad. He could turn it on and turn it off like you couldn't believe. The one thing you never wanted to do was get the wrath of Bob Devaney. Well, Tom Osborne had a completely different personality than Bob. His idea of fun and Bob's were 180 degrees apart.

Tom Osborne was always well respected because he was very talented as a coach; he was smart. And the one thing everybody knew they were getting was somebody very honest. I mean, he wasn't going to do anything that wasn't above board and he wasn't going to tell you anything that he wasn't going to follow up with. That was the big positive—the consistency. Bob had a different way of getting things across, but they both were very honest with you, and fair.

It was different under Tom, but there were a lot of similarities for the players, because most of the assistant coaches were retained. So defensively we didn't do a whole lot different. Position coaches, a few of them were different. There was a little bit of a change there. I think the ability Bob had to break things up, in his own way, was probably the thing that was most different. Tom was more serious. And I'm not saying that to a fault. But that was a little different as far as the players having to get used to it. It was just where we were at. That's what we saw. Probably things were a little more serious and more businesslike with Tom.

I don't remember who we were playing but one time we didn't have a great first half, and Tom got real fired up at halftime. I think he even used a couple of cuss words, and the whole place went absolutely nuts. Then he goes, "I don't ever want to have to use those words again." It kind of deflated me. He's got us pumped up. We're going to go kick somebody's ass. And then he brings us down to reality because he's really disappointed in having to use words like that. With Bob Devaney, you heard blue streak coming after blue streak. He'd be throwing them out there. If it wouldn't be on the sideline, it would be in the locker room. Certain things worked better for me. Sometimes, you've got to get people's attention. That's the only time I can remember Tom getting excited to the point where he said something he wasn't very proud of.

We were pretty much on the other side, only dealing with the defensive coaches most of the time. For most of us, it was easier to stay out of the way of the head coach. Not that you couldn't talk to Tom Osborne or Bob Devaney. But most of the time, most of us didn't. It was easier not to, I think, for us. I don't want to speak for my kids now, but I think they probably have more interaction with the head coach than we had. It may be the size of the squad, too. But all coaches are a little different, personality-wise, with what they're trying to do. The one thing that was consistent with the coaches who have been here the last 35 years is that if you had a problem, you could go talk to them. I know that Bob and Tom, they cared about the kids in the program. And I don't think that has changed. There's a lot of interest in the student-athlete. They ask a lot of the athletes, and I think they realize that.

Obviously the head coach is involved in any kind of success you have in the classroom. But I think kids also have to have some pride in how they do. Coaches can't go to class and do homework for you, and yet if you're not there, they're definitely checking on it. We had academic advising that was in the infancy stage. The adviser, Ursula Walsh, was very talented. I think she was the start of what they're doing today. It was a heck of a lot more than what was done in the early 1970s. They've taken it by leaps and bounds, and I think that's part of the reason they've had a lot of success with their academics. I think the current coaches, as well as Tom Osborne, are to be commended. But he was a big part of it.

There were a lot of people who weren't very happy with teams that went 9-2 or 9-3 because of the standard that had been set. Following a legend the way Tom did and then having 25 years of success, I think that's real hard to do. I don't know that anybody else has ever done it.

Bob Lingenfelter (1974-76)

Bob Lingenfelter was a big farm boy from a small Nebraska town, Plainview. He was on a tractor at age five and planned to return to the farm when his football career ended—which he did. A member of Devaney's final recruiting class, Lingenfelter played defensive tackle on the Cornhusker freshman team then was moved to offensive tackle. He was the team's biggest player as a senior, listed at 6 feet, 7 inches and 277 pounds, and earned first-team, All-Big Eight recognition and All-America honorable mention. His father, Russell, played on the Cornhusker freshman team. His son Newton walked on at Nebraska and earned a scholarship in 2005, following in his dad's footsteps as an offensive lineman. Lingenfelter's brother Bruce was also a Cornhusker walk-on.

Coach Osborne took over and there was some pretty strong rocking of the boat, you know, some comments made that maybe we weren't dedicated enough. But we were thinking the young head coach made a few mistakes, too.

Between my sophomore and my junior year, that spring a lot of us grew beards. Some of the guys were having trouble shaving with their faces breaking out. So the doctor gave them permission to grow beards. Well, if they got to grow beards, some of us other guys figured we ought to have that same problem, too. You can't just ask some of us to shave without all of us shaving, with or without a doctor's excuse. And so we started growing beards. That was in the winter, see? Well, in the winter, there's nothing going on, so Coach Osborne comes up and says that would be all right but come next fall, "we want those shaved." Well, we showed back up in the fall and none of us had shaved. So he made a deal with us that if we would shave for the team picture, we could grow our beards until we got beat.

We all shaved before pictures, and then Tom told us all we could grow beards. By us growing beards, we could go ahead and play the best kind of football we knew how to play and still take a shot at Coach Osborne, because we knew how much he didn't like that. When he told us we could grow beards until we got beat, now instead of just the guys that were raising beards, we all grew beards. That meant guys like Chuck Malito, who didn't have six whiskers on his whole face, started growing beards, and even Don Bryant grew one. Coach Devaney walked up to me after the Missouri game and said, "Would you let Don shave, man? He's only got about eight gray whiskers there." But you know what I'm getting at? It gave us a way to win and still take a jab at the coach, which sounds kind of funny or mean, but you just had to know the situation. Back in the '70s, you had a lot of free love, free spirit, and we kind of all fought authority a little bit, and it was our way of fighting authority.

In 1975, we were supposed to be lucky if we were in the top half of the Big Eight. We had a tough schedule, starting out with LSU. I think Miami of Florida was in there and maybe Texas A&M. And the first five games were at home. We didn't get beat until Oklahoma, the last game of the year, and by golly, those six whiskers were kind of long by then. What it did was it let us take off the differences of opinion that we maybe had with the new coach and concentrate on just trying to win. It was something we could all focus on that was really kind of taking a jab at the coach but not a mean, ill-spirited jab.

We were blessed at that time, too, with, in my opinion, probably the best quarterback to ever play for Nebraska in Vince Ferragamo. He could read defenses. I mean, Coach Osborne only had to tell him once and it was locked in. The thing was, Coach told Vince, "If you see this, this is what's going to happen, and you want to get in this kind of a play. Well, Vince would go ahead and call it."

Back then we had probably four offenses running plays against four different defenses in practice. We ran the plays over and over and over. And so Vince, if he saw a particular defense, he'd automatically switch to another play. He knew by looking at the defense whether or not we could block it. But then come film session, you'd hear Coach Osborne say, "Dadgummit Vince, I know what you saw here and I know what we told you, but we haven't run that play since the spring."

We got lucky because it would score or get us our first-and-10 or it would accomplish what we were hoping for. It worked, but by the same token, he was trying to chew Vince out for calling it. Well, Vince knew we could block it. Hell, he'd run it a lot of times before; just because it wasn't lately didn't mean anything. Vince pulled a lot of rabbits out of the hat and automaticked to things that got us out of trouble a lot of times.

Coach Osborne was notorious for coming in the locker room after the game and in that first breath telling us we did some things right and we won the game, but if we didn't do things better the next week, we were going to get beat. You might have been playing the School for the Deaf, but he never complimented you more than that first breath before he started telling you how you needed to do better or you weren't going to win the next week.

He was still trying to be a very balanced coach back then. If we got a yard running, we needed to get a yard passing. He wanted us to show balance above all. And I kind of felt as I watched him and listened to him as he went on, he became a lot better coach at trying to get the most out of the talent he had. Some teams could run better. Some teams optioned better. Some teams ran the fullback better. Some teams worked the I-back better. He seemed to adjust his offense to what his talent was, whereas, back when we had him, I think he was trying a lot harder to make the talent produce the offense he wanted, rather than the other way around. He kind of got away from the option a little bit. Of course, Vince ran about a 5.5-second 40-yard dash. The coaches said, "Dadgum, aren't you a little slow?" Vince says, "No, every one of my offensive linemen is faster. That's just the way I want to keep it. They're out in front."

I would have loved to have our team and have Osborne as a coach as he was hitting his stride, rather than having him as a coach when he was just trying to feel things out, kind of working through his staff. His attitude became "this is what I've got and this is what it can do, so I guess I'll do what it can do rather than try to make it do what I want it to do."

Mike Fultz (1974-76)

A defensive tackle, Mike Fultz was the team's strongest player as a senior. He was as hard-working as he was strong, buying his first car with money he saved from a newspaper route begun when he was in the fourth grade. He was a state heavyweight wrestling champion at Lincoln High School in Nebraska and the Lincoln Journal and Star *prep athlete of the year, even though Lincoln High won just one football game during his senior season. He earned All-America recognition at Nebraska in 1976. The New Orleans Saints drafted him in the second round, and he played five seasons in the NFL before returning to Lincoln High to teach and coach. In the Cornhuskers' final regular-season game in 1976, a 68-3 victory at Hawaii, the 6-foot-5, 275-pound Fultz lined up at free safety on the final play of the game, a brief change of position he regrets to this day. "Don't get me in trouble with Coach again," he said. "Boy, I took a lot of heat for that. He never did like somebody showboating. Those were the things he just didn't let you do."*

It was kind of a difficult move for him. But Tom did a good job in the transition from an assistant to a head coach. He did do a good job. I had Tom in his early years. He really grew with the job. The longer he stayed, the better he got at what he was doing, he got an opportunity to grow with the job and became a great coach. I saw the changes that he made when he first started, when I was a graduate assistant with him, I could just see the changes.

You do get to know Tom better when you're on the other side of the fence. And, you know, he really did run things. It was amazing that he had his hands in everything. He knew what was going on. I think he was detail-oriented, and that's what made him a good coach.

He had a sense of humor, especially when he was working with those older guys around him. They got to laugh together. He might not have laughed too much with the younger coaches, but with the older coaches, they had a little clique, and I think that was pretty good. They kind of had that little thing going.

At times, Tom was distant. But if you had a problem or something was going on, you could approach him and visit with him. But most of the guys usually would go to their position coach first, because they were used to him. If you didn't get a satisfactory answer, you could go to Tom, and he'd give you an answer. The door was open.

Losing to Oklahoma bothered me. And I don't care what they say, it bothered Tom. It bothered everybody on that staff. It was a difficult thing when we didn't beat Oklahoma, because we pointed to that part of the season. That WAS the season. We drove through the whole season and we got to that game. I don't care what anybody will tell you; that was it. And it bothered Tom.

We had success. It was just that old nemesis Oklahoma that used to ride us. The opportunities were there until Oklahoma reared its ugly head. But we were in the thick of things. I always enjoyed it because we were in the thick of the hunt. As long as we were in it and had an opportunity, it was up to us to do the rest. That's what Coach's teams had; they were in the hunt all the time.

When I was recruited, Tom had actually taken over for Bob, but he wasn't going to be the coach until the next year. I knew that. But I was excited about playing for Nebraska. I grew up in Lincoln. That was it as far as I was concerned. I wasn't going anyplace else. It wouldn't have made a difference who the coach was as long as I got to play at Nebraska. The first time I met him I think it was in the old Coliseum, when the coaches had their offices over there. I was sitting in Bob's chair. He was taking a picture of me. As a matter of fact, I still have that picture somewhere. Everybody took a picture; they brought all the freshmen in there and took a picture sitting in Bob's chair. Coach Osborne was there. All of the other coaches were there. That's where they used to do it. It was a big deal for me.

I went straight through, four years without redshirting. I don't know if it was typical or not. A lot of guys got redshirted. I didn't. I had my goals kind of set so I wanted to play.

I coached with the freshman team as a graduate assistant. Tom usually kept his hands off that. He let the freshman coaches run it. He didn't say, "Play so-and-so." He may have told that to the head freshman coach. But he never told it to the assistants. I think the freshman program was a good little tradition. That's something missing now. We went down and beat Oklahoma in the "snake pit" when I was a freshman. That was a big deal, I thought. We were still playing other Big Eight freshman teams then. By the time I was a senior, they had kind of started moving away from that. But Tom kept the freshman program going.

You wouldn't know it if you just met Tom and visited with him, but he's a very competitive person. You'd sit down and talk to him and watch him coach and see that he really got into the game. That was all part of it. He may have kept it in, but he'd give you a couple of "dadgummits" and get mad at you. He'd say, "Dadgummit, Mike, you can't do that." I'd say, "OK, I won't do it anymore."

He wouldn't say it, but he'd beat your eyes out if he got the chance. A very physical approach—that was his philosophy. We never did any cheap shots, but we'd just pound them and pound them. The whistle would blow, and we'd stop. But until the whistle blew you had to go all out. That's the way he approached the game.

He had surrounded himself with some great coaches, too. That's also what made him good. He wouldn't bother his assistants too much. He turned them loose. Tom was low-key, but then he had some nuts around him who weren't low-key. And Tom knew that. People like Monte Kiffin and all those folks, Cletus Fischer, and "Iron Mike" Corgan, those guys were kind of wild. He knew what to tell them. He had people who would get on you. You've got to have those kind of guys.

Tom treated everybody with respect. If a guy was fifth-string, whoever it was, he would call everybody in and meet with them. That was in the days when we had about 200 kids. But Tom would call everyone in and speak to each one as an individual. He gave you a sense that you were an important part of the team. Even when I was a starter, I had to go see Coach. You'd go in and visit with him. He'd ask a few questions about how school was going and how you felt about the season, things like that. Everybody would visit with him in his office, every year. You didn't miss a year, no matter what.

He remembered everybody's name on the team. I don't know how that man did it, but he did. He would also recall other things. I got to know him pretty well, so he knew my name. But the other kids, it was amazing what he could recall. That's probably what made him a good coach, too. He had good recall—what play worked before that—and could think ahead. That was part of his success. He did it on the fly. He had a good offensive mind. But he didn't just have the Xs and Os. He was consistent. That's what you have to be if you want to be a good head coach; you have to be consistent. And he stayed consistent all those years. It wasn't an up-and-down thing. It wasn't a rollercoaster ride with Coach.

I'm teaching at Lincoln High now, and he comes and visits with me every time he gets over there. He stops in my classroom and we visit, talk a little bit. Am I surprised by his success in politics? No, because once he starts something, he'll just keep going, get better and better. It doesn't surprise me.

Lee Kunz (1976-78)

If not for Osborne, Lee Kunz would have gone elsewhere, probably to Notre Dame. When Osborne visited him in Golden, Colorado, he knew Nebraska was the place for him. Though he might not have been able to articulate why he responded to Osborne then, time has revealed the reason. Osborne possessed "bedrock principles," said Kunz. "He had a moral compass."

Kunz, also a Big-Eight discus champion, played weak-side linebacker, earning All-America honorable mention as a senior. He was a seventh-round draft pick of the Chicago Bears, for whom he played three seasons before returning to Colorado, where he is involved in many things, including real estate development, charter schools, and political fundraising.

He also has done some coaching, but after reading Osborne's book On Solid Ground, *he stepped away to devote more time to his family. "A lot of coaches say things, but he lived whatever he was telling us," Kunz said of Osborne. "He really was a rare coach."*

Coach Osborne was very mild-mannered, very quiet. But his character was extremely loud in the sense that he meant what he said. You could read in his body language that he was sincere. He radiated character. Out of high school, I was looking at going to Notre Dame or maybe Texas. But as soon as Coach Osborne came to my house, he's the one who sold me. He was a closer in the sense that as soon as he left, I was going to Nebraska. And it wasn't anything he had said to me.

In fact, we didn't talk about football very much. We kind of sat in the living room and discussed a few things. I liked him as a person. I liked his character. I didn't think he was very inspirational in the sense of his verbal communication. But his character was extremely loud and closed the deal for me. I didn't even know much about Nebraska football at the time. I didn't know anything about Lincoln. But when he left, I had pretty much determined that's where I was going to school.

I was extremely impressed with the loyalty the players and the coaches had toward each other at Nebraska. I was amazed at how close the coaching staff appeared to be and the positive comments the players were making about Nebraska and the coaching staff. That kind of surprised me, because I don't think I had seen that on any of the teams I had played on. A lot of that was Tom, absolutely.

The coaches always talked about how Coach Osborne started every coaching meeting off with a prayer. I've never heard of that happening in any organization. Here's a group of guys you would say really did walk their talk, because what coaching staff have you ever seen that stayed together as long as the coaching staff Coach Osborne put together? These guys were together for, what, 25 years? That's unheard of. That's really a gift Coach Osborne gave to those assistant coaches who were so loyal to him. They were able to raise their families in one spot. If you go into coaching, it's kind of like the military sometimes. You're moving from city to city, and your kids have to be pulled out of schools, pulled away from their friends. So it was an amazing situation with Coach Osborne and the assistants. That speaks a lot about their loyalty to Coach Osborne. His assistants had opportunities to become head coaches, but they chose to stick together, because I think there was an incredible amount of loyalty to each other.

Coach Osborne did the things he said he was going to do. For example, I don't think he ever inspired anybody with his talks—and I say that in a positive way because that wasn't Coach Osborne. He was always himself. But he did the things that were supposed to be done. He did things correctly. He didn't try to win games based on emotion. He tried to win by doing things correctly.

There's a book that kind of reflects Coach Osborne, *Good to Great*, by Jim Collins. It talks about "Level Five" leaders. They're not the ones with the charisma. They're not the ones who have incredible communication skills. They're the ones who love the organization and do things that are supposed to be done, correctly. That really sums up Coach Osborne. He wanted to be consistent and focus on strong fundamentals, doing things that were supposed to be done. His character reflected that. If he said it, you could bank on it. There wasn't any rhetoric, where you felt you were being manipulated. People appreciate that. People appreciate honesty when it's thrown at them. You don't see that a lot at the higher levels of athletics. I sensed that immediately.

There might not be such a thing as an intellectual in football, but Coach Osborne really was a student of the game. I think he played the percentages and continued to fine-tune it. He used to have an expression: "You either get better or you get worse; you never stay the same." At the same time, I don't think his character ever changed. I think he became a better coach with the years. That's obvious with his records and the national championships.

I know they went with that 5-2, bend-but-don't-break defensive philosophy for a long time, but then when speed started coming into the game, they went to a 4-3, attack style. Of course, coach Charlie McBride did a great job on that, too. It was a radical change.

He had the ability to adapt to change, like when he had Milt Tenopir go look at what some of the professional teams were doing with their offensive linemen as far as blocking. Coach Tenopir came back, and they went to the inside-outside zone blocking schemes, which was a pretty big transition to make. But they adapted that and mixed it in with their option game.

They just did an incredible job with what they had. They always were a physical football team, no matter who was in their recruiting class. I can never remember a Tom Osborne-coached team that wasn't physical. The coaches somehow taught a form of toughness every day. They might not do it in obvious ways, but they had their little selling points of bringing toughness into the game. That was really important. I think Nebraska always defined itself under Osborne as being physically tough and dominating on both sides of the ball.

Tom's teams would normally run the ball from tackle to tackle, straight at you. And there's nothing as demoralizing for a defense as when they're coming at you north and south, moving the ball down the field. I think the offense reflected the character of the people in Nebraska. They liked that. In Tom's case, it wasn't three yards and a cloud of dust. It was more like six or seven yards. Then he took it a step further. Once they were pounding the defense and getting it tired in the third and fourth quarters, they'd use the option game to get the ball to the outside. The system would be really effective when it was clicking, and that was most of the time. Smash-mouth football, physical football, really reflected the character of the people of Nebraska, getting up early in the morning before the sun rises, working past dark, just a hard-working group of people. Coming from Colorado, I loved the people in Nebraska.

A lot of people define vision as the ability to see the invisible. Well, nobody could read defensive alignments better, or secondary coverages better than Coach Osborne. I remember talking to some of the quarterbacks and they would say it was just amazing how he could look and see a coverage and see the weakness. "OK, here's the strength and here's the weakness. This is the area, obviously, we want to attack." He did it in a simple manner that everybody could understand. But he also did it in a sense where he played the odds, what made the most sense. He had that in his head, I guess, from experience. He really had the ability to see the invisible. He could look at those defensive alignments and grasp the weakness, where to attack. I think he just loved it. I'll bet anything he misses that.

I always thought he was pretty much down to business and pretty serious. That's probably a good message to send to a bunch of young kids who need a sense of direction. I would say he developed more of a sense of humor over the years.

Most people probably would say Xs and Os are what made him a great coach, but I would say it was his ability to deal with people, bringing the right people in, coaches that didn't require a lot of discipline, oversight, or direction. He would bring in the right people. Because he had a lot of character himself, he tried to bring in players who reflected character more so than a lot of other teams did. That's maybe why Nebraska has had so much academic success.

I don't think his system was overly complicated. His main skill was bringing people together to work toward a common goal, doing the right things, kind of like how he lives his life. He was great in being able to attack defenses, but you've got to teach players to do that on the field themselves. It's really a transplanting of knowledge to players, getting people to work together.

I've never seen anybody maintain their cool in the game of football like Coach Osborne. And I've been around a lot of coaches and players. It's amazing he was able to never use any bad language. As strange as that sounds, it impressed me the most, under all the emotion and the toughness of the game, and the heat of the moment, to have that kind of discipline and character when it's naturally around you. Tom never bought into it. When coaches scream and yell, they lose their effectiveness because people just stop listening. It doesn't mean anything. Some of the old-school coaches—Woody Hayes might be an example—would scream and yell, almost act violent on the field. But there was always a certain amount of dignity and respect that Tom and his assistants used to implement their system.

I was influenced by Tom a lot more than I initially realized when I was there. That was a big part of our lives, and he was a father figure to a lot of the team. He always set a good example. There's a lot of pressure in coaching. Tom was held accountable every single game day, year after year, and of course we saw how much pressure there was in those early years. That's a tough place to coach, Nebraska. He felt it was important for state pride, and you could take it all the way, even economic factors, people coming into the town. I think actually there was more pressure on him coaching than even in running for governor. He truly was one of the greatest coaches ever to coach the game.

Kerry Weinmaster (1976-79)

True freshmen rarely played for Osborne, particularly early in his tenure as head coach; the NCAA reinstated freshman eligibility prior to the 1972 season. Kerry Weinmaster was pressed into back-up duty his first season because Oudious Lee, another middle guard, suffered a broken hand. He was only the third true freshman to earn a letter at Nebraska in the modern era, playing primarily in goal-line situations. He relied on strength and quickness against bigger offensive linemen, starting for three seasons and earning first-team, All-Big Eight recognition as a senior. After completing his eligibility, he worked as a graduate assistant on Osborne's staff.

Growing up in Nebraska, you heard so much about the Devaney era with all the things they accomplished, the two national championships. Tom, I think he was trying to come out of the shadow of Coach Devaney. I remember when it would come down to Oklahoma and Nebraska. Coach Osborne's first couple of years, Oklahoma pretty much beat the tar out of us. So I think Coach Osborne was trying to fight that and trying to fight the success that Coach Devaney had. And you had a lot of assistant coaches who stayed on the staff when Devaney left, so Coach Osborne had to win them over, too.

Coach Osborne was very serious, I think, when he was younger. You see him now and you saw him in the '90s with the national championship teams—he kind of loosened up. You'd see him cracking a smile, laughing, stuff you just couldn't conceive of when we played. He kind of joked around a little bit. But in our era, I think he was very serious. When we were playing, he took losses very hard.

The only time I really saw him just totally blow a gasket was my sophomore year. We were playing North Carolina in the Liberty Bowl, and they were getting the best of us that first half. I remember halftime him just going ballistic, the red-veined, red face. He totally lost it—"dadgummit"—or something to that effect. I can't recall. He said we weren't playing to our potential, and we were pretty much an embarrassment to the program. He didn't say it in those words. But you knew where he was coming from. I think we got our crap together, put it that way, in the second half, and came back and won. And I remember after the game he said he was proud because of the way we had come back.

You had Coach McBride pretty much laying it on us, too. Charlie's words were always colorful. I think Charlie was in charge of doing that for the defense even when we had Lance Van Zandt for a defensive coordinator. Pretty much, Charlie was the one laying into people. Charlie was the one who got you fired up and ready to play. He would rip you to shreds. He'd put the fear of God in you.

We didn't have the greatest talent, if you compared us to Colorado and Oklahoma. Colorado always had great athletes. Oklahoma had great athletes. I think the thing that made us so good was that we were a bunch of overachievers. We had great coaches. It started from the top down: Coach Osborne, Coach Van Zandt, Coach McBride, Milt Tenopir, Clete Fischer. We just had better coaches.

Talent-wise, Colorado looked like supermen on paper. But we'd go out every year and kick the crap out of them. They'd go up by 14 points and it was, "Big deal." We'd come back and just wax them. Colorado had a ton of people in the NFL off those teams. I'm not saying that we were a bunch of dogs, talent-wise. They maybe ran a little bit faster or were a little bit stronger. But technique-wise, we were soundly coached. The coaches always put us in the right positions. You always had a sound game plan. More often than not, we were always in position to make plays, always in position to win a game.

Oklahoma was in a whole different class. They scared the crap out of you. You'd be watching them on film and you'd be like, "Can we stop these guys?" In 1978 we did slow them down. We didn't stop them completely, but we beat them. The '78 Oklahoma team was probably the greatest team not to win a national championship. In that backfield you had Kenny King, David Overstreet, Thomas Lott, Billy Sims; that was probably the greatest backfield ever assembled. I'd tell that to anybody today: Match a backfield with that much speed. Kenny King would have been a star halfback at another school, and they had him playing fullback. They were that talented. He'd hit that crease, man, and he was gone. I still remember that day. You knew something good was going to happen. It was a cold day, and they normally didn't play well on cold days. And the crowd, everybody was jacked up.

The whole week before the game the coaches got us ready to play. They put the game plan in, and it was a pretty sound game plan. There were times we missed tackles, things like that. But if you look at the film, we pretty much stopped them. There was the time we had them down on the goal line when John Ruud knocked Kelly Phelps out. Phelps fumbled, but the officials said he didn't. I think if we had gotten that ball, we would have gone in and scored and put them away. But we made things hard on ourselves, too, I guess. That was a fun day, because that was the first time we had beaten them since 1971.

Tom can crack a joke. We've been at some functions, in a group of people, and Coach Osborne has come up and said, "Did I ever tell you about the time I tried to get the scholarship back from this guy?"

What happened was, my senior year in high school, around the state wrestling tournament, during districts and conference, I got pretty sick. I was wrestling at 185 pounds, but I lost all this weight, so I was like 160, 155 pounds. The tournament was in Lincoln, at the Coliseum, and Coach Fischer told me about a week before that he and Coach Osborne were going to come by and watch.

They came to the meet. I had lost all this weight, and Coach Osborne said, "We gave this guy a scholarship?" So that was always the big joke. He would say, "We tried to get the scholarship back from this kid." I'm out of shape, in my early 40s, and he brings that up.

He's a jokester now. He can tell a good story. But at that time I played, I guess he put up a defense that he didn't want anybody to know. You always kind of feared him. You were scared of him more than anything else. You'd try to go up and talk to him and lose your nerve, whereas your position coach, like Charlie, you could pretty much tell him what was on your mind, and he'd listen.

With Coach Osborne, it was like, "This guy is unapproachable." At least it seemed that way. Coach Devaney, you could joke with him. But with Coach Osborne, you kept your distance basically.

After practice he'd run laps. So you were dead tired, and you're running and you'd hear these big, plopping feet coming up behind you. He'd run with you, make sure you kept up the pace.

The good thing about Coach Osborne was, he'd look you right in the eye. Some people won't look you in the eye. They'll look at your shoes, won't keep eye contact. He always would look you in the eye.

I guess one thing I'm disappointed in is that he left coaching when he did because I think there was still a lot of football left in him. You look at the other coaches, Joe Paterno, Bobby Bowden, guys like that, and you think, "Osborne could still be coaching."

Isaiah Hipp (1977-79)

As a sophomore in 1977, Isaiah Hipp became "college football's most famous walk-on" after rushing for a school-record 254 yards in the fourth game of the season, a 31-13 victory against Indiana. He had gotten his first collegiate start because junior Richard Berns was injured. Hipp and his sister were raised by their great-grandmother in tiny Chapin, South Carolina. His interest in the Cornhuskers was based on watching them on television against Oklahoma in the 1971 "Game of the Century." He contacted Nebraska about walking on and had to borrow money from a girlfriend in order to pay for airfare to get to Lincoln. His full name, Isaiah Walter Moses, was shortened to the initials I.M. Running backs coach Mike Corgan called him "Zeke." He was such a dedicated weight lifter he had to be barred from the weight room on game days. Trainers Paul "Schnitzy" Schneider, George Sullivan, and Jerry Weber were responsible for making sure he wasn't in the weight room, which was adjacent to the training room. Hipp alternated with Berns in 1978. He was hampered by injuries as a senior and never achieved his goal of winning the Heisman Trophy.

I've always had that "life is great" theory, always, because life is great. If my mind-set was "life is whatever is given to me," I wouldn't have made the effort to go to Nebraska. I would have had that medium mind-set. I would have gone to South Carolina State or Wofford, which did send me letters, or someplace like Hawaii. But I said no, because I felt the best in me was still to come out, and in order for that best to come out, I needed to go to the best school in the nation to allow that to happen.

I had a burning desire to go as far as that desire would allow me to go. I wouldn't let myself be discouraged. It was the same thing with the letter I sent to Nebraska. My mind-set was if they said no, I was going to send another letter. I sent one letter, and Don Bryant sent a letter back and said, "Yes, we would be glad to accept you." They asked my high school coach if he would send some films.

Coach Osborne sent me a letter and said I needed to submit my academics to the admissions office. So I wrote a letter to the admissions office, and they accepted my grades. Then they asked how I was going to pay for it. I said through financial aid. So they sent me all the information. Because of growing up with a grandparent who didn't have a lot, I was qualified to have financial aid.

The first time I met Coach Osborne was in August of 1975. I was the "lowly kid" amongst all those blue-chippers. All of the freshmen were meeting with him in the main auditorium. I didn't feel like, "Oh, I've only got a one-way ticket and no way to get back home." I had everything, every possession, with me. I had told my great granny, the lady who raised me from an infant, "I'm going to make it. I'm going to put Chapin on the map." I was going to make her proud. I didn't have any thought of saying, "They don't know who I am, so I might as well find a way to get back to South Carolina."

Anyway, we were sitting there, and when everybody left, I was still sitting there. Coach Osborne started to walk out the door. He saw me and said, "Can I help you?"

I said, "Yes sir, I came to play football for the University of Nebraska."

He said, "Well, who are you?"

"My name is Isaiah Hipp, sir."

He said, "Come with me." He took me downstairs and introduced me to Bryant—"Fox." They had to pull all of my information. Guy Ingles and Jim Ross were the freshman coaches, and Coach Osborne took me into his office and said, "This is what you're going to have to do, work with Coach Ross and Coach Ingles. If you can prove yourself, that you can make the freshman team, then we'll work it out."

I said, "Thank you, sir."

I didn't have that sit-still mentality. George, Coach Osborne, Schnitzy before he retired, and Jerry had a big sign by the weight room that said, "Zeke, keep out. You're not allowed." That was on game day. They used to take turns looking out the training room window to see if I was in there, because they knew I'd come in and work some part of my body before I got dressed or got taped for the game. While they were taping someone else, I'd be working out.

Coach Osborne would come down and look in, too. "Isaiah…dadgummit, gosh darn it, I don't know what I'm going to do with you." But I had some of my best games when I did that. I was a lifter before I came to Nebraska. I work out at least four times a week still. I'm about at my playing weight, 205.

Coach Corgan used to call me "Lowly Kid." He'd call me Ezekiel, Hezekiah, Israel, and Coach Osborne would say, "Mike, his name is Isaiah."

"Oh well, I'll call him 'Lowly Kid.'"

If Mike Corgan liked you, he would tease you with nicknames. When he was serious, he'd call you by your name. But when he was joking with you, he'd say, "Hey, Lowly Kid, get over here."

Coach Corgan was the first and Coach Osborne was the second who rode with me in my car, just rode with me. We had this sports psychologist come in. I can't remember the name of the guy, but he came in and talked about coach-and-player relationships, that we should have a mentality to be as one. When we're on the field, we're one. And off the field we should be the same way.

Mike said, "Hey, Lowly Kid, let's go for a ride."

I said, "Who's driving?"

He said, "You are."

So we got in my car, a Cutlass Supreme, and I had an eight-track tape player. He just casually reached over and put in a Barry White tape. I kind of leaned back, "Coach Corgan, do you know what you're doing?" And he said, "Whatcha think, I don't know about Barry White?" After that, I was like, "Yeah, you're OK with me, Coach Corgan. You're cool."

Then, Coach Osborne did the same thing. He put in a Kool and the Gang tape, and I said, "Oh, isn't this something?" I believe Coach Osborne had heard the music before. Regardless of what the man said, he had a feel for music; you can believe me he did.

Those two men, they took the time and we rode down O Street, all the way out to 56th and O and came back down to the stadium, just kind of talking. That's when I was a sophomore. They said, "This is something we normally don't do, but we're trying to find time."

I had my normal routine of running steps at Memorial Stadium. I would do the south side one day, and then I would do the north side, one side each day. So one day I was out doing the south side, which was the highest, and Coach Osborne was out doing his normal routine, running around the field.

I said, "Coach, I see you go around that field a lot. How many times do you go around?"

He said, "Oh, I put in probably two miles a day."

I said, "Well, if you really want to get yourself in good shape, come on up here with me."

I guess he was feeling good that day because he said, "OK, I'm ready, let's go."

I used to go up fast and then come down in a cross-step, zig-zag. He said, "I'm not doing that because I'm not going to trip and hurt myself."

I didn't count up and down as two. I counted it was one. I did the whole south stadium. I think there were like seven stairways, and I'd do every aisle. I'd go up and come back down the same aisle. You're talking about 100-plus steps going up. I wouldn't do every one. I would skip every other step, which makes it tough, because when you get up to that third tier, it's not as easy as the first one. And he did two with me.

He went up, came down and went back up and down and said, "That's enough for me."

I was impressed. I said, "Coach, I'm proud of you. You did good. You did very good." I tried to get Coach Corgan to do it. But he just did his normal walk.

Sports Illustrated wrote about the Indiana game and called me "I.M. Hipp." Several papers did, too—Washington, Kansas City, Denver, papers from everywhere. Fox came up with the name, using my initials. He said, "Why don't we just use 'I.M.' because there is no name like that." It was catchy.

"Are you hip?"

"I'm hip," I said. "Go with it, Foxie. You're the man."

So he went with it.

Coach Osborne didn't like it too well. He said, "His name is Isaiah, and I think we should call him Isaiah." But then he said, "OK, whatever he thinks. Whatever he wants to use, that's fine with me." I wasn't too big on how they spelled it, as long as they called me by my name.

I saw Coach Osborne as a great innovator, a great technician. He knew how to design a play. I felt that in order for me to be the best, I had to go to him sometimes and ask questions, or even just sit and talk with him. When I was feeling homesick, away from home, I would go in and sit down and talk with him. I would be feeling a home-yearning and then he would make one of those strange jokes and you couldn't help but be like, "What was that?" It was funny the way he said it.

I believe that's how I got to know Tom Osborne, by him walking through the hallway or out on the track or the football field and then taking the time to work out with me. He would go through the conditioning circuit sometimes. And we would play racquetball, stuff like that. He'd take the time to say, "I believe in you." Being almost 2,000 miles away from home and having a person who was a good role model, in my opinion, helped me and guided me. And at the same time, he was a good friend.

I can still say Tom Osborne is a good friend. He cared in a way coaches don't normally do. He tried to put an emphasis on every person. Even if there were 101 players, he made an attempt to connect with every one. He had a great ability to relate to people. The guidance and direction he gave me as a head coach and a man, as a person, stays with me. I believe that's the reason I am what I am today.

John Havekost (1977-79)

Even though he was an offensive guard, John Havekost carried the ball once during his Cornhusker career, gaining 11 yards against Oklahoma in a 17-14 loss at Norman, Oklahoma, in 1979. The carry came on one of Osborne's imaginative trick plays, the "fumbleroosky." On the play, the center snapped the ball to the quarterback, who immediately set it on the ground for the guard to pick up and run the opposite direction of the flow of the other linemen. Later in the game, Randy

Schleusener, the other guard, scored a touchdown on the play. Havekost was a scholarship recruit from a small high school in Scribner, Nebraska. He was a first-team, all-conference selection and earned All-America honorable mention as a Cornhusker senior. A knee operation ended hopes of a professional career, and he returned to Scribner to farm.

People still ask me, "How was it playing for Tom Osborne?" Well, at that time, he was just a coach. He was a good coach. He treated us fair. He worked very hard and you respected him for that. But he wasn't a legend back then. He's a legend now. I think the kids at the end were caught up in everything he had done. Well, we were on the other side of it. We were the ones who were at the beginning of his career. It was different for us.

My experiences with Tom Osborne were all good. He always treated me fairly. He expected you to work hard, and that's the way he was from the very beginning. That guy worked harder than anybody. He'd do all this stuff, go through all the practices, and when you came out, after you practiced and did your hour's worth of lifting, he was always doing his stuff with the reporters. And when he was done with that, who was out there jogging around the field? It was Tom Osborne, running and running and running.

He was very close to going to Colorado in 1978. We were aware that he was thinking about going. That goes through the locker room pretty fast. Some of us went up and talked to him about it. He just said he hadn't made a decision. I'm pretty sure he was tired of being compared to Bob Devaney. And at that time, he could never beat Oklahoma. There were a lot of things going on back then.

We practiced the "fumbleroosky" every day for maybe two weeks before the game. It was probably illegal the way we first did it. You could get away with it because the officials let it go. The center would snap the ball and fall down to a knee and keep the ball in his hand. The guard would just reach behind him, pick up the ball and take off the opposite way of what everybody was going. The center's supposed to snap the ball and the quarterback's just supposed to drop it. But if that would happen, it could be anywhere. I think they changed the rule a couple of years later so it had to be done correctly. Now it's illegal all together. It was pretty easy. You went down, picked it up and kind of stuck it in your gut so people couldn't see it.

Randy Schleusener and I were built the same. He was probably an inch taller than I was. I weighed probably 235, 240, and he probably weighed about the same. We were tall, lanky guys. We had good hands. And we could run. Both of us could run. So it wasn't like a 270-, 280-pound guy that was running a 5.2 40 out there. We both probably ran 4.7, 4.8 40s. So we had a little bit of speed and good hands. I think it just happened to work out that way, nothing special.

Remember, Oklahoma a couple of years there, beat us with gimmick plays. They had this play or that play and when they ran them, it seemed like they always worked. The plays always went for a touchdown, and Oklahoma won the game with them. I think it was a deal where Tom said, "Hey, if they can do it, we can do it." So that didn't surprise me at all. If Tim Smith would have blocked his guy, I probably could have run forever, because everybody was flowing the other way.

Where Tom came up with some of those plays…we had the kickoff where the one guy caught it and threw it all the way across the field to another guy. And then we ran one with the pitch and the throwback to the quarterback. There were just a ton of them. We didn't practice a lot of them, but we'd use one and we probably wouldn't use it again, so we'd practice another one.

Back then I don't think the conference was quite as competitive as it is now. We had Kansas, which was traditionally pretty bad. And Colorado, we beat Colorado all the time. No matter what happened, when we went out there, we beat them. I think it was my junior or senior year and they scored the first two touchdowns in the first quarter. And their fans out there were just going crazy. Everybody was going, "Well, we're going to beat them this time." And we ended up winning.

I look at the Big 12 now and think, "Wow, there aren't hardly any gimmes out there anymore." We played some of those teams and I hate to say they weren't very well coached, but they weren't. When we ran our pitches and played some of these teams, you could hook their ends all the time. And you were like, "This is too easy." Then you played Oklahoma or someone like that, and they just refused to let you hook them. They practiced and practiced and practiced, and you just knew. Some teams were very well coached. And some weren't. And those coaches didn't last very long.

Tom Osborne, competitive? I think anybody who is out for football, most of the guys out there, are that way, some more than others. I know I'm that way. I don't want to lose in anything, with my kids or whatever. They know I'm not going to let them win. Tom was that way. That's the way he coached, and I'm sure that's probably the way he played in high school and college. When you play Division I ball, you'd better be that way, because that's the way everybody else is.

I'm sure he probably had a sense of humor. I can't say I ever remember him doing anything overly funny. He would pull a joke on a coach or do something. You knew Tom had a sense of humor. You just didn't see it that much.

We were behind at halftime of the Liberty Bowl and that was the only time I ever heard Tom Osborne swear. And I don't remember; it was "hell," something like that. We all had our position meetings and he came out right before we went on the field, and that was the most worked up I've ever seen him. I think it was something like, "Now, get the hell out there and do something," something to that effect. We went out and won the game. And everyone said, "I can't believe that." He was pretty upset that whole halftime. He let us have it, and we needed somebody to let us have it.

I can't really say one game sticks out. Of course, the Oklahoma game where I ran the "fumbleroosky," even though we got beat 17-14, that's something I can always tell my kids: "Hey, I was a lineman and I ran the ball." They go, "Oh, really?" I enjoyed all the games. You came running out of the tunnel and there were 78,000 people yelling. If you can't get excited about that, you shouldn't be playing.

Everybody was always upset about Tom not beating Oklahoma. You know, not only was it frustrating for him, but it was frustrating for the players, too. There were years where we were probably as good as Oklahoma. We just didn't seem to win. And there were some teams, probably when we beat them in 1978, that we probably weren't as talented as they were. They had Billy Sims and a bunch of great players. There were other big games, and not all of them we won. But every time we walked out on the field we expected to win. And if we didn't, it was a big disappointment.

Tom worked really hard. That was one thing he always told us. When you went out to play, he'd talk to you. You were usually stretching and he would come up, look you in the eye and tell you, "I want you to go out there and do your best today. If your best isn't good enough, well then, so be it." He would always say, "Go out, leave it all on the field." I always think that's what he expected out of himself, too. He did what he could and after that, that's all he could do. The guy always prepared for everything so well.

Kelly Saalfeld (1977-79)

Kelly Saalfeld was the center when Nebraska used the "fumbleroosky" for the first time, against Oklahoma in 1979. The Cornhuskers used the play twice more before a change in NCAA rules made it illegal after the 1992 season. Dean Steinkuhler scored the Cornhuskers' first touchdown in the 1984 Orange Bowl game loss against Miami, and Will Shields carried for a 16-yard gain against Colorado in 1992. Saalfeld walked on from Lakeview High School in Columbus, Nebraska, as a 215-pound offensive tackle and earned a scholarship as a sophomore, after moving to center. He was a two-year starter and a first-team, All-Big Eight selection as a senior. After a brief NFL career, he returned to Nebraska. He began officiating football in 1991.

People who don't ever have the opportunity to be involved in athletics don't understand what a mentor, coach, and role model Tom Osborne was. The academic part of the university can't understand how big of a role somebody like Tom plays in athletes' lives, how he influences them when they're presented with decisions later on in life, how they deal with it.

His priorities were always in order. You get coaches that, man, if you don't have athletics at the top of your list of priorities, you're not going to be the type of player they want. But he understood that your faith and your family came before athletics, and your academics were very important.

My appreciation for Tom extends into my refereeing life. Every year as I read the collegiate rulebook, there are rules that were made for things that Tom did as a coach. Every year I come across a new one. For example, in 1978 when we played Oklahoma, I think Coach Osborne maybe thought that Uwe von Schamann, their kicker, was soft. So he asked Randy Schleusener on every kickoff to not do anything but smack von Schamann right after he kicked off.

I'll never forget when we went into the film meeting after that game, after we beat them when they were No. 1, and the first reel that the coaches showed was the special-teams reel. After the first kickoff, von Schamann was going into the fetal position immediately after he kicked the ball because Schleusener was smacking him. Shortly thereafter they made it illegal to contact the kicker until he's had five yards after he has kicked it off. They protect those guys nowadays. They really do. Tom wasn't the only coach to do it. But he certainly did things to intimidate guys that he thought could be intimidated.

Honestly, I don't know that he ever said it, but he probably scripted plays way back when and would just plug them in and go back to them. One of his favorite plays was our "44 iso pass." The quarterbacks would hold the ball on their thigh. Vince Ferragamo really carried out that fake well. He would have the ball on his thigh and everybody would be collapsing on the run.

My blocking assignment was to go play-side, give the run fake and then go back-side because the tight end was vacating that spot. I'd check to make sure there was no blitz. If there was, I'd pick the guy up and then I'd come back. Many times our line was blocking so well there would be nobody to pick up. I would always stare through and try to pick up that strong safety coming up for run support. I'd see his eyes get big when he figured out the tight end was behind him and the quarterback still had the ball. I'd burst out laughing because I'd see that strong safety come up, and his eyes would get big, like "Oh, man, I'm beat." It was so much fun playing in that kind of system, knowing that Tom was trying to get that safety to bite on that play after running an iso so many times.

In the 1978 Oklahoma game, my responsibility on a lot of those isos was right seam, left seam, and then backside linebacker. But Oklahoma's linebackers, George Cumby and Daryl Hunt, were so fast that if I checked to those two first and neither one was threatening my gap, I'd go back-side and that guy would be gone; he'd shoot the gap so fast. Barney Cotton, the guard, probably really got his first offensive coordinator's role in that game. We decided we were going to double team that back-side guy into the linebacker and then let Andra Franklin, the fullback, read it and cut back.

You feel pretty good after you beat the No. 1 team and they tear the goal posts down. But to be quite honest, that was my lowest grade ever as a Husker. I graded about 30 zeros because we didn't follow through on our blocking responsibilities. I think Coach Osborne thought Coach Fischer or Coach Tenopir had made the blocking adjustment, and they thought Coach Osborne had. After the game, they realized we had just done it on the field. It ended up working. So on all those Franklin runs in the middle, Barney and I were racking up zeros. The grading system was zero if you didn't know what to do, one if you knew what to do but didn't get it done, and two if you knew what to do and got it done.

It was one of those deals where you gave up the personal grade to get the result. With a veteran line, you tried to do that because the other thing really wasn't working. But we didn't do a good job of communicating with our coaches what we were doing. They would have maybe said, "Yeah, that's a good idea." But as it stood, they didn't sign on during the game. So we ended up paying with our grades.

As players we knew the Oklahoma games were big, but maybe we didn't understand how big for Coach Osborne. I remember standing on the sideline as a redshirt in 1976 and seeing Elvis Peacock on that flea-flicker and getting a sickening feeling. I remember the 1971 game, obviously, the "Game of the Century." I remember how excited my mother and my grandfather were. My mother had to take my grandfather out of the house and walk him because she was afraid he was going to have a heart attack. Being from Nebraska, I understood how huge beating Oklahoma was.

Obviously, the "fumbleroosky" is no longer allowed. I think the NCAA said, "Hey, Nebraska is always scoring with this play. We've got to get rid of it." Tom used to send in plays via messenger and then bring the guy out without him ever playing. They made that illegal. I see his hand in a lot of things the NCAA Rules Committee has done. Tom knew the rulebook pretty well. Those things you don't appreciate until you really get in the rulebook. Every year I find a rule and think, "We used to do that all the time. Now you can't do it anymore. I wonder when they made that switch." He knew the rules better than any other coach. I've been out 25 years, and I'm still recognizing some of his brilliance.

Tom always had an affinity for anybody with a pulled hamstring, because he had pulled a hamstring in the pros, I think. So if you ever wanted his sympathy, you "pulled a hamstring." That was your injury. One summer I went home to Columbus and ended up messing around on some playground equipment. There was this big old barrel kind of thing and I got thrown out of it, landed on my tailbone. It was sore. I think it happened in the early spring and I went through spring ball with a badly bruised, and possibly cracked, tailbone. But boy, he didn't have any sympathy. He couldn't understand how somebody could hurt their tailbone. It was really an excruciating injury. I knew I should have said I pulled my hamstring. He could relate to a hamstring injury. But you couldn't really say it was a hamstring when it wasn't, because Paul Schneider and George Sullivan would have seen through that.

At the Liberty Bowl in 1977, we had screwed around during the week, and a bunch of guys missed bed check. We really didn't have good practices down there. It was noisy in the locker room at halftime from all the music. I think Roy Orbison was there. That was the year Elvis had passed away. They put his cape and guitar in the middle of the field, under a spotlight, and people were going crazy. The combination of it being noisy and the fact we hadn't had a good week of practice and a lot of the players had maybe partied a little harder than they should have, Tom ended up losing his voice in about 30 seconds. He was yelling. Of course, no swear words or anything like that, but he got everybody's attention.

Tom must have had a phone to God, because every time it would be snowing or pouring rain in the morning, we would walk out for practice at one o'clock, two o'clock, whenever we would hit the field, and the clouds would part and here would come the sun. We were like, "Well, how does this work?"

You knew it was going to be a good day of practice and we might get to go in shorts, or just shoulder pads, if the offense had had a good practice the day before. The defense could have gotten just killed and the defensive coaches would be looking at each other like, "This is not good." But if the offense had a good day, we had a good practice. If the defense really stepped it up, though, that was not a good practice, and we could look to do a lot of running the next day.

I knew Tom was a good coach even back then. He was a good person. He just kept working at it, kept building on it. One thing I think Tom, or Coach Osborne—I never really did call him Tom—did that most coaches don't do was make changes. He was not afraid to make changes. When he was getting beat by Oklahoma with their Wishbone and their fast quarterbacks and running backs, he said, "Hey, we're going to go to that, too." And right after I got out of there they started getting guys who could run the option, Turner Gill and those kinds of quarterbacks. When I was there, we were about 50-50 pass-to-run.

Tom encouraged us. He made us grow up. He turned us into men. He was a strong influence. It's not a shot at Nebraska's academics, but Tom was head and shoulders above any professor I ever had at Nebraska as far as being influential and what he meant to me in my development as a person later on.

2

Changing
Philosophy

(1980-85)

A foolish consistency is the hobgoblin of little minds, according to Ralph Waldo Emerson. Tom Osborne was consistent in character. He wasn't foolish about that. But he was flexible as a coach, willing to adjust his approach in order to keep up with the times and old nemesis Oklahoma.

Offensively, Osborne's early teams had tried to balance run and pass, with quarterbacks more comfortable in the pocket than tucking the ball and taking off. With Dave Humm and then Vince Ferragamo under center, the Cornhuskers led the Big Eight in passing in 1974 and again in 1976. But their inability to beat Oklahoma caused Osborne to consider a change. The Sooners relied on athletic, option quarterbacks, who could make plays in critical situations and often did.

By the late 1970s, Osborne was looking for such quarterbacks, and in 1980 he recruited one who would establish the standard by which those who followed would be measured. He won a head-to-head recruiting battle with Oklahoma to get Turner Gill, a dual-sport athlete from Fort Worth, Texas, who was drafted by the Chicago White Sox as a shortstop out of high school. Gill, who was told a black quarterback would never have an opportunity at Nebraska, grew up following the Sooners and might have ended up in Norman, Oklahoma, if not for Osborne. He was the first in a succession of run-pass quarterbacks that included, most prominently, Steve Taylor, Tommie Frazier and Scott Frost.

Gill's arrival coincided with a break in the Sooners' spell over Osborne. His teams lost eight of their first nine games against Oklahoma before they finally won three in a row beginning in 1981. Gill didn't play in the 1981 game at Norman because of a calf injury suffered against Iowa State two weeks earlier. Even so, during the three seasons he played for the varsity—Nebraska still fielded a freshman team at the time—the Cornhuskers won three Big Eight Conference championships and lost only twice when he started. And they could have been national champions in each of those three seasons.

Nebraska recovered from a 1-2 start in 1981 to win its first Big Eight title outright under Osborne, climbing to No. 4 in the Associated Press rankings going into an Orange Bowl game matchup against No. 1 Clemson. No. 2 Georgia and No. 3 Alabama both lost that day, but the Cornhuskers, minus Gill, dug themselves a hole with penalties and turnovers and couldn't climb out, losing 22-15.

In 1982, a controversial 27-24 loss in the third game of the season at Penn State effectively cost Osborne his first national championship. The Cornhuskers took the lead late, but watched in frustration as a Penn State pass to their 2-yard line was ruled in-bounds when the receiver was clearly out-of-bounds and then, on the next play, a touchdown pass was ruled complete even though photographs showed the Nittany Lion receiver picking up the ball off the ground. Had replay been used then, Nebraska almost certainly would have won.

Afterward, Osborne told his players they might feel like blaming the officials for the loss, but successful teams had to be able to take games out of the hands of officials. Despite losing to Alabama a week later, 42-21, Penn State would be voted national champion after defeating Georgia in the Sugar Bowl, while Nebraska would finish 12-1 and No. 3, its highest final ranking under Osborne to that point.

A national championship was his for the taking in 1983, had he been willing to compromise his principles. The theme of Nebraska's schedule poster for 1983 was the "Scoring Explosion," featuring Gill at quarterback, Mike Rozier at I-back and Irving Fryar at wingback. Oklahoma coach Barry Switzer nicknamed the three seniors the "Triplets," and they were the prime movers in an attack that ranked first in the nation in scoring and rushing offense and second in total offense.

The 1983 team was No. 1 in the preseason rankings and held the top spot until the night of January 2, when it lost to Miami on the Hurricanes' home field at the Orange Bowl, 31-30. Nebraska scored twice in the fourth quarter to cut the deficit to one. The consensus was, had Osborne been willing to settle for an almost-certain extra-point kick and a tie, the Cornhuskers would have been voted national champions. But, without hesitation and 48 seconds remaining, he elected to go for two. Miami defensive back Ken Calhoun got a hand on a Gill pass, which glanced off I-back Jeff Smith incomplete.

Nebraska would be in position to give Osborne his first national championship the next two seasons as well. In 1984, the Cornhuskers were ranked No. 1 in mid-November before losing to Oklahoma, and in 1985, they were No. 2 in late November before losing, again to Oklahoma. Until they finally won a national title for Osborne in 1994, however, they would never come closer than that night in Miami when, wrote George Vecsey of the New York Times, *"Osborne showed that he and his team and his college and his state loved winning so much that they would take the chance of losing."*

Turner Gill (1981-83)

Turner Gill established the standard for option quarterbacks at Nebraska while breaking the stereotype that black quarterbacks were only runners. Other schools tried to make race an issue during his recruitment. However, "I had the approach that one day Nebraska would have a black quarterback, so why not me?" Gill once said. "I wasn't saying it would be me, just that it could be."

He was a three-time, first-team All-Big Eight selection and finished fourth in voting for the Heisman Trophy in 1983, when teammate Mike Rozier won the award.

Osborne was a significant factor in Gill's picking the Cornhuskers over Oklahoma, and the two developed a close relationship. Osborne would be a groomsman at his wedding and would bring him back to coach the quarterbacks in 1992. Gill remained on staff through the 2004 season, when he coached the wide receivers for Bill Callahan. He also served as assistant head coach to Frank Solich in 2003. He is currently head coach at the University of Buffalo.

I thought Coach Osborne was very genuine. I knew he really cared about me as a person, even more than he did as a football player. Yes, he recognized me initially because of my football talents and all that, but I knew he cared about me deeply as a person. That meant a lot to me. I wanted to go somewhere that someone was going to help me become a better person through those four years of my life. I knew he was going to be able to do that for me, no matter what happened football-wise, baseball-wise, or whatever. I just knew he was going to make me a better person when I was done playing. We were very similar in our personalities. Absolutely, that's what we hit off on. That was a key, too. I felt I could really relate to him, and he could relate to me because of the similar personalities. We hit it off really, really well. Definitely Coach Osborne was the main reason I chose to come to Nebraska.

I did hear the stories about African-Americans, that they had not had an African-American quarterback at Nebraska. Actually, I believe they did, but I guess I would say they didn't have one who had started for any length of time, or maybe had not started a game at that time. So I knew about that. Obviously at the time, Oklahoma was playing African-Americans at quarterback, and that was the place people said to go. Growing up, that's where I said I would love to play. I grew up watching Texas and Oklahoma, and I always said if Oklahoma gave me an opportunity to have a scholarship, that's where I was going to go. So it was interesting.

But Coach Osborne, just the way that he was, he really won me over. I should give some credit, also, to Lance Van Zandt. He was the main guy recruiting me. Lance, I know the last week or two, he didn't see anybody else. He didn't recruit anybody else. He was at my school just about every day, giving me attention, being there and showing me they really needed me, they really wanted me and they were going to help me be the best I could be in every aspect of my life.

I remember it snowed when I came for a visit. It was my first time on an airplane when I came to Nebraska, and I think they had about four or five inches of snow. But that didn't bother me. I wasn't going to base my decision on the weather. That wasn't even an issue. I know when I got here, everybody thought, "Well, it ain't going to happen with all this weather." But I was looking for deeper things to make a decision on. The people, that was one of the key things, how the people were here as far as the coaches and the players, just the people who were going to surround me, help me become a better person. I knew they were going to help me become a better football player, but really, how were they going to be able to help me become a better person, help me learn as much as I could, grow in a lot of different ways?

Deep down inside it was always Nebraska and Oklahoma. I visited Nebraska, Oklahoma, and Texas. My high school coach, Merlin Priddy, convinced me to visit Texas. High school coaches down there sometimes get their arms twisted a little bit and say, "You need to talk them into doing this." I respected him; he did a lot of great things for me, too, as a coach and also as a person, teaching me things. So he was definitely a guy who was helping me. He also was protecting me, looking out for my best interests.

The day before, maybe two days before, the signing day, I had called and made my announcement that I had made a decision and was going to Nebraska. I had an appointment made for Enos Semore, the Oklahoma baseball coach, and Scottie Hill, the Sooners football recruiting coordinator, to come to my house that night. I called to tell them they didn't need to come. But they came anyway. I know Coach Van Zandt ended up calling Coach Osborne; he was somewhere else. Coach Van Zandt said, "Hey, I think you need to come to Fort Worth and be here because the Oklahoma coaches are going to be here, and I think it would be appropriate for you to be here." So Coach Osborne came to Fort Worth.

I went with Coach Van Zandt to pick up Coach Osborne. He had flown in. The Oklahoma coaches were there, waiting at my house. I didn't say anything to Coach Osborne, and Coach Van Zandt didn't say anything to him, either. We drove into my driveway, and Coach Osborne said, "Hey, Turner, you've got a lot of people here." I said, "Well, I've got a few cousins and aunts and uncles, who just want to meet you." That's probably normal, anyway, people coming around to meet Coach Osborne. But we walked up to the door and he sees Enos Semore and Scottie Hill; they're in the house. He kind of looked back at me as if to say, "What's going on? You didn't say anything about this." I said, "Well, Coach, they're here. But I'm not going to Oklahoma. They want to get one more opportunity to talk to me. It's going to be okay."

So we ended up going into my bedroom and they talked to me there a little bit. They were good about it. It was nothing harsh or anything of that nature. They just gave me respect. I told them, "My mind's made up. There's nothing you can do or say that's going to change my mind."

Coach Osborne gave me the opportunity to play as a freshman and compete for the starting job. But I guess I wanted to make sure I went somewhere that I got some experience first. My goal was to be the starting quarterback my sophomore year. I guess that was kind of in my mind when I got there. Yes, he was talking about bringing me up on the varsity, practicing with the varsity, competing and all those things. I just really felt good about myself going with the freshman team, being with a group of freshmen and playing with those guys and just getting myself ready, really ready, to compete for that job my sophomore year. That's kind of what I had in my mind. He did bring me up to the varsity a few times in my freshman year and I got the chance to play in games late. That was good experience.

I felt that I was ready to play at the beginning of the season my sophomore year. As a matter of fact, I remember going and talking to Coach Osborne the week before the first game about the depth chart and where I was at. He had already kind of told us who was going to start. He had mentioned that Mark Mauer was going to be the starter, that Nate Mason was going to be the second-team quarterback, and I was going to be third team. I was a little bit hurt by it, but I understood and respected him. He had to make those decisions. I just thought maybe I should have at least been the back-up guy. But I remember him saying, "Turner, one day you may be in a similar spot that Mark Mauer is as a senior. I really feel like I need to give him the opportunity. He's done a good job in practice. And I believe he deserves to at least start this first ball game. Then we'll just go from there." A guy has his opinion. I'm glad he let me express mine. I wasn't in there to try to change it. I just wanted to express what my thoughts and feelings were.

It worked out well for me. It was truly a blessing from God. Unfortunately for Mark, maybe he didn't play as well. Nate had an opportunity, but it was definitely unfortunate for him. He got hurt, then I got an opportunity, and things worked out very, very well for me; it just kind of fell into place. If Mark plays well, if Nate plays well or he doesn't get hurt, I don't know if I would have had an opportunity to play. Nate Mason was an outstanding quarterback. When he got hurt, he was playing real well, so he may have been the guy that was playing those next three or four years.

It was very, very gratifying to me, deeper than just wins and losses, that I got a chance to meet a lot of great people at Nebraska. I have a lot of great friends that I played with during my four-year career, coaches too. They taught me a lot about life, not just football, and those things are really meaningful.

I think the 1983 Orange Bowl game against Miami, my last game, represents what Nebraska football is all about. There are definitely some other games that represent it, too. But I think it's all about going and doing the best you can and trying to win every single football game. You want to go out on top; you want to do the best from that standpoint, not necessarily tying. Not to say that wouldn't have been okay, but it just represented what Coach Osborne, what the Nebraska football program, is all about. It's about class. It's about how you handle things, how you handle adversity. That's the key thing in life. We're all going to have adversity. The question is how you handle it. Coach Osborne, with his approach, his motivation and his perseverance, taught us about life through football.

Dave Rimington (1979-82)

How good was Dave Rimington? Consider that he was chosen as the Big Eight Offensive Player of the Year in 1981. And he was a lineman, a center. He was the most decorated offensive lineman in college football history—in fact, the only player to win two Outland Trophies. He also won the Lombardi Award. He was a two-time All-American, a two-time Academic All-American, a National Football Foundation & College Hall of Fame Scholar-Athlete and a three-time, first-team all-conference selection.

He considered leaving Nebraska after his junior season, declaring for the NFL draft. As it turned out, however, he would have had to challenge NCAA rules at the time, because even though he had been forced to take a medical redshirt as a freshman, he wouldn't have completed a degree before the draft. He was a first-round NFL draft pick the next year and played seven professional seasons. He is a member of the College Football

Hall of Fame and the Academic All-American Hall of Fame. He serves as president of the Boomer Esiason Foundation, a sponsor for the Rimington Award, presented annually to the nation's top collegiate center.

Coach Osborne was consistent, consistent with his effort, consistent with his play-calling; he was just a guy you could count on. If you watched him on the sideline, you couldn't tell if his team was winning or losing if you were focused on him. He had the same expression. That was the remarkable thing about him, his consistent effort and calm under fire.

He wasn't flaky like some coaches. He was a guy who knew what he was doing, knew what he wanted to accomplish, and I think the coaches around him knew him very well because at that time the stability in the coaching staff was remarkable, that he could keep a coaching staff together as long as those guys were together. So there weren't a lot of surprises. We went out and did what we had to do. I don't think he had a lot of hobbies other than fishing. He fished and probably thought about football when he fished. That's probably where he dreamed up all those crazy trick plays.

There weren't the emotional swings that you see with some coaches. I believe, personally, that he was one of the best coaches ever. Once you stepped on the field, you knew, from the academics to the training table to the weight training, that everything was geared to win. When I got into pro football, I didn't know why we were there some of the time. Coach Osborne would tell us what we needed to do on Monday or Tuesday, whenever we came back for practice after a Saturday game. I can't remember what our day off was, or if we even had one back then. Anyway, we'd come in and he'd say this is what we needed to do. He would write down the number of yards we needed to rush for, the turnover difference, what we needed to do. It was pretty cut and dried.

You could trust Coach Osborne. He didn't sugarcoat a lot of things. He'd tell you how it was going to be. If you were going to win, you had to do this and this. There wasn't a lot of screaming and hollering. But some of the assistant coaches were screaming and hollering. Somebody had to, but it wasn't Coach Osborne. He was the one you always felt was under control and knew what he was going to do. When you watched him on the sideline, if you weren't playing, you could see that he was always a play ahead. He wasn't on the play that they were calling. He was on to the next, "OK, this is what's going to happen. If we make the first down, this is the play we're going to run next."

The one thing about playing at Nebraska, everybody knew what we were going to run. It was never a surprise. But we did it out of different formations. He changed little things, but he pretty much stayed with what got us there. He would change the formations, and as an offensive lineman, that didn't really affect us much because our blocking schemes didn't change. If the defense saw a formation, they couldn't really zero in on exactly what we were going to do. They probably had a good idea that maybe we'd run three or four plays out of it, but with Tom moving guys around a little bit, it kind of made it hard for them to zero in on exactly what we were going to do.

I loved it because he liked to run the football. As a lineman, heck, he just put it on us. And he spread the risk around. That was the thing I liked, playing for Nebraska; the offensive line knew that if we didn't perform, the team wasn't going to succeed. In the new type of offense, if the quarterback doesn't perform, they can't win. The offensive line facilitates. When you're throwing the football, no matter how well you block, if that receiver drops the ball or the quarterback has a bad pass, you can block your guy all day long and it won't matter. So that's what I liked about it. We beat teams up, and he allowed us to really stick it to people. There was a point in the game where you could see the other team had had enough, that you'd beat 'em up enough. You would take one or two plays and the guy would get blocked and then there goes Roger Craig or Mike Rozier for 40 or 50 yards. We'd throw an occasional pass, but it was all based on the play-action. He had a good system, and Coach Osborne used his players as well as could be expected. It was just a lot of fun to be on those teams.

We had bread-and-butter plays. We had plays that the other team had to prepare for, like the trap, the isolation, the pitch. There weren't a lot of them. There were just 15 pages of plays. Every team we played knew what they were going to have to do, what they were going to face. We weren't fooling anybody. We'd just pound them and pound them, and it might not work right away. But pretty soon you run enough traps and they get sucked inside and you throw a pitch out there, and the guy runs down the field. I think Coach Osborne figured out football is a game of 10 yards. And he really did a good job of getting us to keep the chains moving and marching down the field. It wasn't pretty a lot of times, but man, it was fun to play that type of football as a lineman.

There were only a few times I can remember Coach Osborne being upset. His halftime speeches were about what we had to do to win. Before the game, he'd tell us we had to have X amount of yards rushing, we had to have X number of turnovers. He'd go through the whole list and have on the board what our goals were for that day. I can't remember a time when he was really flustered, even in games we lost. The only game I really remember him getting kind of emotional was against Auburn in 1981.

We'd had a bad stretch. We'd gotten beat by Iowa in the opener. We'd gotten beat by Penn State in a close game. And we just weren't playing very well on a sloppy field the first half against Auburn. He came in the locker room and was pretty emotional. I guess people were booing us, and he was upset. He got us pumped up, and we came back and won that game. It wasn't pretty, but we ended up getting through. During a season, there are going to be a couple of games you've just got to get through, find a way to win. That was one of the games we found a way to win and it really propelled us to greater things down the road. We turned the whole thing around off that one game, pretty much, and ended up having a pretty decent year. But that's the only time I can really remember him being emotional.

He wasn't going to win any awards with his pregame speeches. But he really prepared the team. I can't remember any time that we were surprised. We may have been surprised by the personnel, but we weren't surprised by the formations, the things the defense was doing. I think he did a great job that way. We just had to go out there and execute his game plan for him.

It was a lot of fun to play for the guy because he was a class act. What you saw is what you got. It wasn't a lot of fancy words but it was stuff that was true. He told your parents, "Hey, we want to give your son an opportunity to get a scholarship and get an education here at Nebraska. We're going to do what we can if he gets injured. We'll make sure he gets his schooling paid for." I think if you talked to anybody who played for him, I don't think he ever reneged on that deal. He always took care of the guys unless they screwed up themselves and got kicked off the team.

I probably upset him a few times. But what the hell, I was young. I remember after the Orange Bowl game against Clemson, I was pretty beat up and I was looking to go play pro football. I thought he was going to kill me. He got upset then. But I understand how it is. I'm glad I didn't leave, but at the time, I didn't know how long I was going to be able to last because my knees were so bad. I just wanted to get a chance to play pro football. I didn't want to screw it up. But it all worked out in the end.

They would have had to set a precedent for me because I still had eligibility left. I think Herschel Walker was one of the first guys who left before his senior year. And I think he may have gone to the USFL first. But I wasn't going to be the test case; let's put it that way. I wasn't that confident.

I think Coach Osborne saw how important Nebraska football was to the state. He's from Nebraska. He understood it. He was a great high school athlete, played a little bit of pro football and saw the good, the bad, and the ugly of what football can do, then tried to give everybody a chance. As long as their heart was in it and they played hard—did what they had to do in school—he gave kids the opportunity. You don't see that too much anymore. The walk-on program was such an important part of it, and the fact that he wouldn't differentiate the scholarship guy from the walk-on guy.

The first year, everybody was in that freshman locker room, and the cream would rise to the top. He recognized the importance of persistence, more so than some coaches do. And he put a lot of stock in improving, working hard. A lot of guys get rid of themselves along the way. Something happens where they screw up in school. There's a place in football for a guy who's willing to run through walls and do whatever it takes because he might not have all the physical talent, but given the time and given the opportunity and the seasoning, he'll become a very productive player.

That's what Coach Osborne did better than any coach I've seen, recognize the importance of sticking with a player and it's not where you start, it's where you finish. It allowed the guys to blossom into decent football players, especially on the offensive line. The home-grown kids who came from Nebraska, a lot of them walked on and did pretty darn well. It took a while. They didn't come in starring right away but they were willing to go to Nebraska, pay their own way and really grind it out. I think he appreciated that and probably had an affinity to guys like that, guys who probably weren't the greatest athletes but worked hard, were smart and did the right thing. He was the same way. He worked his way up from a volunteer coach. He got released or quit the NFL, came to Nebraska and went to school there. Hell, how many coaches have a Ph.D.? That should tell you something about him. He did things the right way, worked hard, and paid the price. Because there is a price to be paid if you want to be great.

L.G. Searcey (1980)

Like so many who walked on at Nebraska under Osborne, L.G. Searcey grew up a Cornhusker fan. He was raised on a farm in southeast Nebraska. His father has had season tickets since the early 1940s, and he attended his first game at Memorial Stadium in the early 1970s, when Bob Devaney was the coach. After a multisport career at Wymore Southern High School, he paid his own way to play at Nebraska, as a defensive back. Knee problems cut his career short, however. Though he was unable to play as a senior, he helped coach. He is a senior vice-president at Union Bank & Trust in Lincoln.

Playing at Nebraska for Tom Osborne was a tremendous experience for me. I was one of those guys who grew up in a small town, on a farm, and always wanted to play football for Nebraska from the very first time I can remember. Just the experience…I saw things and did things that I thought were never really possible, coming up here, meeting some great people.

The biggest thing I probably took out of that was, I got to see a great organization at work. Tom Osborne had a great organization—how he handled people and how he delegated things, how he did things. I can use those things in the business world today.

I got to experience him both as a player and as a graduate assistant coach for about a year and a half. I got to sit in the coaching meetings, and one semester I worked on the offensive side of the ball. I got to go to Ozzie's quarterback meetings, got to hear him talk. I can remember him talking to all the coaches about, "OK, let's be positive out there today. If the players need correcting, let's correct them, but let's correct them in a positive way."

I just learned so much. The things you learn as a 20-, 21-, 22-year-old, you take with you to the business world. I saw Tom's work ethic, his consistency, the way he handled himself. You felt very close to him. You'd do anything for him because you knew he was working hard for you. I don't know this for sure, but I think maybe he got closer to his players later on. I'm sure he got close to some quarterbacks and some offensive guys when I was there. The second- and third-string defensive backs, he knew us and talked to us, said hi to us always. But I sensed from what I heard that he got closer to all of his players later on in his coaching career than he did early on.

You sensed he was pretty good in what he did. You believed in what he did. You always thought you had an advantage in coaching when you went into a game, even back then. I didn't know it, maybe, at the time, but I think I realized it once I became a graduate assistant and maybe five or 10 years later when I got more involved in the business world, probably. I think he could have taken his organization and set it in a bank or an industry and how he ran things and did things would have worked very well there, too. He understood how to motivate people and how to get people to work to reach a common goal. I think that's what he got through all that psychology. That's just my theory. I don't know if it's right or not.

He didn't have to do much, just communicate with you. He made me feel important, and it wasn't like I scored any touchdowns or anything. I spent more time in the training room than on the field. But I always felt important around him. It's too bad he didn't stick around to coach another five or six years. He really had it going toward the end there.

Tom started the Unity Council and he got Jack Stark involved as a team psychologist. We always had an edge at Nebraska. You go back and think, even under Bob Devaney, it was like that. We were the first school to start winter conditioning, the first school to start the weight training stuff, the first school to have an Ursula Walsh as an academic counselor. We were always kind of on the cusp. It seemed to me that either Devaney or Osborne could come up with that one thing maybe we had—the walk-on program is probably an example, too—that no other school could match. They all eventually copied us. But that may have been part of Ozzie's brilliance. He was always a step ahead.

He was competitive in his work ethic and how hard he poured himself into the job. And I think his brilliance was thinking of some of these things to give him an edge. From what I've always heard, and from hanging around as a graduate assistant, he was exceptional once the game got started in making adjustments. Tom was exceptional at coming in at halftime and saying, "Okay, here's what they're doing, and here's what we're going to do." And if he got on a roll, I mean, he just buried the other team.

That's something unless you were actually coaching with him, you wouldn't maybe grasp—not that I even was able to grasp it as a graduate assistant. It seemed like he always thought of certain key plays in big games that he hadn't used before, like throwing it to the tight end against Colorado in 1994, when Brook Berringer was the quarterback, and the play with Scott Frost—the quarterback draw—he used against Washington in 1997. He must have been a brilliant offensive mind. We probably don't know how brilliant he was.

He had a very dry sense of humor, but he didn't use it a lot. I think he developed it more and used it after I was there. I saw it in meetings when I was a graduate assistant more than I saw it as a player. He had that dry, real quick-witted sense of humor. He'd squint that one eye. He used it in some of the coaches meetings, making fun of himself or some of the coaches, like Mike Corgan, every now and then. He had some pretty neat guys in that coaching staff. And they were loyal.

He hired some people who weren't really like him, like Lance Van Zandt. We, the defensive backs, still tell Lance Van Zandt stories. Lance was the defensive coordinator and coached the defensive backs. He was a funny guy. That's all we talk about when the old defensive backs get together now, the one-liners. Boy, Lance worked us hard.

You'd go, "Why did he do that?" Lance arrived the year before I got there. I think he understood the intricacies of being a defensive back, the angles and steps. But he just said, "Go knock that guy's socks off." And if you didn't, you were on the bench.

We tell a lot of stories about him. One of the toughest practices we ever had was when we went to the Cotton Bowl in 1979. We got off the plane and went right to the stadium to practice. Lance was from Texas and he had a bunch of his buddies hanging around there at practice, and we just knocked the crap out of each other, the defensive backs. He was going to show his buddies how he worked us.

At practice, Lance would always look around, "Well, the offense is way down there at the other end of the field. We're going live." He wouldn't do it if Tom came walking down the hill, though. The poor scout team guys would just get killed. He had a different mentality than Tom and some of the other assistants. That was part of Tom's brilliance, hiring assistants like Lance. You look at players, too. How did he keep Turner Gill, Mike Rozier, and Irving Fryar all happy? How in the heck did he keep those guys all on the same page? Tom was able to do that. His system made it work.

For the first five or 10 years I was away from Nebraska, I wanted to go back. Every fall, I would say, "What am I doing in a business suit and a tie?" I wanted to go back. If Tom Osborne called me today and said, "Hey, I'm thinking about going back into coaching," I'd probably jump in a second. My wife would probably divorce me. I don't know if I'd really do it, but I'd want to. There would be a big part of me that would be tugging. It must almost be like a drug or something, you get that high and you always want to kind of be around it. I think Tom probably struggled with that. But maybe it was a good thing.

I know I had a good work ethic from the way I grew up, but Nebraska taught me that if you work hard, if you persevere, if you believe, stay with it, things will work out. That's what all the walk-ons believed. And that's what I've carried with me as much as anything, in the business world: If you believe, if you work hard, if you persevere, things will work out. Tom convinced us of that. If you think about it, that's kind of what he did. It took him 20 years to win a national title. He believed. He worked hard. He stayed with it. And it worked out for him.

Kris Van Norman (1980-82)

The play was memorable, certainly. A blitzing Kris Van Norman was ready to tackle Bo Jackson as soon as the Auburn freshman took the handoff—except that he didn't wrap up and Jackson broke free for a good gain. "I'm mad," Van Norman recalled. "I jump up, chase him and spear him on the ground, tack on another 15 yards, not the highlight of my career by any stretch of the imagination."

There were plenty of highlights, however. For someone who grew up in Minden, Nebraska, just playing for the Cornhuskers qualified. As a high school senior, Van Norman was the Class B Offensive Player of the Year. But he played monster back (strong safety) at Nebraska. He was a two-time Academic All-Big Eight selection and a second-team Academic All-American as a senior. Van Norman founded a real estate investment-development company in Houston.

Tom was young when I played, and he was still, you hate to use the word "green" with Coach Osborne, but he mellowed out quite a bit after that from what I could tell. He really did seem to calm down or mellow. You talk to guys who have been around for a long time, and they say the first few years after Tom took over as head coach, it was almost painful to watch him at a press conference or giving a speech because he was pretty uncomfortable. But there aren't many better presenters now than Coach Osborne. He's very comfortable, very confident, very funny, actually. I've seen him give some talks the last four or five years at alumni events, and he's very entertaining, which, when I first met him, you would never get the impression that he'd be the keynote, after-dinner speaker that would keep the audience in stitches. You would see his sense of humor, but you would see it in subtle ways.

He was involved with the offense a lot more than he was the defense, so we were exposed to the real low-key coaches like Lance Van Zandt, people who never said anything quotable. I'm kidding. But we saw a lot less of his humor. I don't know who came up with the phrase, but we had a kicker who was not necessarily real reliable as a backup. Somebody cracked, "Such and such put the excitement back in the extra points." Coach Osborne thought that was real funny.

We were down in the Orange Bowl after the 1982 season and a couple of linemen were on a little fishing excursion after one of the practices, before we were supposed to go to one of the evening functions. And they got back and the discussion was, "How was your fishing trip? What did you catch?" They said, "Well, we didn't catch anything because a couple of the guys ate all the bait." Tom thought that was pretty funny, too. He wasn't necessarily a jokester, but you could definitely tell he appreciated things like that. Coach Osborne wasn't David Letterman by any stretch of the imagination. But he had his own kind of subtle way of getting you to laugh, knowing he wasn't as serious as you sometimes thought he was.

At the time, for me and every kid in Nebraska like me, it was a dream come true just to be offered the chance to come there. I played most of my high school career just thinking, "Geez, I don't know if I'll ever play another down after high school football." And to have the opportunity, based on what Bob Devaney built and what Coach Osborne followed with, was enormous. I got a fair amount of letters, but let's face it, coming from Minden, Nebraska, in the days before the Internet and all this other stuff, press conferences for a high school student to announce who he's going to sign with wasn't even in anyone's imagination. It was an honor for me to be considered for a scholarship to play there. But certainly having Coach Osborne there was a huge bonus. Even though he wasn't as established as he soon became, he was a guy everybody looked up to and had tremendous respect for, and my high school coaches considered it a real honor for any of their players to be considered for a chance to play there.

It was pretty clear early on that if I didn't play defense, I might not be playing. Athletically, I was a very good high school player. But I was going to have to give it everything I had to play in college. I guess that was the Nebraska small-town, classic overachiever mentality. But it was pretty clear. We were loaded with world-class talent at running back. And so defense seemed to be a better fit for me. At a small school, you pretty much played every down. You didn't have a whole lot of depth.

He came to my house. I think that's the first time I met him. I may have met him on a recruiting trip. But in typical Coach Osborne style, he pulls up to my house in a station wagon, by himself, comes in and sits down in the kitchen and has a cup of coffee, talks to me and my mom and my dad and my high school coach. He was very low-key, very unassuming.

Ironically, this last season, I was up for a game and I was parked in the garage across the street from the stadium. I had my family with me. I parked the rental car. And I see a solitary figure come walking across, through the garage, by himself. I looked at him and thought, "Man, that looks like Coach Osborne. It can't be. He's a congressman; he's got to have an entourage." But sure enough, it was Coach Osborne, all by himself. It's amazing…he'll remember me. He'll ask how my dad is. He's got some phenomenal recall for names and faces and probably a lot of other things. You think of the thousands of players and families, alumni and people he's been exposed to, he seems to have an unbelievable recall for these sorts of people and things.

He was always able to make you feel like he knew who you were and what you were all about. That's a very unique quality of his. When you're trying to earn a position on the team, my perspective was, "Man, I'm just trying to make the team. I'm not worried about whether he knows too much about me as long as my name is still listed on the depth chart."

He definitely was competitive. But you never would hear him swear. Maybe I've just blocked it out selectively through the years; he may have used one curse word the entire time I was there, and there were many heated halftime discussions and sideline discussions. He was unbelievably unique in that he was always able to keep his perspective about things. His philosophy was, "Let's not let the highs get too high and the lows get too low, and just try to keep things on a pretty even keel." That works in business and sports and relationships and whatever else you need to apply it to. I saw him get animated, but never to the point where he was not in control of what he was doing or saying. He has a very good perspective, a very balanced perspective on things.

It was pretty clear when he was unhappy. But he was always able to keep it in perspective and be constructive. You'll see some—a coach, a teacher, a boss—that will dress you down and never offer anything positive. He was always able to round the whole package out. If you were going to criticize somebody, tell them what they were doing wrong and then tell them what they needed to do differently to make it positive and constructive, not just a total destructive, diminishing comment.

Defensively, he didn't get that involved on a play-by-play or scheme-by-scheme basis. But I think we were playing at Colorado my senior year, and we kept giving up one play repetitively, and it just so happened to be yours truly who maybe should have been in coverage on that particular play. I came running to the sideline and got a pretty thorough dressing-down by some of the guys, my coaches at the time.

Coach Osborne comes over and says, "You need to be telling him what to do, not what he's doing wrong. Tell him what he needs to do to do it right." It was very clear that he had a little different perspective than some of the folks did.

Football's a brutal sport, but he basically showed everybody that you can compete at a very high level with the best and do it the right way, do it in a way that you're proud to talk about it years later, not like some other coaches who want to win at all costs. He's gotten a bum rap in some places, after the Lawrence Phillips thing. People who really knew him knew he did things not because he wanted to win games but because he wanted to be a positive influence in the life of a kid who maybe wouldn't have a chance otherwise. I was living in Texas at the time—the media here is about as brutal as it is anywhere—and the negativity was mind-boggling. "It's win at all costs." I'm thinking, "If they just knew him, ever even met the guy, that was the last thing he was thinking." He had Ahman Green on the sideline. Do you suppose Ahman could play a little bit? It wasn't like he needed Phillips. He had plenty of depth there. That's a really bad rap Coach Osborne got. It was frustrating to hear the negativism.

You could tell he would be successful. No one could predict the future. There are so many variables that come into play. You've got to have a lot of things come together in addition to having great coaches and players in order to win the national championship. But it was clear to me that he had all the basics. I don't have a huge frame of reference. I haven't been exposed to a lot of different coaches, like guys who played in the pros. But he definitely had the whole package. Later in his career, he was pretty much legendary, so it probably came a little easier to him in terms of recruiting and everything.

He was very competitive, but all I have to think of is one play: going for two points against Miami in the 1984 Orange Bowl the year after I got out. He probably wins the national championship if it's a tie, if he goes for one. To me that was a pretty big statement. He was playing to win the game. He wasn't playing to tie. You're out there to win or lose, not settle for anything less.

He was unbelievably prepared for everything. You would never say, "Gee, we lost, but we weren't prepared, we weren't ready." You never felt like you were going into a game where you weren't ready to play. I think all the coaches got that from Coach Osborne. Maybe they couldn't afford not to, I don't know. But he was somebody who caused you to try to be the best you could be, and for the right reasons.

Mark Mauer (1979-81)

Mark Mauer, a passing quarterback from St. Paul, Minnesota, got caught in the transition to an option offense. He was chosen to be a co-captain as a senior and began the season as the starter. He was replaced by Nate Mason following an opening-game upset loss at Iowa but regained the starting job for the fourth game against Auburn after Mason suffered a season-ending injury.

Again Mauer gave way, this time to Turner Gill, after a lackluster first half against Auburn, in the rain at Memorial Stadium. When a calf injury in the next-to-last regular-season game sidelined Gill, however, Mauer came on to direct the Cornhuskers to their first victory at Oklahoma since the 1971 "Game of the Century," and only their second victory against the Sooners under Osborne. He completed 11-of-16 passes for 148 yards and one touchdown as Nebraska beat its rival 37-14.

Mauer is the head coach at Concordia University in St. Paul.

John Melton recruited me. Back then you took a lot more visits. So I visited Wyoming, Wisconsin, Missouri, and Minnesota. Really, it just boiled down to having a real good feel for the program. Coach Melton is a great guy. He was a lot of fun, got to know my family. And I just fell in love with Nebraska. Going down there and seeing everything, recognizing how important football was in the national spotlight, as a 17-year-old, it had a huge impact. I considered going to the Air Force Academy. I even got my letters from the congressman and everything. But Nebraska was just right. Plus, it wasn't far.

Coach Osborne came to my high school, and we met in one of the administrative offices. Other coaches had come in. Coach Osborne walks in kind of stoic—the consummate professional, straight, flat-out businesslike, but a really nice man. He talked about football, talked about academics, talked about the program and really made me feel good about myself as an athlete. At that time I played linebacker and quarterback and didn't know what I'd end up doing. I just remember really liking him. John Melton was the character, coming in smoking cigars, talking a little smack, having fun, a joke-ster. They complemented each other.

I was pretty much recruited as a quarterback the whole way. Vince Ferragamo was a senior and they were throwing the ball around, which was another reason I chose Nebraska. Of course, after my first year, going into my second year, is when Coach Osborne, philosophically, made the huge switch. He went to option football. We went to running the football.

I got caught a little bit. I wasn't a great runner. I wasn't your Turner Gill-type, your Tommie Frazier-type or Eric Crouch-type, all the great ones who could fly, even Jeff Quinn. Jeff was a great runner. He could move. So it caught me a little bit because we went to throwing the ball probably nine or 10 times a game, as opposed to when I was recruited. But I hung in there because I loved the offense. I loved winning. And I didn't bat an eye at the change.

The change was really a credit to Coach Osborne. He played in the NFL. He knew the importance of throwing the football. But he was sharp enough and smart enough to take into consideration the elements. He knew that in Nebraska they were going to play a certain part of the season in bad weather. So he put together an offense taking that into account. He complemented it with great defense, and look what happened. I think it was extremely wise, to be honest with you.

I don't think I got to know him any better personally than any of the other players because of being a quarterback. But I think we spent more time around him, got to know him maybe as a whole person. Shoot, we got to appreciate his intelligence. The guy would talk football with us. The quarterbacks always met a half- hour before the rest of the team; we had extra meetings with him.

We spent more time with him, so I guess we saw a little bit of a lighter side. Believe it or not, the guy had a sense of humor. There were times that we'd enjoy it. We'd get a kick out of him. He didn't discourage us from having fun. Also, he would take phone calls during the meetings sometimes and we would get to see how he dealt with other people. I don't think too many people really knew him personally, other than his immediate family and close friends.

All of us, eventually over the course of time, had an incident or two when we got in trouble and had to go to his office or got called in for whatever reason and got to know him that way. There were some things I regretted. I got called into his office. He would try to educate you on how to do things right. "That's not the way to conduct yourself." That was the biggest thing about the guy. He didn't just look at you as a football player and try to develop you. He really tried to develop you as a person. He showed you how to do things right, how to conduct yourself.

He led by example. You had to watch the guy and see how he dealt with people. He was so honest and fair. He never got angry. The guy never yelled. All of us who had anger problems, we got better as a result of being around him. I never saw him really mad. His mad would be, he'd shout out, "Dadgummit, my gosh." That's the truth, too. Never, even in the locker room, would he yell or scream or throw a tantrum.

He might be a little bit more tense in practice or in meetings the week we played Oklahoma. There may not have been a light side to him then. We noticed that in the staff. When we played Oklahoma there was just an intensity during that week that was a little bit different. Maybe as players we were the same way. You just locked in a little bit more than when you played someone else. There was a different mind-set the week we played Oklahoma. But he still conducted himself the same way. The routine, the way we did things, never really changed much. We didn't practice any longer. We didn't do anything differently. There was just a different aura amongst all of us that week.

The 1981 Oklahoma game was special to me because it seemed special to the whole state, special to all Nebraska people. You realized how big it was to be able to beat those folks down there, when Nebraska wasn't having much success against Oklahoma. So it was a big win. Nobody likes to have a rollercoaster season like I had. You're a starter. You're a captain. You get set down on the bench. You get put back in. You're playing in a back-up role. But beating Oklahoma was fun.

The way Coach Osborne helped me through my senior season was, he didn't do anything differently. He didn't go out of his way to be different. He called me in and talked to me. He let me know the change was going to occur. To this day, I appreciate that.

I come from a coach's family. My dad was a high school coach. I've always been around athletics. Even though I competed and I worked my tail off, I was no idiot. Here was a guy, Turner Gill. We practiced against each other; I knew he could run faster than me. I knew he ran the option better than me. I knew he was more skilled than me. I was a senior. I knew the offense better than he did, and I did a couple of things in the short passing game better. But he was unbelievable. I saw it. I knew it. When we got into conference play, they made the change. Looking back on it, that was wise. They didn't want to throw him in there earlier. He wasn't ready mentally then.

We struggled as an offense in the first four games. We had graduated a lot of people. We were young in the offensive line, and I was a first-time starter. So we had our problems. But when Turner came in, he did things I couldn't do in terms of making plays. He was so gifted. I struggled with it, because who wants to get sat down? At the same time, I was a captain and I knew this guy could do some things that could help us get back on the winning track. Coach Osborne, it was quite evident he wanted to option the football, run the football. And I couldn't do the things Turner could do.

It wasn't as bad as it seems. Maybe it should have been, would have been, for other people. But, my gosh, I wanted to win as bad as the next guy. And when you think about the history of Nebraska quarterbacks, in my opinion, he was the best. I really believe that. I know Eric Crouch was as fast as the wind. But as a complete quarterback, running the ball, throwing the ball and leading, there wasn't anybody better. I don't think Eric Crouch was. I don't think Tommie Frazier was. I don't think Scott Frost was. I think Turner Gill was the best. Shoot, I saw how good he was.

Ed Burns, Randy Garcia, Tom Sorley, and I, we were the guys brought in to run the offense, and boom, the switch was made, that more athletic, more mobile, option-type quarterback came about: Nate Mason, Jeff Quinn—he was before me. They made that change and it proved to be fine.

The best one of all of us was Bruce Mathison. He was from Wisconsin. We played against each other in high school. He broke his leg in a high school all-star game so he didn't join Nebraska until January. You talk about an arm. He was a phenom. It doesn't get any better. He was 6 feet, 4 inches, 210, 220 pounds. He could run. And he played in the NFL for five or six years. But he never played much at Nebraska, because he was backing up Turner Gill.

In our option offense, passing was sprint out to the right or sprint out to the left—very, very basic to be honest with you, because when you practice, you only have so much time to go to certain things. And our deal was option football. That took a lot of time because we ran it 15 different ways.

If you had put Bruce in an offense where he was throwing the ball 40, 50, 60 times a game, it would have been interesting to see what his college career would have been like. He had all the tools. But you don't complain. You do what the coach tells you to do. You do what the team needs. You play. You compete.

I modeled myself as a coach after Coach Osborne. I think it's human instinct. It's natural. We do it as young people. We pick up things from our elders and parents. Shoot, as I developed as a player and as a young coach, absolutely I picked up a bunch of things from him: his honesty, his fairness, the way he treated people, his spiritual way of going about things. He's a great family man. This is the strongest statement I can make about the guy: Coach Osborne is, in the top three, with, obviously, my father and Dennis Claridge who played at Nebraska. Those are the three men who had the biggest influence, the biggest impact, on me as a person, all the good things anyway. The bad things I did on my own.

Dennis Claridge was from Robbinsdale. It's like a suburb of Minneapolis. When I went to Nebraska, they had a "Lincoln parent" program. It was the best program you could ever establish, but the NCAA cut it out. The program was for all of the out-of-state athletes—those a long way from home. They would put you in touch with a family in Lincoln, and the family would have you over for dinner, just keep in touch with you to make sure the homesickness didn't set in, to make sure you had a family there.

Dr. Claridge and his wife, Rhoda, took me underneath their wing. It was such a neat connection because they were Minnesota people. I still consider him one of my best friends. The guy's one of the best human beings, period. He's as solid as they come. He's a real humble guy, like Coach Osborne.

Coach Osborne surrounded himself with tremendous people and then he worked with all those people to create an environment, an atmosphere, that was so positive, from meetings to practices to off-the-field things. He created an aura around that place. Nebraska already had the fan support, tradition. But he surrounded himself with good assistants and secretaries, and then he just continued to be himself, and I'm sure that rubbed off on me, rubbed off on everybody. There was a chemistry among the staff members, the players, the equipment people. Everything was operated on a professional basis.

We knew as players that we were the most important thing. And he saw to it that the players were taken care of. I should say the athletic department made sure that we were taken care of, that we got tutors when we needed them; academics were important. As a player in that atmosphere, that environment he created, we just knew we were important. It was a combination of everything, recruiting, the knowledge of the game, getting talent. It's kind of a neat story. There haven't been too many like him.

To be a good coach and to be as good of a person as there ever was, that's what makes Coach Osborne so special. That's what makes me so proud to have played for him. I tell people, everything you see publicly about this guy, he was like it behind closed doors. And that's a unique quality. There are a lot of guys we see publicly that we like, but get them behind closed doors and they may be entirely different. But not this guy. So I was pretty fortunate.

It started to hit me probably when I was a senior and then a graduate assistant coach. I didn't appreciate it when I was a freshman, a sophomore and a junior. You don't appreciate it really until you grow up. Everybody hits that point a little bit differently. But boy, when it hit me, I really came to appreciate what the guy was like, what he stood for, what he was all about.

Politics is perfect for Coach Osborne. He's so well-read. The guy is so doggone intelligent. He could have been a doctor, a lawyer; he could have been anything he wanted.

Jamie Williams (1979-82)

Osborne's influence is probably best represented by Jamie Williams'
doctorate in organization and leadership management. That Osborne

had a doctorate and encouraged his players to look beyond athletics "is one of the reasons I sincerely believe that I have a doctorate today," said Williams, a self-described free spirit. He came to Nebraska from Davenport, Iowa, where he was a high school teammate of Roger Craig, also his Cornhusker teammate. He was a two-time, first-team, All-Big Eight tight end and finished his career at No. 18 on the Cornhuskers' receiving list. He was a third-round draft pick of the NFL's New York Giants and played 12 professional seasons, primarily with Houston and San Francisco. Williams is the founder and CEO of San Francisco-based YMotion Media, Inc.

Tom Osborne's presence, his demeanor, his ethics and values and his work ethic had a tremendous impact on me. He always seemed to be a man who was looking to the horizon. He had a vision.

I remember having a conversation one time with him when I was young, a freshman or sophomore; it wasn't really about me, more so about dropping some knowledge on me, how a lot of people go through life and they get one thing done in a day and they think they've done something. But there's time to get many things done in a day. That never left me.

He didn't even look at me my freshman year. I think it was part of his coaching style: "There's a tradition here, and before you can be part of that tradition, you have to arrive as a player." He'd walk by and he'd nod his head and keep going. He was like, "Who are you, kid? Until you make a play, I don't know who you are." I knew there was a method to that madness. I knew that Junior Miller was the All-American and made it look easy. I knew he thought, "Kid, you're still skinny. You're young. You've got a ways to go to get in that league."

He's the head coach and you're thinking, "I need to do something to get this guy's attention." I think I got it pretty quick. I was always kind of a cerebral athlete anyway. So I got it pretty quick. "I've got to show him something. I've got to earn my stripes." So I went on a mission to do that. As I got bigger and stronger, started to meld into the system, started making plays, before we got to the big games—I'm talking about making plays in practice—he'd come over and talk to me.

That wasn't my freshman year. My freshman year I'd make diving catches and I'd beat a varsity guy, block somebody good, and he'd just nod his head. But once I got out of that freshman year and I started doing my thing, he'd come over to me and say, "That's going to make you a player. That's what we expect from you, Jamie. That's going to help us this season." They were things you wanted to hear from your head coach. What I'm trying to get at is, he didn't give you anything. He'd let you know in subtle ways that you had to earn his respect.

I'm just talking about things that I kind of carry with me through life, that I impart to my kids and other young people I run into. Tom Osborne had that aura about him. He was never disrespectful to you. But he let you know that to be a Husker—just having that uniform on—didn't mean anything; if you did something with that uniform, then it meant something.

I owe him a lot in that respect, in helping me make the transition from high school to college. A lot of people never make it. They get the scholarship, but they don't really make the transition and become something. He never got in the way of his assistant coaches. He didn't micro-manage from what I could see. He let Gene Huey, my position coach, develop me the way he felt he should. Gene was instrumental in my development into a pro athlete, and Tom never got in the way of that, never got in the way of his defensive coaches either. I always thought that was pretty interesting. They talk in business school about visionaries and charismatic leadership, servant leaders, and Tom was already doing it. He kept his eye on the prize and made sure his lieutenants got us ready for where he wanted to go. That, to me, was amazing.

Another thing that happened on the academic side, I would hear people call him "Dr. Osborne" or "Dr. Tom." And he and I had a really good relationship that evolved over my time there—from when

I was just a lowly freshman to a person he talked to often. I remember asking, "Why did you do that? What does that mean?" And he told me he had to develop his mind, too. He was a good athlete. He played pro ball. But he said, "I always felt I needed to do more, Jamie." So it was like I needed to do more, work out my mind. I did enough that I earned a doctorate. I always kept what he told me in the back of my mind, which is one of the reasons, I sincerely believe, I have a doctorate today. Tom Osborne was the only person I knew who was an athlete and a coach and had a doctorate. I always thought about that in class. I was trying to live up to Tom Osborne's standards.

Tom has a really quirky sense of humor. But it's precise, I think because he's such an intelligent man that his wit is profound at times. He'd use me sometimes as the butt of a joke, my having three girl-friends. I kind of marched to my own beat. He said one time in front of all the players, "Jamie, you're kind of odd." And then he walked off. Everybody laughed because I guess they knew what he was talking about. I thought it was funny a coach could get down on that personal of a level.

I watched the Super Bowl with a couple of other players at his house. I played tennis with him. Of course, I let him beat me so I didn't get demoted. But he was very comfortable with coaching me and then playing tennis with me. I thought that was cool. And he would call me into his office, and this, to me, is the true mark of a leader: He knew he was the figurehead, the Lion King, but yet he'd call a cat like me in off the field and ask me a question about information he needed. He didn't care where he got his information. He brought himself down to my level to get information.

Sometimes leaders are all-knowing. They can be wrong and run right into the wall. But I remember him calling me into his office and saying, "I've got a question for you, Jamie. You seem to be pretty hip and a lot of the guys follow you. I'm not communicating real well with my son. You know my son pretty well. What do you think?

What do you think I need to do?" So I talked to him about what I thought. I can't remember what it was, probably something pretty corny. But I remember him talking to me about it. He said, "Thanks, Jamie, that helps a lot."

Then when Mike Rozier, Irving Fryar and some of those guys from New Jersey came in, he called me in again and asked me about the music we listened to. At that time the music was really kicking, I think, early '80s, and he was like, "I want to make sure I understand these guys." I remember telling him, "Look, as black guys we kind of grow up with music, so that's kind of oil to our engines. The fact that we're jamming to the music is what helps us go do our thing on the field." He was like, "Oh, okay." And you know what, I remember that year he loosened up a lot. To me that's amazing because I've been around some coaches who don't get it. Tom seemed to be the kind of guy who always wanted to make sure he got it. But in the middle of that, he never left or got away from his own system. My last couple of years, I had a lot of fun with Tom Osborne.

Tom Osborne was definitely the closer in recruiting. He had that Bear Bryant-type of persona. "This is the guy." So when Tom would come to see me in Davenport, I always respected that. I remember looking outside once; it was snowing and he was standing outside my house. "That's the cat I've seen on TV."

I remember Notre Dame came in and played this holier-than-thou deal. That never resonated with me. Tom was very much on the personal level with me. He was the reason, the guy, what you see is what you get. I saw that. I was like, "I can trust that." I was the first one from my family to go to college. So I was like, "I'm getting ready to embark on a serious adventure here, whom do I trust? Which way do I go?" And outside of Penn State, Tom was the only one who really talked to me about academics and how I could get a degree. Most of the schools, because I was a top guy coming out of high school at my position, just wanted to play music for me. Tom actually talked about my future, what it meant to be the first one in my family to go to college. Besides football these were the things I could do at Nebraska. That had a profound effect on me, to say the least.

I didn't get to play early because I had some upperclassmen in front of me. And I remember thinking about the prospect of transferring. It was like, "I need to be on the field. I just want to play." There was a game that I didn't play in and I felt like I should have played. It was actually a pretty tight game. We ending up winning but I didn't get to play. After the game I was sitting there feeling sorry for myself. I wasn't one of those guys who went to the press or started bad-mouthing people, getting vocal. I never did that. But inside I was kind of hurt. I knew I could have done some good things in that game if I had gotten in. I remember almost immediately after the game, in the locker room, Tom Osborne comes up to me and says, "Your time is coming. Don't worry. Your time is coming." That buoyed me. You think you're getting lost in the shuffle and they don't really care about you. All athletes go through it. But Tom knew I was part of his future and he made sure to let me know, "Young kid, don't give up."

When we lost to Penn State in 1982, I think he was a little bit shook initially because he felt we were a better team, and we all felt we were a better team. In my college career, that game is the one that sucks the most. That year, we should have been undefeated. We had a good defense but not a great defense. Our offense was sensational. The only way you could beat us was by keeping our offense off the field.

Penn State got some calls that still defy logic. But Tom didn't belabor it. He moved on. A lot of us didn't. He had a way of keeping us focused. That's what I liked about him. He always had big vision. He could always keep us focused on the prize. "OK, we lost to a good team. But if we're going to lose, we'd better lose early, because we're still going to be in the hunt." And, of course, we rocked everybody's world the rest of the season. Then it came down to votes. That would have been a nice time to have a playoff. In the system we have today, we probably would have gotten a shot at redemption because everybody had lost. There were some great Nebraska teams that followed us, but we were pretty sensational for a couple of years. The 1983 team was the same except that you don't have Dave Rimington, Jamie Williams, Roger Craig, or Todd Brown. People still ask me, "How did you guys lose?"

Tom Osborne defines leadership. Leadership, the field in which I have my doctorate, comes in a lot of different packages, but I think Tom encompasses what they call the transformational leader, the adaptive leader. He had his core style. But I watched him adapt, and when it was time for him to get on us and to prod us, he would do it. When it was time to encourage us and inspire us, he would do it.

He's larger than life. You hear about people like that and go, "Sure." But he was really a guy who was larger than life. You look at John Wooden, Bear Bryant, Joe Paterno—guys larger than life. Tom was definitely one of those. All of us who played for him were blessed.

I think a lot of head coaches pale in his presence. Tom understood himself. A lot of coaches don't. That's why they flop around. Tom was consistent, but yet he could adapt to the situation. A lot of coaches do not. There is so much to be learned from Tom Osborne.

Mitch Krenk (1981-82)

Mitch Krenk, an uninvited walk-on from Nebraska City, Nebraska, was still playing on the scout team in his third season. But he climbed the depth chart as a junior, alternating with Jamie Williams at tight end. He played his senior season after the middle toe on his right foot had to be removed because of cancer. Krenk caught 18 passes during his Cornhusker career, the most memorable from wingback Irving Fryar on the "bounc- eroosky" against Oklahoma in 1982. Quarterback Turner Gill passed to Fryar, but because the ball hadn't crossed the line of scrimmage, it was a lateral and as such remained live even though it hit the ground and bounced into Fryar's hands. Fryar then passed down the field to Krenk, who, presumably, had been ignored by the Sooners' surprised defensive backs.

Krenk played briefly in the NFL and was with coach Mike Ditka's Chicago Bears when they won the Super Bowl in 1985. He is a homebuilder in Nebraska City and active in Nebraska's N Club.

If I were a high school kid today, I would never be allowed to walk on because of the NCAA taking away all of those undergraduate assistants, limiting coaches, limiting scholarships, limiting the number of players. The kid in Nebraska like me can't walk on anymore. He just can't.

I was recruited essentially by no one. I was offered maybe a little bit of a scholarship at Peru State because I'm from down there, in Nebraska City. And in the summer after my senior year in high school—luckily when you're 18, you're pretty naïve—I got in my car and drove to Lincoln. I just went to the South Stadium and asked a secretary if I could see Coach Osborne. She kind of looked at me and said yes. It's amazing. Coach Osborne came out of his office, and I said, "Hey, Coach, my name's Mitch Krenk. I'm from Nebraska City, and I was wondering if I could walk on."

You know, the first thing he asked was about my grades. And he asked if I was enrolled in school. I said, "No, I'm not, Coach. I'm kind of an A and B student, once in a while maybe a C, but an okay student."

He said, "You get enrolled in school and you can walk on." He wrote my name down. That's how it started. Some coaches wouldn't even have come out of their office.

I had gone to Nebraska's football camp the summer before and obviously, there must not have been a lot of interest in me from the camp because I wasn't really recruited. But maybe naively, I thought Coach Osborne remembered me. That was 1978.

Guy Ingles was the freshman coach, and we had 150 freshmen. So I guess Coach Osborne told a lot of other kids they could walk on, too. Anyway, I thought I should have been an outside linebacker. And the first practice I was with the linebackers, with Jimmy Williams, Tony Felici, all the guys in the stand-up outside linebacker days. I thought that might have been my spot.

The next day, Coach Ingles calls me over. He says, "Hey, what's your name?"

I say, "Mitch Krenk."

He goes, "You ever play tight end?"

I say, "I did a little bit in high school my senior year."

He goes, "Well, what do you think about playing tight end?"

I say, "Coach, I think I'd be a better linebacker."

He says, "Let me tell you something, son. We've got 30 line-backers. Look over there."

He points to Jamie Williams and Dan Hill. They're both scholar-ship guys. And he says, "They're my only two tight ends. And Jamie is going to redshirt, so I've only got one tight end."

I tell him, "Okay, Coach, I'm a tight end now."

That's how I got to stay as a freshman. It bought me a year. I always tease Ingles. "I owe a lot to Coach Osborne for letting me walk on, but I owe a lot to you for changing me to a tight end."

At that point, I didn't have any bargaining power. The coaches tried to go through the first practice with 150 guys. Can you imagine? They had a meeting the next day and Coach Ingles said, "You know, guys, by the end of the week, we're going to cut 50. We can't have any more than 100."

So when he said, "Hey, do you want to change to tight end?," I thought I had better change or I would be one of the 50 guys gone. And there were still 100 guys practicing.

Then, of course, we went from there to winter conditioning, and they cut some more guys. Boyd Epley and Mike Arthur, the strength coaches, liked to tell this story. I was the only guy who made it from what they called the "dirt group." They had all the recruited guys, including the recruited walk-ons, and they had all the rest. So they took all the varsity guys and the recruited guys in the fieldhouse for winter conditioning on the artificial turf. And they had the "dirt group" in the old indoor dirt track, the "mushroom gardens." We were jumping rope in the dirt, doing up-downs.

Looking back on it, they just wanted to see who would make it. I remember about the last day of winter conditioning, some of the coaches came in the mushroom gardens. I looked over and thought, "Man, there's something going on here." So I busted my tail. Some guys dogged it and I was like, "Boy, I don't know if I'd be doing that."

Sure enough, one of the coaches said, "You, what's your name?"

They didn't even know our names. I said, "Mitch Krenk."

He said, "Come over here. The rest of you guys can leave. Thanks for your time."

I never saw them again, in spring ball or anything.

For a good portion of my junior year and all of my senior year, Jamie Williams and I were running in plays. So every other play, I was standing next to Coach Osborne. Mike Rozier would be running the ball, and it seemed like before he even hit the ground after being tackled, Tom would grab me and be telling me the next play, while I'm almost jumping up and down because it was such a good run by Rozier. But Tom's grabbing me, saying, "Okay, 'I-right, 49 pitch.' Now get in there." He was so intense and focused that he knew what he was going to call next while the play was going. It was just amazing to me.

The other thing I noticed was, very early, right after that ball was snapped I could see Tom's facial expression. He might be saying, "Dadgummit," right away, before the running back even hit the hole. He could see something that had broken down. He could see the play wasn't going to go anywhere before any fan or any player could tell. Or, on the reverse side of that, I could see some real excitement in his face. I'm thinking, "This guy isn't even to the line of scrimmage yet and Tom's excited because he sees everything ahead, the hole that is open, the whole play developing." There's a reason he was such a great coach. He was way ahead of the curve on all that.

Gene Huey was my position coach. My wife and I went to high school together and dated through college, and I remember saying to her, "Man, Coach Huey is on my butt every day. I can't stand that guy." But looking back on it, he must have seen something in me.

My junior year, I was just playing in double-tight-end situations at the beginning of the season. I wasn't running plays in and out yet. Jamie was the starter, and he really wasn't coming out of the game.

I can't remember what game it was. But it was fairly early in the season. We were playing Oklahoma State, I think, a big game down at Stillwater, and on the opening kickoff, Jamie got hurt. I look over there and he's on the ground, holding his knee. I think, "Oh, crap, I'm in there."

The first play of the game—this was Coach Osborne coming up with a genius play—was an "iso" pass. Coach Osborne would always open the game with just an "iso" or a pitch play, every game. Well, this game, you've got Mike Rozier in the backfield, and everybody runs "iso," everybody blocks "iso." The quarterback fakes to Mike Rozier, the lead fullback goes through. The tight end blocks for a couple of counts and then slips out into the flat. The idea is everybody flies up on the "iso." The tight end is supposed to be Jamie. Well, Jamie's hurt.

I didn't know this until years later because now I'm good friends with Coach Huey; we stay in touch. So I'm in the game, not Jamie, and Gene's up in the coaches' box. And he says, "Hey, Tom, run the play, run the 'iso' pass." Coach Osborne says, "But Gene, Mitch is in there."

Coach Huey says, "Mitch can run it. Just run the play."

Heck, everybody sucked up on it, and if I had had any speed, I would have scored on an 80-yard touchdown pass. I went for about 35 or 40 yards, I think. The stars must have been in line. I played the game of my life, caught a bunch of passes—for a Nebraska tight end, that was three or four passes—and I caught a touchdown pass. Plus, I blocked pretty well. Jamie was hurt for a while. And when he came back from the injury, we ran plays in and out because they wanted to keep Todd Brown, the split end, in the game all the time, which made sense. That was a real turning point for me.

It does show how coaches are, even Coach Osborne. They want to see somebody perform in a game situation. They might have confidence in you in practice but until you do that in a game…then all of a sudden, heck, he had all the confidence in the world.

The bounce pass against Oklahoma my senior year still surprises me to this day. Coach Osborne calls the bounce pass, lets me run the bounce pass. I always thought it worked pretty well in practice. We practiced it quite a bit. But Dave Rimington was upset when I came in the game. We were taking it at Oklahoma on the ground, and he still says to this day, "Hey, that play didn't work half the time in practice." So anyway, we're just running it right up the gut, around the end, whatever. And, of course, Nebraska linemen, that's what they want to do. They want to shove it down the other team's throat. But I came in with the play and I was all excited. I told Turner Gill to call the bounce pass. It was such-and-such bounce pass; it wasn't called the "bounceroosky." And Dave goes, "We're not running that blankety-blank play." I turned to Dave and said, "Dave, I'm just the messenger, man."

So Turner calls it. Irving was not supposed to throw the ball if anybody was close to the tight end. Of course, the safety was Scott Case, who played 12-14 years in the NFL. And he wasn't fooled, really. He was right on my tail. But Irving threw it anyway. Luckily I made the catch of my life.

One of the attributes of a great coach is when he causes rules changes. Tom got many of those trick plays from high schools because he would watch all that high school film and he'd see a play. I think it was in the Orange Bowl game against Clemson, and who knows, maybe it would have made a difference in the game. I thought this was genius, too. When you line up for a field goal, or even a punt, but I think this was a field goal, the tight end-type guy is up on the line of scrimmage and a back is lined up outside of the tight end but behind the line of scrimmage. What we were supposed to do was, I would step back and the back would be there also. Then I would step forward and I'd say, "Get out of here, too many guys, get out of here." Essentially what that did was put him in motion toward our sideline.

Then we would snap the ball and throw it out to him. Nobody on defense would be there. Coach Osborne would always tell the referees before the game about these plays so they wouldn't have an inadvertent whistle. He came over to me and said, "The referee said, you cannot say 'Too many guys,'" because he felt that was deception. But I could say, "Hey, get out of here" or something like that. So we run the play and the fullback is wide open. We throw it and it hits him right in the chest and he drops it, poor guy. Who knows if it would have made a difference in the game if he had caught it.

I don't know where Coach Osborne saw that or if he came up with it himself. But I thought that was genius. How many times do you see special teams have too many guys on the field? So you yell at a guy, tell him to go out, and he's running almost backward, going in motion, and you throw him the ball.

I'd definitely say Tom was an offensive genius. But many times it went to simplicity. I remember we'd run the old pitch play. And the next time, he'd go, "They didn't stop it. Run it again." I guess you could say that was the genius of it. If he got something that worked, he would beat that horse until it was dead and then go to the next one.

I didn't really respect a lot of those things until I was lucky enough to play in the NFL with the Chicago Bears in some championship years. How lucky can you get? I have a Super Bowl ring. I've got Big Eight championship rings. I got to play for Tom Osborne and I got to play for Mike Ditka. Talk about two people who are totally opposite as far as personalities, but two people who are very much the same competitively. Coach Ditka was brutally honest. Coach Osborne was obviously more reserved, but just like Coach Ditka, he expected you to be prepared, expected you to know your assignments and expected you to do them right, all the way down to the smallest detail, which he would pick out and say, "Hey, we need to work on this." At Nebraska, we would go over and over things: "Okay, on this play you take a six-inch lead step with your right foot"—every little detail to make it work.

When I was in training camp in Chicago, and this shows you how Mike Ditka was, he came into a team meeting and slammed the door. Of course he's yelling and cussing, and he says, "I am so pissed off. You know what I just had to do? I just had to cut two players that have more heart and more desire than half the guys in this room. The sad thing is they don't have the ability." He just let us have it.

As a player, you knew how much Tom wanted to beat Oklahoma. One thing that always makes me laugh is, we'd be getting ready to play Kansas and on Monday at practice, the defense would be working on the Wishbone, which Oklahoma ran. But Tom would say, "Hey, one game at a time, fellas. We've got to stay focused. We're just playing Kansas this week." And all the players would go, "Yeah, but we're working on the Wishbone." Obviously, that was the game we were preparing for.

Coach Osborne had a great sense of humor. I don't know if he thought he was being funny; maybe we just thought he was. We'd always have meetings on Sunday morning to watch film, and it was the week before the Penn State game my senior year. Coach Osborne said, "Hey, everybody sit down. Okay, we're not going to have meetings on Sunday." Of course, everybody was excited. "But we're going to get together on Monday," he says. And then he says, "I'll see you all on Monday."

I could hear some guys talking, "Hey, let's go hunting. Let's do this and that." All of a sudden, Coach Osborne goes, "Hey, hey, huntin' smuntin', we play Penn State next week." Like I said, I don't know if he meant to be funny, but we all got a kick out of that.

I would say the maddest I ever saw Coach Osborne was in 1981 when we started the season 1-2. We got beat by Iowa and we got beat by Penn State. We weren't playing well, and here I was, hardly playing, just in double-tight-end situations. I hate to say I did it, but I did. He grabs me like he always would do to send in a play and says, "Mitch, Mitch, 'double-tight, 49 pitch.'" And he starts to push me out. Then he goes, "No, no, no." It was one of the few times he was indecisive. He changes the play and he goes, "Get out there." And he pushes me. My foot catches his headset cord and jerks his head down. I look back and my foot catches it again. I see his head go down. He grabs that headset and throws it to the ground. I just take off running. I remember thinking, "I can hardly remember the play. And I don't think I'm ever going to play here again." That was the maddest I've ever seen him. I almost pulled his head right off his shoulders. Now I think the headsets are wireless. Anyway, if Tom didn't swear when I jerked his head that time, he was never going to. You could see that redness coming up on his neck.

Coach Osborne would always come in the locker room at halftime very calmly. He'd say, "Go to the bathroom, get a drink." And he would get up there with the coaches on the chalkboard. Sometimes we weren't playing very well and I remember sitting there, thinking, "I can't believe he's not yelling at us."

But he would just go over and say, "This is what we need to do." I can't remember Coach Osborne talking about winning very much.

What he always talked about was, "If we play to the ability that we're capable of, we will win. That's just what we need to do, guys, just play to the level that we're able to and we'll win." And he was exactly right. It's funny. I've got two boys, and I tell them, "Hey, the challenge is not for you to be the best." That's what Coach Osborne instilled in me. All you can control is yourself. And if every player gets the most out of his ability, you're going to be successful. That's what I've always preached to my kids. You may not be the biggest guy or the strongest guy or the fastest guy, but if you get to be as big and strong and fast, the best athlete you can be, that's all you can do.

It was every play. That was instilled in us. You didn't take a play off. From the time you snapped the ball to the end of the play, you went as hard as you could and did your best. And then you went back and did the next play the same way. It wasn't trying to win the game. It was trying to do your best every play.

I was at training camp with the Dallas Cowboys, we were watching film, and Coach Tom Landry said, "Our wide receivers have got to start blocking better down field. I want to show you a film." What he showed was a Nebraska film. And I was on there. He said, "This is the way wide receivers and tight ends block down field." He got film from Nebraska.

You talk about extremes, Coach Landry would walk around the field and he had a megaphone, an electronic one. He was real soft-spoken. He wouldn't yell at you. He'd just hit the volume on the megaphone. "Mitch, you're supposed to run a 10-yard out." I was like, "Can that guy yell at anybody?" At least Coach Osborne would give you a few "dadgummits" once in a while. Coach Landry wouldn't even raise his voice. He'd just hit the button on the megaphone.

Coach Osborne, so many times we had a conversation that impacted my life. Finally, I'm playing my junior year, I'm getting minutes, running plays in and out with Jamie Williams. That was a big turning point, my junior year. The spring practice after that is when I had that toe problem.

I was running a route and it popped. I went over to the trainer, George Sullivan, and I go, "George, I think I broke my middle toe on my foot." He says, "The hell you did."

I'm like, "I don't know, it's killing me." The toe is flopping around. George pulls off my sock and says, "I think you broke it." So I get an X-ray. They think it's a decalcified bone; the end of the bone looks like honeycomb. The doctors meet with me and say, "We're going to take your middle toe on your right foot off. It won't affect your balance." I said, "What?" They said, "You'll be back pretty quick."

So they took the end of my toe off. Toward the end of spring ball, I was back practicing for about a week and a half. You spend all that time to get up on the depth chart and you don't want to miss time.

I remember I was at the training table, eating, and this gal comes over. "Is Mitch Krenk in here?" she asks. "Coach Osborne needs to see you." Of course everybody at the table goes, "Ooohhh."

On the way over there, I'm like, "Oh crap, what did I do? Was I out too late?" I'm thinking of all this stuff I could have done. I remember walking in his office and Coach Osborne was white as a sheet. The first thing I thought was something bad happened—my parents.

He told me to sit down and then said, "Well, Mitch, they had to do a biopsy on your toe, and it came back and it's malignant. You have cancer." I could tell it was hard for him to say.

At that point, being young, I didn't really understand the ramifications. "Well, what do we do?"

He said the doctors were waiting for me at their office. He said, "They need to talk to you." I've always respected Coach Osborne for that. He was the first one who told me. When I went to the doctors' office, that's when I got scared. They told me, "This is called Ewing's sarcoma," which is a bone cancer. It's often fatal. It's usually in a big, major bone in your body like a thigh or a hip, a back or a shoulder. They said they were very concerned that the toe was a secondary location and they said, "You're going to fly out tomorrow morning to the Mayo Clinic."

I was like, "Oh, my gosh." I can remember leaving there and bawling like a baby. I was like, "Oh, man, I'm done dealing here." Well, to make a long story short, I went to the Mayo Clinic, where doctors took some more of my toe. I played my senior year, didn't go through chemotherapy, and it never re-occurred. I was really lucky. My doctor at the Mayo Clinic had just come back from Europe, where he spoke about Ewing's sarcoma. He was an expert on it, and he wrote an article about it in the *New England Journal of Medicine* on how a patient (they don't use your name) had Ewing's sarcoma in an extremity, not a major bone. It was just a freaky deal.

The Spring Game was a day or two after I found out about the Ewing's sarcoma, and Coach Osborne said, "We can get you up to the Mayo Clinic and you can still play in the Spring Game." I said, "I just don't feel like it, Coach." So he said, "Fine, everything's secure here, Mitch. You go take care of yourself." Coach Osborne touched my life in a lot of ways. And that was a big one.

The first year, I had tests about every three months. I went up to Mayo Clinic for them. After that, for like five years, I went up there every six months. And finally, they just said, "We're going to cause more problems trying to find something. So get out of here. You're okay."

So I had quite the rollercoaster ride between my junior and senior years. But it all turned out well. It was a scary deal, that's for sure. I've often said I wish a lot of people could go through that experience and then end up being okay, because it really puts things in life in perspective. A lot of times I get upset, like we all do, and then all of a sudden, I go, "Naw, it ain't that big of a deal." Looking back, I didn't go on and do things like Lance Armstrong, but I can relate to what he went through. Luckily, I didn't have to go through as much as him. I just had some further surgery and a lot of scares and testing.

It really gets you on a different plane—a different level—I think. Like I said, you almost wish people could experience that and then be able to live their lives. Many times, people experience that at an older age and then live life like maybe they wish they had before. I was 20, 21 years old.

Coach Osborne has had a lot of influence in my life. When I was done playing football, after I got released by the Seattle Seahawks, Coach Osborne said, "Are you done with your school?" I said, "No, I've got one class to take." So he made me a graduate assistant on the freshman team and I coached the tight ends. That paid for my school and I finished my degree. Of course that's the kind of guy he was, too, making sure to give you every opportunity.

What a great era, to be able to just show up. A lot of guys showed up and didn't make it. But at least they had a chance. You just don't have a chance now, a lot of those kids, what I call the late-bloomers, kids like me who graduated high school at about 6-foot-2 and 180 pounds. You can't get recruited now. You're not a linebacker or tight end with 5-flat speed. You just don't get recruited now.

Personally, I wish Coach Osborne was the type of person who would say, "You know what, I think I'm ready to fish and go to grandkids' games, kick back." But obviously that's not Coach Osborne. I'll support him in anything he wants to do, because he supported me. I'm a huge Tom Osborne fan.

I think Coach Osborne was probably competitive in about everything. I bet he was competitive in recruiting. I bet he was competitive on the floor of Congress, when he was trying to get something through. He's going to do his research, I bet. He's going to do everything he can to the best of his ability.

Roger Craig (1980-82)

Nebraska has never had a more enthusiastic, team-oriented player than Roger Craig, who followed his brother Curtis (1975-78) to Lincoln.

He scored 15 touchdowns and averaged 7 yards per carry as a sophomore back-up, rushed for a team-high 1,060 yards as a junior and then agreed to move from I-back to fullback as a senior so that he and Mike Rozier could be on the field at the same time.

While Rozier was breaking the school single-season rushing record, which he would break again the next season, Craig battled injuries as a senior. Even so, he finished fourth on the Cornhuskers' career-rushing list and was a second-round NFL draft pick of the San Francisco 49ers, where he became the definitive West Coast offense back. He was the first player in NFL history to gain 1,000 yards rushing and receiving in the same season, totaling 13,100 yards and 73 touchdowns for his career. More significantly, he contributed to three Super Bowl championships. He is a director of business development and marketing for Tibco, a Bay Area computer software company.

What sold me on Nebraska was Tom Osborne, his character. My junior year in high school, Jamie Williams was getting recruited by college teams from all over the country. No one was really talking to me, and I can remember Coach Osborne telling me, "Roger, I'm coming here next year to get you to come to Nebraska." That just made me feel really good. It changed my life. I could have easily given up and made excuses because I got my leg broken the first game of the season of my junior year in high school. I didn't play the whole season. But Coach Osborne knew how hard I worked out because I had gone to Nebraska and worked out with my brother, Curtis. He let me train with him and the guys a little bit.

So, anyway, my leg was broken my junior year and I had this big cast on and all these recruiters were coming in, all these different scouts, talking to Jamie. I'm hanging out with Jamie, and not one of them said to me, "I'll be back next year and talk to you." Coach Osborne was the only one who said that. It told me a lot about him as a person, and just by him saying that, it motivated me to want to work harder, to come back stronger than ever from the broken leg.

My senior year, I was a high school All-American. In the playoffs, I set a record, ran for 354 yards in one game, made a name for myself. All the schools were coming back then to recruit me. But it was hard for me to look those guys in the face when I knew that Coach Osborne was the only one who had been honest with me and said, "Hey, we'll be back here to get you next year." I respected that.

At Nebraska, it was such a great program, great tradition, and there was a lot of pressure for us to win. We were well prepared, from spring football through the summer all the way through the fall. He ran a first-class organization, with great assistant coaches—smart assistants.

Tom Osborne was a Christian coach. He wouldn't raise his voice much, and when he did raise his voice, he caught our attention real fast. He'd get mad, but he'd always keep his composure. He'd say, "Dadgummit." He'd never cuss but he'd say, "Dadgummit." That's when we knew we'd better get it in gear. He'd get beet red. "Dadgummit, we've got to go to work," he'd say.

We had a lot of respect for him. I have a lot of respect for him still. He could do whatever he wants. That's how smart he is. I thought he was one of the smartest coaches I ever met. Early in my career he definitely schooled me and got me going in the right direction. If you had a problem, he talked with you. I was going to transfer from Nebraska my freshman year because I wasn't playing. But we talked it out. He said I really wasn't ready to play on varsity. And I wasn't. He did the right thing by not pulling me up to varsity. I could have gotten hurt. I wasn't ready to take that kind of pounding as a freshman.

All the freshmen wanted to get in there and play right away. But sometimes you had to listen to the coach. He'd tell when you were ready. It was a smart move that I didn't transfer, because it could have been a disaster. Coach Osborne stuck by his word. He told me to work hard in spring practice and we would see where I was. I worked my butt off and moved up to third team. I was the best third-team running back in the country my sophomore year. I scored 16 touch-downs and had almost 1,000 yards rushing, and I was third-team. So, you know, Coach Osborne got me in when he had to, when I was ready. He knew exactly when to play me. I thank him for that. You had to have the trust in him.

That's why I agreed to move to fullback my senior year. Coach Osborne said to me, "It's going to hurt us to keep you and Mike Rozier both at tailback. If one of you guys gets hot, the other one gets cold, and if you go back and forth, it's going to hurt the team. So would you be willing to play fullback?" I said, "Sure, I'd be happy to." I made the switch. As long as it was going to help our team win, that's all I cared about. I was a team player. There I was, a candidate for the Heisman Trophy and it was my senior year, but I was willing to change positions because Coach Osborne asked me to.

I knew how important it was for him to beat Oklahoma at that time because I watched my brother go through the system. My last two years at Nebraska, we beat the Sooners, and it was a big deal. I wanted to make a statement when we played those guys, because I knew how important it was to Coach Osborne. Barry Switzer had his number for so many years. We got a chance to slap Barry in the face my last two years and that really made me feel good. We didn't win national championships, but that made me feel good to win two Big Eight championships where we beat their butts to do it. It was a big deal for us to beat Oklahoma.

Coach Osborne was organized, very intelligent. His preparation was unbelievable. You look up to guys like that. I took that same atti-tude he exuded. He got me ready for the NFL. He got me ready for dealing with preparing for games, preparing in the off-season, things like working out, being in great condition and just being a good person. That's how I try to conduct my life.

I thought about him a lot throughout my professional career. He really helped me a lot. I was prepared to go to the NFL. I was accus-tomed to studying plays and preparing for games, not making mistakes, being a perfectionist, all those things that make you a great athlete. I was prepared. I was a smart football player, basically. I was a student of the game. Coach Osborne made me a student of the game. That's why it was easy for me to make the transition to being a professional athlete.

He's a genius as a coach; he's definitely a genius. They called Bill Walsh "the genius of the West Coast offense" and "the genius of building the 49ers' dynasty." I think Coach Osborne did a great job of building a dynasty out in Big Red country. He called the plays for Bob Devaney. He was the man for that. Coach Osborne was behind the scenes. I would say that he built that dynasty for years, throughout the '70s, '80s and '90s. That was just unbelievable, 30-some years of great, great football.

You know another cool thing about Coach Osborne? He knows everyone's name in my family. Whenever I see Coach Osborne, he always asks, "How's Raslyn doing?" That's my baby sister. How does he remember her name? It's amazing. He's so great with names. That's what I respect the most. People mean a lot to him. For him to remember stuff like that is incredible.

I saw Coach Osborne recently. We talked for a long time. I was telling him some things I want to do for former players who might be having problems. I want to create a website where we can generate some revenue, bring players in for games, pay for their flights and figure out jobs, like job placement. I've got some other players involved, too. So he said, "Hey, count me in. Just let me know." He's still committed to helping us after we're out of the game. He doesn't have to do that. But he said, "Count me in. I'll do whatever I can. Let me know what I can do for you guys."

Woody Paige (1983, 1985)

Had it been up to him, Woody Paige would have stayed on the West Coast. He was from San Francisco and wanted to play football at UCLA. The decision wasn't his alone, however. His dad was concerned about the stability at UCLA, specifically that Bruins coach Terry Donahue might leave for the NFL. His dad also was impressed by Osborne. So with a promise that he could earn a scholarship if he worked hard, Paige, a high school teammate of Cornhusker scholarship recruit Anthony Thomas, walked on. Paige earned a scholarship, playing on special teams and as a back-up defensive back. He served with the U.S. Army Reserves in Saudi Arabia during Desert Storm and has made his home in Lincoln, Nebraska, working as an assistant on an open-heart surgery team at Bryan LGH East Medical Center.

Clete Fischer came to my high school to recruit Anthony Thomas. That was the connection. We had a scrimmage at a junior high field, actually, and I guess I did pretty well in the scrimmage. They were pretty impressed with it. Coach Fischer asked, "What year is he?" My coach told him I was just a junior, and Coach Fischer said, "We'll be back." That was my first contact with the University of Nebraska.

It was interesting, growing up in San Francisco and being recruited by a lot of schools in the Pac-10 and then coming out here. The relationship Coach Osborne had with my father, I think, was pretty much what locked, signed, sealed, and delivered for me to come to Nebraska. I thought I was going to UCLA until my dad had something to say about it. He and Coach Osborne developed a nice little relationship and they thought Nebraska would be the best place for me.

Due to a lot of the things my friends were into, I think it probably worked out. I couldn't complain. I enjoyed the time I had here. I made it my home.

George Darlington did most of the recruiting on the West Coast. Coach Darlington and Coach Osborne visited my house. That's how the relationship between my father and Coach Osborne got started. They also were recruiting Jack Del Rio at the time. He was from the Bay Area, too. He went to school in Hayward. Jack was a cool kid. He wanted some assurances that he would get a chance to play varsity right away. Coach Darlington emphasized, "No, you guys have to play junior varsity. We have a junior varsity program. We'll evaluate you that way and then we'll put you on the varsity." Jack told them, "USC told me I'm going to get a shot to play with the varsity." So that pretty much sealed his decision to go to USC.

I was going to UCLA. Coach Osborne and the Nebraska coaches were pretty cool. They said, "We're going to be around for a long time. We've been at Nebraska this long." That's what pretty much sold my dad, because Terry Donahue, at the time, was kind of a young coach at UCLA and there was always talk of him going to the NFL. On the West Coast that's what the talk was. He never did. He ended up staying at UCLA for almost 20 years. I also had a nice relationship with Don James at the University of Washington. Those were three pretty significant coaches.

But my dad, Woody Sr., wouldn't sign a letter of intent for any place but Nebraska. It was cool. I enjoyed it. I couldn't complain. It was one of those things where father knows best. You may not want to do it. You may think, "This is my decision." But it isn't. Or it wasn't for me.

They gave away the last scholarship before I got here. But Coach Osborne assured me I would be listed as a walk-on, like Jimmy Williams and his brother Toby, but said, "We'll put you on scholarship if you earn it." I said, "I have no problem with that." Eventually, I got a scholarship. He didn't make any guarantees, any promises, at least to me, that I was going to play or anything like that. He said, "You're going to have to earn your playing time." And I said, "I understand that."

Several of us were going to leave Nebraska at one point in time, guys that weren't too happy with the situation. But my father made me realize that there were a lot of things in my corner that I could have changed. I didn't realize what big-time college football was about when I got here. I thought it was going to be like high school. You get your playbook. You go over the plays in practice and you just practice that way. When I first got here, they gave us like 15 plays, with six different formations. Then the next day they gave us 10 different plays and another five different formations. I figured we were going to go over it in practice. The stuff we went over in practice was the stuff today, not what they gave us yesterday. And the stuff we did yesterday, we were supposed to know.

I'm out there thinking, "Well, we'll go over it in practice." When they called the play, you were supposed to know it. Don't be out there running around like you didn't know it. I was unhappy with that situation. I wasn't climbing the depth chart. I was pretty much doing a descent. So I went in and told Coach Osborne that I didn't think this was going to be the best place for me anymore. He called my dad. And my dad told me, "You'd better open your playbook and open up your school books, buckle down." Once I did that, things started changing.

I hadn't thought I was being accepted too well. But Coach Osborne made me realize that the only thing I wasn't doing was learning my material that I should have learned. Once I started picking that up a little bit better, I started seeing the field a little bit more.

I came here as a wingback and punt-and-kickoff-return specialist. I was one of the top high school kickoff returners in northern California. My freshman year, I played wingback and returned punts and kickoffs. When we lost Ric Lindquist and Allen Lyday—they were seniors and defensive backs—the coaches wanted me to be a defensive back, a cornerback. Coach Osborne approached me in the hallway and said, "Woody, we'd like you to play defensive back."

I said, "Sure, I'd be interested in playing safety."

He said, "We don't need any safeties, Woody. We need corners."

I was like, "Well, Coach, I want to play safety."

That was another little thing we went around about. He had to make another phone call to my dad, who then told me, "If this is going to get you on the field a little sooner, you need to be thinking about cornerback." So I was a cornerback after that. Me being strong-headed as I was, Coach Osborne would make a call to my dad and my dad would clear things up for him.

Before we got here as freshmen, they told us who our roommates were going to be. I was going to room with Guy Rozier, Mike's brother. So I called him in advance and talked to him and his family. Once we got that squared away it was pretty cool. We knew each other before we even got together. Guy was the social one and Mike just kept to himself. They were like the brothers I never had. They can't do any wrong in my eyes.

I couldn't complain. I had a lovely time here. I believe if it wasn't for Coach McBride, Coach Darlington and Coach Osborne, I probably wouldn't have played a down here. I had a great time here. It was a beautiful experience.

Coach Osborne was down to earth. He was a wonderful man. He was a good leader. The first time I suited up for a varsity game, I think we were playing Penn State, my freshman year. We're in the locker room and I think we were down at halftime. I consider myself one of the old-school players, when coaches used to grab you by the facemask, throw you on the ground, punch you in the helmet, "Go out there, get mad and kill somebody." We're sitting on the offensive side of the locker room and Coach Osborne comes in, and the first thing that comes out of his mouth is "Dadgummit." I'm like, "What did he just say?"

Coach Osborne didn't swear or cuss, anything like that. But down the hall, you hear Charlie McBride, "Flim, flam, flam, flim, flam, flam, flam." The bombs were flying. I'm hearing Coach

Osborne, but I'm not getting motivated. I'm hearing Coach McBride and I want to run through a wall. So that probably meant I needed to be on the defensive side of the ball.

I never heard Coach Osborne swear—never, ever. I saw him get red, though. But then he calmed down. Nothing came out of his mouth that was foul. After the 1984 Orange Bowl, he got frustrated with reporters who were wondering why he didn't kick the extra point and tie Miami. He said, "Our boys came down here to win the game." And we should have won the game. We could have kicked the extra point, tied the game and been crowned national champs. But how were we going to live with that? We had to go down there and win. No way in the world were we going to leave with a tie.

I enjoyed Coach Osborne. Practice was great, the way he would conduct it. We had this option drill, and it seemed like every time Tom Rathman and I would get matched up, we would do this one-on-one option drill where we tried to knock the heck out of each other. And Coach Osborne would be like, "If you keep this up, you're not going to have anything left for practice." He was a real card. He was a great head coach.

3

Great Expectations

(1986-92)

The position was perfect for a national championship run, No. 2 in the rankings. That's where Nebraska began the 1987 season, and that's where it remained until mid-November. After an off-week, the Cornhuskers moved to No. 1, trading places with Oklahoma, which had beaten Missouri 17-13. The timing couldn't have been worse. The Sooners came to Lincoln for what was hyped as the "Game of the Century II," and the reversal in rankings provided additional incentive. Not that they needed anything extra. They controlled the game, which lacked the drama of the 1971 "Game of the Century," winning 17-7.

That was the next-to-last time Tom Osborne would coach against Barry Switzer, whose final season at Oklahoma was in 1988—with Nebraska winning 7-3 at Norman. The victory ended the Sooners' 31-game conference winning streak and gave the Cornhuskers the Big Eight title. Osborne would coach only one more loss against Oklahoma, in 1990, and finish with a 13-13 record against the Sooners.

Outside linebacker Broderick Thomas and quarterback Steve Taylor, among the seniors on the 1988 team, were members of a 1985 recruiting class rated by one analyst as the nation's second-best. The class held together even though Osborne underwent double-bypass heart surgery a week before letter-

of-intent signing day. His presence and the esteem in which he was held by parents and guardians as well as the athletes themselves were important elements in the recruiting process.

Osborne's teams won 10 or more games each season from 1986 to 1989. But the Cornhuskers managed only the one conference title and struggled in bowl games. In fact, after defeating LSU in the 1987 Sugar Bowl, they lost seven in a row, including four by 20 or more points.

Nebraska was a combined 68-16-1 from 1986 to 1992 but slid in the national rankings. In 1989, the Cornhuskers dropped out of the top 10 in the final Associated Press poll, and in 1990 they dropped out of the top 20, finishing No. 24, the lowest during Osborne's career. Two of their three losses that season came against teams that split the national championship, Colorado and Georgia Tech. In 1991, they were never higher than No. 9 in the AP poll, even though their only losses were to co-national champions Washington and Miami. And in 1992, they were never higher than No. 7.

Osborne's run-oriented offense was criticized for lack of imagination. Nebraska, which completed barely 40 percent of its passes in 1986 and averaged fewer than 100 yards passing per game, needed to throw more, critics said. They also said Osborne couldn't win the big game, pointing to the bowl-losing streak as evidence. Such reasoning was circular, however. Any Nebraska loss was big, so by definition, Osborne couldn't win the big one. Plus, critics didn't take into account the fact that six of the seven bowl losses were against Florida teams, Miami and Florida State, in Florida, at the Orange Bowl.

During a news conference prior to the 1992 Orange Bowl game against Miami, which was ranked No. 1 in the AP poll, Osborne talked about what he perceived to be growing disaffection with his coaching. "There are people in Nebraska who would like to see somebody else try it, probably," he said. "And there are some who are willing to go along with me a little longer." Even though the Cornhuskers had gone 9-1-1 in the regular season and shared the conference title with Colorado, his 18th season as head coach had been "unpleasant" and had "given me a little bit more jaundiced view of the whole situation."

He was the winningest active coach in NCAA Division I-A, with a 186-42-3 record. The Cornhuskers had been ranked as high as third by the AP as late as November in 11 of his seasons. And they had won or shared eight conference championships. But expectations were exceedingly high. "Last year drilled some things into my head about how things really are. You can get lulled to sleep," he said.

Osborne never so much as dozed, however. He continued to evaluate what he was doing defensively as well as offensively and began to change his focus. He had always emphasized controlling what could be controlled, winning the conference title, and never talked about the national championship unless asked. That couldn't be controlled, he said, so it shouldn't be a goal—at least not one to be discussed. By the early 1990s, he had become more open about the national championship.

Early in his tenure as head coach, Osborne had changed his offense, patterning it after Oklahoma's. To beat Oklahoma, he concluded, Nebraska had to play the way Oklahoma did. Colorado took the same approach and won a national championship in 1990 with a run-oriented offense similar to Nebraska's. Kansas State did the same thing during its rise in the Big 12's north division in the late 1990s.

In the late 1980s, as the bowl losses mounted, Osborne began to consider how he might change his defense to deal with the passing attacks of warm-weather teams. The changes he decided to make would have a significant impact on the remarkable finish to his Hall of Fame career.

Broderick Thomas (1985-88)

Broderick Thomas, the "Sandman," was brash, his personality seemingly more suited to Oklahoma than Nebraska. And he probably would have gone to Oklahoma if Coach Barry Switzer hadn't insisted on playing him at defensive end. Thomas was determined to play outside linebacker; he wasn't interested in being a down lineman, as he had been at Houston's

Madison High School. "If Barry was a lying guy, he would have got me,"
said Thomas, a first-round NFL draft pick who played for the Switzer-
coached Dallas Cowboys, among other teams, during his 10 professional
seasons.

Thomas adjusted—though he continued to speak his mind to
reporters—and Osborne adjusted. And they both benefited. Thomas
played as a true freshman, outside linebacker. He was a two-time All-
American, as well as a three-time, first-team all-conference selection, and
a senior co-captain. He never hid his passion for the game or for Osborne
and Nebraska.

Tom was quiet. Really, I have never been scared of much. But Tom
almost scared me. He has a calm about him that will make you alert
right away. Tom walks in. He's a tall drink of water; you can see that.
And he's just so calm. You're like, "Man." There were people standing
outside my house when they heard that Tom Osborne was coming to
my neck of the woods. My God, it was a buzz. We had 11 Division I
recruits at my high school, and the buzz was, "Tom Osborne is
coming to get Broderick Thomas."

That buzz was all through Houston. "Hey, man, they say Tom
Osborne is coming to get the kid from Houston." You've got these
other schools coming in and everybody's in awe of Tom. They're not
even paying attention to these other guys' signing. It was me and
Tom. He has that effect everywhere he goes. There aren't many—
Barry Switzer, Joe Paterno, and Jimmy Johnson at the time. When
they show up, everybody starts getting antsy, putting their hands in
their pockets, like, "Man, is that him?"

Tom didn't just influence me in recruiting. He influenced my
mom and my high school defensive coordinator. When he walked out
of my house, my mom told me, "That man who just left here, that's
where I want you to go to school because he's a God-fearing man, a
godly man, and he's a trustworthy man. Out of everybody I've lis-

tened to, I trust that man right there." And that was it. Me and my mom are very close. You know how it is; I'm Momma's boy. And she said, "That's the one I trust."

If not Nebraska, it would have been Oklahoma. The problem I had with Oklahoma was they wanted me to play defensive end. I was a defensive end in high school. I came to Nebraska and learned how to play outside linebacker on the run. I had never played linebacker in my life, but I had no desire to get any bigger. I didn't want to play any more defensive line. I said I wanted to move to linebacker.

I had two issues with Nebraska. I didn't want to redshirt. I said, "I'm coming right in and I'm going to play. Give me the four years and I'm good." At that time, everybody at Nebraska was redshirting. Tom said he would give me a chance to come in and play right away and if I could handle it, he would let me. When he said that, the whole deal was over. I turned down my visit to Oklahoma. I had scheduled a visit, but I thought the pressure would be too much to even visit Oklahoma and come out of there not saying, "I'm going to Oklahoma." I've always been an Oklahoma fan. You don't tell Tom you're going to Nebraska and the next thing you know, you come back and say, "Oh no, I'm going to Oklahoma."

Tom was real cool and you could just see trust on his face. You could feel it. Tom has a presence. And that presence is hard to beat, even when it comes to Barry Switzer. I wouldn't have played for Barry in the pros if he wasn't a trustworthy guy. Barry told me, "You'll be an All-American as a sophomore at defensive end." I said, "Coach, I don't want to play defensive end anymore. I'm done with it."

Barry's a man of his word also. He's my kind of guy. But Tom is THE guy. You're going to 1A or 1B, Nebraska or Oklahoma—two of the best universities in America, two of the most competitive, two that the national championship is going to go through your backyard.

Tom is a very careful person. You're not going to get him to jump on anything. Tom is going to research everything. He's very intelligent but real reserved. He didn't talk about winning national championships. He just talked about winning games and being in position at the end of the year to be able to do whatever you wanted. He never talked about it, but you knew it was on his mind. For three years straight it was between Oklahoma and us who was going to play for the national championship. He just made sure he was preparing us for it.

I played in the pros for Tony Dungy and Dennis Green, two of the smartest coaches ever. And Tom Osborne was sitting right there with them. He had us totally and fully prepared for everything. He went over everything. What are you going to do? What call would you make? Tom would ask in front of everyone, "Broderick, if we block a punt and the ball goes over the line of scrimmage and you get a chance to run it back, what are you going to do?"

"Well, I can run it back because it's our ball." You'd better have the right answer, or he'd be looking at you kind of different.

Tom seemed very soft-spoken. He spoke calmly but aggressively. I'll never forget him telling us, "At the end of the day when I look across that field, I want to know, to be able to tell my team, that they have quit on the other side. We play four full quarters of football. Come the fourth quarter, they should quit."

I saw Tom get mad and show emotion one time. We were getting beat up by Iowa State. I think it was my sophomore year. That's the only time I really, truly saw him mad. Normally, even if he's mad, you don't know it until he says something to you. At halftime, if we weren't losing, we were close to losing and we were physically getting beat up by Iowa State. And he came in and said, "Dadgummit, you're the No. 1 team in the country and you're getting beat up." He snapped his palms together and said, "Dadgummit." And his watch came loose. I'll never forget that. "Boy, I ain't ever seen Coach Osborne even talk aggressive." So we went out there and just finished up. "The 'Redhead' is mad. Hey, let's go." We went ahead and took care of it. Everybody in the locker room knew he was mad. If he was going to say a curse word, he would have said it that day. Other than that, he was just real cool and reserved and collected. He was a smooth operator. He'll let you know that his attack is aggressive, but he's not going to get out of character to sell you that. He and Coach Dungy are a lot alike. They're just real reserved. They're going to express themselves very sternly, and that's it. Tom is just the coolest dude. He's a brilliant person.

It took me to leave Nebraska to know why he had Charlie McBride as defensive coordinator. He didn't have to get out of character because he had Coach McBride to strangle somebody. Tom would sit back and manage everything. And when anything got out of line, Charlie was going to attack it head-on anyway. So all he had to do was back Charlie down. Charlie was still spitting and cussing and Tom would be like, "Now calm down, Charlie. It's going to be okay."

If it got to where he thought Charlie couldn't handle it—and there wasn't anything Charlie couldn't handle around there—then Tom would step in. Other than that, he would let Charlie choke somebody. And they'd finish it up like that. The thing about it is, if you meet the two of them, you'd be like, "How in the heck can they work together?" But they worked like a charm. They were perfect together. Tom had a wonderful staff. Milt Tenopir was one of the best offensive line coaches I ever met. And I've met some good ones.

Tom has a sense of humor. I've been in the big meeting room when he hit a line and the whole meeting was falling out because, "Hey, the 'Redhead,' he don't smile. He don't laugh. He don't joke. The 'Redhead' is just serious." It was always good to see him with his sense of humor, because we didn't expect it. But he's a fun-loving person.

Tom is always thinking. All those times he was running around that field after practice, there was something on his mind. That's the only time you hoped that he didn't stop jogging, and come over to pull you aside. You hoped he kept running. We might still be on the field but you noticed it would kind of clear out when Tom got to jogging because he might just slow down and say, "Hey, excuse me, meet me down there at the corner." That meant some issues.

Tom knew how to put things together. If I got a head-coaching job somewhere, I'd call Tom. "Coach, I'm going to put you on speed dial. I need to know how to run a program. I'm going to talk to you, Coach." I've seen some things in Tom that other people might not see.

He is a special guy, a father figure. I got a chance to know him because I was having issues and I was thinking of leaving Nebraska when I was a freshman. We came within one meeting. I just didn't think I was being treated fair. Inside I was on fire but I was burning myself down. If it wasn't for Tom being fair, I would have left. I should have started my freshman year. And I made it known.

Another thing was, I was so strange to the rest of my teammates, they didn't understand me. They didn't understand my fire. They didn't understand where I came from. It took them a while. Through that time, I had to talk to Tom a lot. I was loud, rambunctious and reckless. I came to Nebraska to win a national title, not one but a couple. And we should have won a couple. But we fell short. When I look back, I had too much fire. I needed a guy like Tom. I needed a guy to calm me down, tell me it was going to be all right. My fuse was always short. I was ready to play at the drop of a hat. If the wind kicked up, I was ready. Tom was real calm. It was like they dropped me off on the moon until I talked to Tom or Charlie. It was rough at first, but all the things I went through just made me better.

I love Nebraska and Tom Osborne so much. If I could say one thing that stands out, Tom always taught and preached that we were family. When I was there, I fought for the defense to get some credit. My thing was, "Listen, we play ball on the other side of the ball, too."

The history of Nebraska has always been mauling people on offense. I had a problem with that. "Are we going to get any credit over here on defense? Hey, you've got to give us some credit. I play for one of the best defensive coordinators in all of college football, and we don't get no credit. Hey, man, we're balling over here." Through four years, that was one of my biggest negatives.

If Tom was coaching right now, I would tell my son, "If you want to take visits, you can. But you are going to see Tom. And you are not just going to see Tom, you are going to play for him, because I trust Tom." I would love for my son to play for Tom. It would be a no-brainer. We wouldn't have to take visits. There is no other man that you would want to raise your son than Tom. He's a wonderful man. He's a man that to this day, if I get into a big situation, I call him right now. "Hey, Coach, what would you do?" You're not only going to get a fair answer, you're going to get the best answer.

I'm sometimes overwhelmed still. People ask, "Did you play for Tom?" I say, "Yes, yes, I did." I'm proud to say that. I watched him deal with situations on our team. Sometimes other coaches would tell you it's time to leave. But Tom is fair. As long as you're fair with me, we're good for life; just don't try to cheat me. I thought Tom was the fairest man; he and my uncle Mike Singletary are the two fairest men I've ever met in my life.

If Tom tells you you're going to get a chance to play, you're going to get your shot. A lot of schools, their deal is they recruit you so they don't have to play against you. But when Tom gives you his word, he doesn't have to swear and promise to God. When he opens his mouth, it's a promise to the good Lord. That's what he's going to do. That's very hard to find, especially in Division I football. I help kids look for schools. I try to help people, use my name as best I can. People will tell you, Broderick is an honest person. I try to do the things that will make Coach Osborne proud.

Steve Taylor (1985-88)

Though he wore a No. 3 jersey at Lincoln High in San Diego because he was a Joe Montana fan, Steve Taylor was labeled the next Turner Gill when he signed a letter of intent with Nebraska. Gill did influence his decision to sign with Nebraska. His skills as a runner were suited to Osborne's option offense, but Taylor also considered himself a passer. Recruiters from other schools tried to convince him that the Cornhuskers weren't interested in throwing. "But they threw the ball, in my eyes," he said. "I thought Turner was a pretty good passer. He was there, so I figured it would be a great place to go." Taylor was a three-year starter and finished fifth in career passing as well as first in career rushing by a quarterback, setting a single-season record with 826 rushing yards as a senior. After playing in the Canadian Football League, he returned to Lincoln and works in real estate.

I remember watching the 1984 Orange Bowl game, the one Nebraska lost to Miami—the way the Cornhuskers came back, the enthusiasm, the integrity, and the character they played with. And then when Coach Osborne went for two points and the win, that was just awesome. He easily could have kicked an extra point and won a national championship. But he went for it. Although they didn't get it, that decision alone convinced me Nebraska was the place for me.

I played the latter part of my senior year knowing that I would most likely go to Nebraska. I took visits to other schools, just to kind of see other campuses and what they had to offer. But the decision was fairly easy. Nebraska had great linemen, great running backs and a great coach. So there was no better place to play than Nebraska. It was just a good fit for me.

The first time I met Coach Osborne, he came to my school, he and George Darlington. I was in class and some girl came and said there were these two guys with red blazers in the gym, looking for me. It's the middle of winter, and Coach Osborne and Coach Darlington aren't tan. They're pale white. They've got that rough skin—weathered skin, cold-weather skin. Coach has red hair and he's 6-foot-4.

Coach Osborne was a big factor in my decision to go to Nebraska. Other coaches promised me a lot of things. But Coach Osborne said, "Steve, I can only promise you one thing: You'll get a good education. You will definitely play quarterback. Don't worry about being switched to a different position."

He had told me they thought I could play relatively early. At that time it was pretty much unheard of for freshman quarterbacks to play at Nebraska, to make the traveling squad. I thought I would play on the freshman team and redshirt, then be a three-year starter, something like that. Things just progressed a lot sooner. I think it caught Coach Osborne off-guard a little bit. Nebraska, at that time, you came in, played on the freshman team, redshirted, and then played on the varsity. Turner started midway in his sophomore year. It was a little different. But I got the opportunity to play in a couple of big games as a freshman.

What made the experience unique was that I was with Coach every day in quarterback meetings, so I got to know him on a different level. Broderick Thomas was my roommate, and Broderick and I used to have conversations about that. Broderick didn't like it. He didn't like that the head coach was also the offensive coordinator, because he thought the offense got special treatment. He always commented about how scrimmages were geared for the offense to look good. He had a little thing about Coach, that Coach favored offensive players. That was Broderick's spin on it.

I think Coach realized he had to treat players differently—Broderick differently than Turner or Tommie Frazier, Lawrence Phillips, Scott Frost or Eric Crouch, whoever it might be. Once he established those relationships, there was a better bond. Then the defensive players loved him as much as the offensive players. That quiet confidence just started to come out. I think he grew as a coach as far as relating to players, motivating them and saying it's okay to go after the national championship. When I was there, our goals were really within the team—win this game, win that game, be Big Eight champs. Our goal was never to be national champions. We never said openly, "Win the national championship." It was kept quiet. But afterward, it came out that it was a goal of his to be national champions. And there's nothing wrong with that. I saw that. It was just a gradual progression. It became more and more of a focus.

It took me a year and a half, two years, to be comfortable around Coach Osborne, because my personality was a little bit different than Turner's. Turner looked at Coach almost like a father figure. I just looked at him as a great guy and a coach. I don't think I was as reserved as Turner, which was fine. I think it took Coach a little time to get used to my personality and for me to get used to him.

My first year or two, people compared me to Turner so much, I had to be quiet and say the right things. That just wasn't me. I'm like that, but not all the time. I laugh. I'm jovial. I really blossomed in my junior year. I didn't want to be Turner. Turner was a great quarterback. But I have a different personality. When I came and started, I think it opened Coach Osborne's eyes, "Hey, you can be a young player at a key position and contribute dramatically to a team." I think that gave him the ability to let Tommie Frazier play so early. And that helped the whole thing.

Coach Osborne was very humble. I was humble, but I was confident, too. I would speak my mind. I needed to do that. You can keep your personality and not be offensive or come across as arrogant or cocky. If you feel you're better and you're going to win, you can say that. But you've got to say it in a manner that's not going to be taken the wrong way. Anyway, we got to know each other quite well.

You don't appreciate how good of a coach he was until you leave and play for other coaches. That's when you start to think, "We really did have something special at Nebraska." You appreciate it at the time. But until you play for other coaches, who weren't that caring, who could be quite rude, quite arrogant, and might not have had your best interests at heart, you don't really appreciate the type of coach you had. He knew about all aspects of the game. Not only did he know offensively what the opponent was doing, he knew defensively. I saw on many occasions where he would consult with Charlie McBride about things defensively. From my experience, you didn't find too many head coaches who had that much command over every aspect of the game, offensively, defensively and special teams, as well as personnel. That's when you really respect him as a coach.

There were only two games I wish I could have over again, the Oklahoma game and the Florida State game my junior year. We were better than what we played. If we had won those games, we would have been national champions. I think we had a better team than Oklahoma. But there were a lot of things that came into play. We had a week off. We said some things—actually not the week before the game but earlier in the year, after we played Missouri—that we were going to kill Oklahoma. That really wasn't what we said. We had beat up on Missouri and were asked about Oklahoma. And we said, "We think we can beat Oklahoma this year." Oklahoma had a good ball club, and once that got out, they got motivated. They played well that day. And we didn't. That's one game I wish we could have played over.

Tom and I used to run into each other quite a bit with his grandkids and my daughter playing soccer together. He would try to be in disguise at games, with a fishing hat and some sunglasses. It's great that he got all of the accolades, but he would have been a great coach in my eyes, regardless. Anyone who would go for two in the situation he did against Miami, speaks a lot about someone's integrity; it does for me. And then the way he handled the Lawrence Phillips thing. I'll never forget that. I was playing in Canada then, and when Coach let Phillips come back to the team, guys were giving me a hard time. They said, "You guys at Nebraska are just about winning." I said, "No, we see it as Coach is giving a guy an opportunity, and whatever happens, happens. He's going to do what he thinks is in the best interests of the player, regardless of what the media or people think he should do or say."

That's why I'm not surprised he went into politics. He wants to have an impact. He is really a sincere individual. I played for some coaches who just looked out for themselves. Of course, they were professional coaches. But they looked out for themselves, said one thing and did another. You don't run into too many like Coach Osborne at the professional level or the college level. He coached because he loved to do it and because he was developing young men. I knew he would be in the Hall of Fame if he won a national championship. But even if he hadn't, he'd still be a Hall of Fame coach to me.

Jeff Jamrog (1985-87)

Even though he had scholarship offers from smaller schools, Jeff Jamrog walked on at Nebraska, paying his own way but with an assurance from Osborne that he could earn a scholarship. Having grown up in Omaha, he was familiar with the Cornhuskers' tradition of embracing walk-ons. He was a running back at Elkhorn Mt. Michael High School but played defensive end from the beginning at Nebraska, backing up Broderick Thomas as a junior and then moving to the other side to start as a senior, when he was a first-team academic all-conference honoree. Osborne was true to his word, of course; Jamrog earned a scholarship. He returned to Nebraska as an assistant coach under Frank Solich (2000-03), working with the defensive line, and is now the head coach at Minnesota State-Mankato, turning that program around in his first year.

I wanted to play football at the highest level possible, and obviously growing up in Nebraska, I went to games at Memorial Stadium from about the fifth grade on. Maybe it was before the fifth grade, but that rings a bell. I always enjoyed the games, just being a part of it, going down by the locker room before the game, seeing the players come out of the locker room and then going over and watching the visiting team come out at halftime. I thought that was a pretty neat deal.

When I went down to Nebraska on an official recruiting visit, Coach Osborne told me if they had one more scholarship, I might be the guy to get it. And I believed him. Cletus Fischer did a good job of selling me on Nebraska, telling me that I would have a chance to prove myself. I played Midget Football in eighth grade with a couple of guys who got Division I scholarships and my mindset was, "I'm just as good as those guys." Going to Mt. Michael, I don't know if that hurt me, but it was a Class B school.

You're not quite as smart when you're 17 or 18 years old, but my mind-set was that I could make it. I was recruited by Iowa State, South Dakota and the University of Nebraska-Omaha; they all offered me scholarships. The coach from South Dakota did a really good job of recruiting me. He played at Nebraska—Jeff Carpenter. He was a captain. He said something I always remembered: "You know what, Jeff, I think you're a heck of a player. In fact, I think you're better coming out of high school than I was."

I put two and two together. "Wait a minute, if this guy ended up playing for a couple of years at Nebraska and was a captain his senior year, maybe I can go down there and play." What he said stuck with me. I don't know if he meant it or he was just trying to be nice to me. I kidded him about that later on.

Coach Osborne told me he was going to treat me just like a scholarship player. He said, "You're going to be able to eat at the training table. You've just got to pay for your education, and when you get on the two-deep, you're going to have a chance to get a scholarship." And that's how it played out. I knew he had put other guys on scholarship. He said he held back a couple of scholarships for walk-ons every year. You get some attrition and other things happen. There was a track record of guys walking on and succeeding, from being All-Big Eight to All-American to Academic All-American, guys getting put on scholarship after a couple of years. He showed me that on paper.

Back when I played, Nebraska had the freshman team. I probably walked on with 60 guys plus the scholarship class. I don't know what the exact numbers were between the varsity and the freshman team, but there were a lot of players. I thought Coach Osborne did an outstanding job of getting to know people. Whether you were the 200th guy on the team or the star, he did an excellent job of getting to know you. It's just natural with him being the offensive coordinator, being in the meetings, that maybe offensive people felt they knew Coach Osborne better, but I think he did a great job of getting to know the defense and watching our side of the ball, too. I thought he did a great job of balancing that because it's a fine line when you're the head coach and you're calling the offensive plays to get enamored with the offense.

He was a tremendous teacher. He made great halftime adjustments and week-to-week adjustments. That always hit home, the adjustments he made, particularly on the offense. And he did a great job of conveying what needed to be done in the second half to win or keep the momentum going. Sometimes he was more adamant about finishing off the second half, even though you might be up 25 or 30 points. It's not always about the scoreboard, basically. As he said in his book *More Than Winning*, it's about playing your best football. It doesn't matter if you're up by 28 or down seven.

He set weekly goals, and if you met the majority of the goals, you had a pretty good game. I remember sometimes winning but not meeting the goals. So even though it might have been a happy locker room after the game, come Monday when you went over the goals, boy, maybe you hadn't played as well as you thought you had. It was evident over the years. He lost to a team that finished the season with a losing record only one time. That's a perfect example of not overlooking people, having a one-track mind, taking one game at a time. Players can sense if you're looking past the next opponent. But whether it was Kansas or Oklahoma or Oklahoma State, it didn't matter. He was zeroed in on the upcoming opponent.

When I was a graduate assistant, I saw Tom play basketball one time, just a pick-up game, and you could tell then that he was all business. He wants to win at whatever he does. The way he goes about it is, he rolls up his sleeves and gets after it. He's just not vocal about it. That's why some people don't realize how competitive he is, how driven, day in and day out, his work ethic. That will always stick with me, the hours he put in, whatever he was doing, recruiting or game-planning, getting ready to win.

Some people will eventually remember a name. They'll say, "Keep telling me your name every time I see you, and maybe by the third or fourth time I'll get it. But I might forget it a month or two down the road." With Coach Osborne, it was amazing how many players he coached over the years and then remembered their names when they showed up to watch practice. He even remembered parents' names. My dad showed up at practice one time, and Coach Osborne said, "Hey, Jerry, how're you doing?" I was like, "Man, that guy's amazing."

I've kept in touch with Coach Osborne. After the coaching staff was fired at Nebraska, I remember calling him early in the morning and asking if he would make a call for me. And I remember him saying, "Well, it's going to be tough to call right away because I have a flight at 8 a.m. But I'll let you know how it goes when I do." I got a call at 2:30 that afternoon and he said, "I got a hold of the guy right before I got on the plane, when it was ready for boarding, and had a nice conversation. I think you've got a chance at the job. Let me know how it goes." To call me right after he landed in Washington, D.C., to tell me, that was pretty impressive.

A lot of what he talked about were principles, what it takes to win rather than about the games themselves, what life's all about, what teamwork's all about. I remember a lot of his speeches being more about life than about what was going to take place on the field.

For me, probably the biggest things that describe Coach Osborne are hard work and perseverance. Those are the things I took from him. You're going to have a chance in life, as well as in football, with hard work and perseverance, just sticking with it. Eventually, good things are going to happen with those ingredients.

Tom Banderas (1985-87)

How's this for efficiency? Tom Banderas caught only 16 passes during his Cornhusker career. But he scored touchdowns on 10 of them. And if more passes had been thrown his way, he would have scored more touchdowns. "That was the beauty of the play-action pass," Guy Ingles said.

Ingles, a former Cornhusker wide receiver and assistant coach, understood the system on which Banderas capitalized. Banderas played tight end. He was the strongest of the receivers and he was big enough to play in the interior of the offensive line, a rugged perimeter blocker. But when an opposing defense committed its safeties to run support, he became Mr. Touchdown.

That was never more apparent, or more satisfying, than in Nebraska's 42-7 victory at Missouri in 1987. Banderas, who was from Oak Grove, Missouri, caught three passes, all for touchdowns.

He has made Lincoln his home, working in insurance.

Consistency—that's the word I'm going with to describe Coach Osborne. He really made hay in recruiting with the consistency of the program. I had been recruited by and took visits to USC, Texas, Notre Dame, and Colorado—Bill McCartney's first year. Those programs were all good. Well, Colorado probably wasn't at the time, but the other three were. Historically, they were powerhouses. I just think it had to do with the consistency of the program at Nebraska and the consistency of T.O. When you came here, when you were recruited by his staff, they liked your style of play for that position, and chances were you were probably going to get to stay there at that position. I was more of a power-blocker, like an extra guard out there. A different coach with a passing style might not have thought my game was very good. I might have had to go, maybe, to guard or defensive end.

I think from that consistency, you knew T.O. and the coaches were going to be there for five or six years. You knew that you were probably going to be in a bowl game. And if you put together a good season, you were going to have a chance to win a national championship.

Coach Osborne had a calming effect, again because of that consistency. He was always there, always the same, always level headed—just consistent. That's going to be my word: consistent. That's what I think of when I think about Coach Osborne and the staff at the Nebraska program.

It was a program that worked. T.O. had a patent on something that worked. What do they say: If it ain't broke, don't fix it? Well, it wasn't broke. It worked. We had a recipe that worked, and he was going to make the biscuit the same every week. It just didn't matter, like Vince Lombardi: "I've got four plays. I'll tell you what they are. If you can't stop 'em, I'm going to keep running 'em."

What's wrong with that? It doesn't matter if you know what we're going to do if you can't stop it. We had so much confidence in our pitches that the fans might boo us when it was third-and-9 and—now I'm not saying it was the best call every time—but when we broke the huddle we thought we could pick up a first down by running a "41 pitch." And it wasn't uncommon for us to pick that up.

When I would break the huddle and we were on our game and knew we were owning somebody, I'd be walking up to the line of scrimmage, talking to the defensive end. "It's coming this way, boys." The offensive tackle next to me would be going, "What're you doing?" I'd say, "I'm letting the boys know it's coming right here. I want to see if they can stop this thing." You want to talk about making people mad, that would do it. Gosh, I loved it. Oh, that was so much fun.

Here's something T.O. told me a long time ago and I never really thought about it until down the road. He always said of Nebraska football, what we had accomplished superseded any actuarial numbers—and I'm probably not saying it correctly—but for our population base, being in the Midwest and all the other limitations, there was no way in the world we should have accomplished what we had for as long as we had. Does that make sense? It's like Class B high schools competing against Class A schools. There are more athletes to choose from in the Class A schools. Well, we were like a Class B school, but we were winning the Class A championship.

Those touchdown passes I caught (Steve Taylor and I always BS with each other, and T.O. knows this, too)—you just look at film after film of the tight ends at Nebraska, forget me, but Monte Engebritson and even before him, Mitch Krenk and Jamie Williams, and after me, Todd Millikan had a pretty good touchdowns-to-receptions ratio—we were wide open. I should have had 50 catches with 30 touchdowns. What happened to us in those years, our quarterbacks were taught to go three-deep reads on receivers. But if that first read wasn't there, they scrambled. That's what I always told Taylor: Don't you think there was a reason you were the No. 1 rushing quarterback? You weren't reading two- and three-deep. If you had, you would have had 10 more touchdown passes and sacrificed 500 rushing yards.

There's a science to it that people don't think about unless you're in the heat of the battle. I told Taylor there was a reason I had only 16 catches. I could show you 15 times when I was standing wide open, waving my hands. It was the design and how we utilized our tight ends. So if there were two chances a game for the tight end, one of those two was probably going to be a touchdown. We blocked so hard that any time I jammed up in there, delayed two or three seconds, and then just took off, I was wide open. So if the line protection held up…we just naturally seemed to be wide open. It was crazy.

As a matter of fact, one of the things I would say to T.O. that would just crack him up, and all the coaches and players, was: "Coach, I can't say this any clearer. You just get me the ball five times a game, and I'll get you the championship." And, of course, it made him laugh. But what I was trying to tell him was, make some plays for the tight ends because they're going to be wide open. I think he just looked at us as kind of a safety blanket and that extra offensive lineman in there. As a matter of fact, we probably would have made better guards than a lot of the guards. I'm not including Will Shields and all of our All-Americans and professional-type guys. But we were probably bigger than some of them were.

T.O. and I were actually at odds to begin with. I didn't get in the trouble some guys did, just ornery stuff, but they were having to check up on me, and there were several times where Gene Huey, my position coach, told me if T.O. had a viable option, he would not want to play me. But then there was a transition period, probably between my sophomore year and my junior year where maybe I changed a little bit and he changed a little bit, maybe understood me better. From that point on, we had a wonderful relationship.

The great thing about T.O.—and I know he did this from start to finish with every class he had—was two or three times a year he drove home the fact that professional football was probably not where you wanted to be. He said, "Even though all you guys think it is, you don't want to do it because there's less than one percent of you who it's drastically going to change your life."

It doesn't surprise me that he's in the Hall of Fame. In my eyes, he's probably the best. No one's going to argue that he's not in the top five, hands down. You've got to give guys like Bobby Bowden and Joe Paterno some love, and then people are going to make cases for Bear Bryant and Woody Hayes. But that's a whole different league. You've got to look at the whole ball of wax, not just wins and losses, not even championships. I know we've got to measure somehow. But I think T.O. is in a whole class of his own. We're not comparing apples to apples here, so what we've done far outweighs what you've done. We've made you guys look like underachievers.

I saw a sense of humor, certainly. It wasn't my type of humor. But he had his own sense of humor, no doubt about it. And I was able to keep up with it, but some of his stuff could go over other guys' heads. "Are we supposed to laugh now?" He always tried to keep everything tactful. I don't ever remember him trying to jam anything down anyone's throat. He was like, "Hey, I'm responsible for me. And if I make sure I'm right, I can help you guys become better men, through work hard and doing some ethical stuff." He walked the walk. He didn't just run his yack. You could tell; you knew what he was about.

If I had gone to Missouri, I probably wouldn't have beefed up to 260. I would have stayed at about 220 and I probably could have had 50 or 60 catches in my career, and maybe had a chance to start four years. But I don't think I would have been willing to sacrifice the wins. At some places you almost have to go for individual accolades because you don't have the team. I'd rather sacrifice some of the individual stuff. Hey, I wasn't a superstar at Nebraska. You look at the quarterback, the running back, the big defensive players—we were just pieces of the puzzle. I never had any issues with that.

When people ask me what I thought about Coach Osborne—and I've told him this is what I tell people—if this isn't as good of an endorsement of Coach Osborne as there is, I don't know what is: You know what? They say hindsight is 20-20. If I had to do it all over again, I would come right back to Nebraska. If you had told me I was going to have 16 catches, with 10 of them being touchdowns, and start for two and a half years, that would have been good enough.

Micah Heibel (1986-87)

A writer for Sports Illustrated *described Micah Heibel as "an unsung yet inspirational fullback who plows holes for the better-publicized runners." The writer could have added "introspective" and "patient" as well. Heibel, a* Parade Magazine *All-American at Lincoln, Nebraska, Pius X High School, was recruited as a linebacker, but he was moved to fullback as a freshman because the No. 1 fullback quit and was still playing on the freshman-junior varsity team as a third-year sophomore. He didn't estab-*

lish himself with the varsity until his junior season and didn't become the regular fullback until he was a senior.

He made the most of the educational opportunity as well, earning first-team academic all-conference and second-team Academic All-America recognition. He teaches high school math in Lincoln, and coached for several years, approaching football the way those who coached him, including Osborne, approached it. "I never had a coach who would yell and scream," Heibel said.

Coach Osborne was under a lot of fire when I was a player. People don't want to believe this, but I used to say you could take the letters people wrote about Frank Solich in his last couple of years as coach and you could get out a newspaper from 1987 and it would say all the same stuff, exactly, just change the names. In a way, I think, Tom was under pressure. I don't think it mattered so much, though. He might have been under that pressure, but I don't think it affected the way he approached things.

He says things many times that are kind of clichés, but they are generally true and he absolutely believes them. He might say if we lose and play the best we can, that's what he wants. And I think he really believes that. That was kind of his way. There was nothing flashy about him.

I was watching a program about the spacewalk on television, and whoever the commentator was, a former astronaut, said they have a saying, "Be overprepared and undertaxed." It's kind of a cliché to say you'll just prepare well and that will take care of it. But that's what it was all about for Coach Osborne. I hate to repeat things I know other people have said over and over, but we ran so many plays in practice. Sometimes people are surprised when I tell them, but we didn't get coached much on the field. We got repetition after repetition after repetition in practice and then we watched films. That's when you did your coaching. Man, there would be four fullbacks and they would all get an equal amount of work in practice. We all alternated plays. We all got evaluated.

We used to run that damn pitch play all the time in practice. With our blocking rules, the offensive tackle would go hard at the defensive tackle, and if the defensive tackle slanted, the offensive tackle would take him. If he wasn't there, the offensive tackle would just let him go, and we'd switch responsibilities. The fullback would block the defensive tackle, and the offensive tackle would go on to the linebacker. We'd run the pitch so much in practice and, I don't know, every 20th time they would throw that in there, with the defensive tackle slanting, even though it never happened in a game. When I was a senior, we played at Arizona State. It was real hot, hotter than heck. They scored to tie it with just a few minutes left. We ran a pitch, and Keith Jones had like a 60-yard run. The defensive tackle slanted and it worked just exactly like it was supposed to. I remember sort of sitting there on the field thinking, "You know…that's why you do that. That's why you throw that in every so often." We had prepared for it so much. We didn't score on that play, but it kind of won the game for us.

I think about that stuff because I used to coach. There's a lot to be said if it's fourth-and-2 and you run a play that you've already done 7,000 times in practice and everything that could possibly happen on the play is in your comfort zone. It's as easy as pie. It's just a matter of getting the job done. Things are not going to pop up to surprise you. That's where the repetition comes in. You're not thinking about what you're doing.

I don't think I saw Coach Osborne outwardly angry at a player. As a matter of fact, I don't remember seeing him outwardly angry, period. I remember him saying to one of my teammates once, when we were watching film, "You know this is *tackle* football." But that was fairly out of character. That was about as nasty a thing as he would say. When I was a junior, we were at Iowa State and we were behind at halftime. It was the only time I saw him pop his cork at halftime of a game. But I didn't really buy it, and I'll tell you why. Because I noticed that as he was yelling, raising his voice, he kept pounding his fist in his hand. And when he pounded his fist, his watch clasp would come undone. It would pop open, and he would close the clasp. Then he'd pound his fist in his hand again and it would pop open. He wasn't too out of control because he kept fixing his watch whenever it came undone. Maybe others did, but I didn't really see a temper. He really was, I think, as a coach pretty much like he seems now as far as his temperament.

He obviously was competitive. It was about winning football games; there's no doubt about that. And to a certain extent at that level it's about who can do the job for you. I mean, I don't think he was going to play a guy just because he liked the guy. But it was probably as non-dehumanizing as it can possibly be. In a way, you're a piece of meat. What can you do for me on the field? But it was probably as little like that as it was going to be. I felt some self-worth even when I wasn't playing. I felt like a man.

Everybody seemed to matter. Walk-ons were treated the same as scholarship guys, as much as possible. They just didn't get their school paid for. I know there are people who didn't pan out as football players who got their school paid for one way or another, whether they were injured or whatever. Nebraska took care of them because they had come there to play. That was an environment where, really, you signed a one-year contract to play. That was all. And you couldn't leave. That meant a heck of a lot to me because I thought I was going to be one of those guys who didn't pan out for a period of time.

I think there was a mind-set under Coach Osborne that we'll take the players we can get and we'll outwork everybody. It's funny what that does psychologically. The time I was there, I think we were 9-3, 10-2, and 10-2. But I still felt like we were the best football program in the country, even though there was some evidence we weren't.

I sort of offended somebody once because they said, "Boy, when you finally got to start a game, I'll bet that was thrilling." I said, "By the time I got to start a game, I sort of felt like that's where I should be, that I had earned it a little bit." They were sort of discouraged to hear me say that. I think they thought that showed a pretty rotten attitude. But there's a lot of truth to it. I started a couple of games as a junior, but even then, that was the fourth year I was there. I'd been around. I had scrimmaged against people who were good. There was no doubt I could at least get by. I didn't know how well it would go. But you understand what I'm saying. That's a program thing. That's an attitude.

When I was a senior in spring ball, they brought in some kid who was supposed to be a hotshot transfer or something. I don't remember his name. He wasn't around in the fall. Anyway, it's the first day of spring practice, and everybody's going a hundred miles an hour. This kid was a big, strong guy and we're doing drills. It's hard. It's physical. It's not that pleasant. And I remember thinking, "What this kid doesn't know is, we will do this every day for four weeks. He's out here trying to impress somebody. But I know that I can do it. I know that I can go and not stop. And I'll win." That kid doesn't have the mind-set.

It was just about getting the job done. Maybe I perceive it that way because that was always my attitude. It really fit me, because it was very businesslike and very methodical. We would be physical. But it wasn't, "Let's go out and kill somebody." It was, "Let's go be physical so they don't want to play anymore." It was a means to an end. And that kind of fit my point of view.

I was not a rah-rah guy. I just wasn't. Tom wasn't a rah-rah guy, either, not at all. He used to say before big games, "You don't have to play any better than you can play to win this game." That was his way. "We don't have to play above ourselves to win."

I think I saw a man of integrity. I have real positive feelings about the guy. I really do, just because I know that whatever it takes to do the job, he will find it out and research it and do it. It will be methodical and boring and painstaking, but he'll do it.

Bill Bobbora (1987-89)

Bill Bobbora played defensive end in high school in Amarillo, Texas. But Cornhusker assistant Milt Tenopir, who recruited him, made it clear he wouldn't play defense at Nebraska. "Coach Tenopir said, 'You come here and play whatever position you want. You can play quarterback if you want to. But if you ever want to see the field, you're probably going to want to listen to Coach Osborne and me,'" Bobbora recalled. He listened and became an offensive lineman. Just as Tenopir told him, he saw the field as an offensive guard, playing as a backup for two seasons and then becoming the starter on the right side in the second game of his senior year.

Osborne was held in such regard that one school's recruiter, with ties to Nebraska, told Bobbora, "Even though I have a scholarship for you, you should go with Coach Osborne."

Bobbora is a banker in Houston.

Nebraska was one of the first schools to recruit me, and I just kind of latched on to them. Coach Osborne's presence—he had built such a fine organization that you couldn't help but love the guy when he walked in the door. And Milt Tenopir—I knew he was the guy I wanted to play for. He was the offensive line coach, the day-to-day contact, and I knew I was going to be an offensive lineman.

Not taking anything away from other programs, but Nebraska was just flat-out, brutally honest, the Big Red machine. Coach Tenopir told me, and I think he spoke for the whole program, "You have a chance to come to the University of Nebraska. You have a chance to be part of something great. If you come here and you bust your butt and you do what you're told, you may start when you're a senior."

You can see through a coach's BS, some of the used-car-salesman types who come passing through town. I just don't understand how they convince kids and parents that they're sincere. You meet people like Coach Tenopir and Coach Osborne; there's no nonsense with those types of guys.

That was the challenge, take it or leave it. It wasn't, "Come here as a freshman and you can play." I really bought into the challenge, the whole goal-setting process that was so much a part of Coach Osborne's program. You laid out objectives; you laid out goals. You put the system in place to achieve them. And then you achieved them. It was kind of no-nonsense in that regard, which I think is a characteristic of any successful organization, whether it's sports or business. You have a leader who creates an environment where people can achieve success beyond what they could do individually or beyond what they could do in a different system. That, to me, is the legacy of Coach Osborne. He was so successful in creating this winning culture. In business, the culture of an organization is probably as important as anything else. It molds people to think different ways. It draws a certain type of person to the organization. It kind of becomes a living, breathing organism. That's hard to maintain over the course of 25 years, whether it's in business or sports. It's a real fragile deal at the same time.

When people ask me, "What was it like?" I don't think about winning games. I think about little instances where Coach Osborne is writing goals on a board and he's kind of got this CEO-meets-professor look on his face; you can tell he's agonizing over the details of specific goals. We're going to get 314.5 yards rushing, for instance. He had it down so scientifically, and all we had to do as players was believe it and do what we were told, just kind of fit into the system and go. As a lineman, that was really a cool deal. You could look out over three, four, or five years and see that if you did what you were supposed to do, where you would fit in the system. There wasn't a lot of guesswork in that regard.

That was Tenopir as much as Osborne—the weekly testing, the depth charts being posted two or three times a week, the grading of practices. It was a grind, but at the same time, you knew exactly where you stood. You don't get that a lot in most organizations. There was constant evaluation. As I look back, I don't know quite how to describe it, but I think it was one of the most competitive environments you could put people in. But it was done in such a collegial, paternal way that you knew it was in your best interests. It wasn't like, "Go out there and smash your heads, and the last man standing wins." It was more scientific evaluation. There was a methodology to it. You were graded certain ways. It was consistent. In some ways it was much more educational than emotional. The goals were laid out there for you. It was your job to meet and exceed them. That's pretty powerful, especially for a group of teenagers.

I remember we were sitting in the old Nebraska Center, and I don't remember who we were playing. It's funny how I don't remember opponents as much as I remember everything going on before the game, the preparation and all that. But it just really struck a chord with a couple of us. It was such a subtle, Coach-Osborne-the-psychologist, Dr. Osborne play on words.

"Now, fellas, it's going to be a tough day, and this is a real good opponent. When you get after 'em and when you knock 'em down, just make sure you pick 'em up, slap 'em on the butt and tell 'em good job, and then tell 'em that you'll be back."

It wasn't, "Go out there and kill 'em." It was an accepted fact that you were going to knock 'em down, and after you did, make sure you were gentleman enough to pick them up. You set the expectation level so high that you don't realize when you're in the middle of it that your expectations are so high. It wasn't a matter of, "Will we win?" It was a matter of, "How will we win? Will we meet our goals?"

There were games where we would win by 20, 30, 40 points, but we weren't happy because we didn't meet our goals. We didn't meet our rushing goals. We didn't meet our grades as linemen. Some people say, "That sucks. You should enjoy the moment." But at the same time, we were playing to a higher level. We were playing to Coach Osborne's and Coach Tenopir's expectations more than we were playing for wins and losses. Tom would say this, and he believes this because it's been proven throughout his whole life with people he's touched: Winning is a by-product of being a successful person.

That probably characterizes the organization of Nebraska football. You won. It was expected. It wasn't really questioned. But you won because of the preparation, because of the system, because of the people you were, because of the people you associated with, because of the way you approached life in general, not just because of the way you approached practice that day.

I don't think his philosophy really separated on and off the field. It was a philosophy of how to approach things. That's why I think things like the violence of it or the wins don't really register as much as the preparation and the expectations that went into it.

I think it was our senior year against Iowa State, and I think it was Coach's 150th win. I don't remember for sure, but it was a milestone victory. He screamed at us at halftime and said something like, "Crap." There was dead silence. "Dadgummit, I can't believe we can't execute. This is just a bunch of crap."

There was silence all across the room. He was all red and mad. And then after the game, whatever milestone it was, he said it didn't mean anything to him because he had treated us the way he did, and men don't treat men that way. He was embarrassed by his behavior and hoped that we didn't emulate it. We were like, "Gosh, Coach, we deserved it. All you said was 'crap.'" He was just such a perfect gentleman. The fact he lost his cool in front of his team meant more to him than getting some milestone victory.

Him losing his cool was still nothing compared to how anyone else would lose their temper. If he had gotten mad at you, just yelled…but he'd say how disappointed he was. I tried that tactic with my five-year-old and it works better than yelling or screaming. I don't know if I got it from Coach Osborne or not.

To play under Coach Osborne, I think, was an honor. It wasn't an entitlement. It was really an honor to be there. You take it for granted in some ways until you get out of school for five or 10 years. Then you look back and think, "Wow, that was really amazing," in all aspects, not just football, but the academics, his attempts at spiritual guidance. You just have to hope you plant some seeds and they sprout later in life.

One of the most important skills any leader can have is that ability to listen, the ability to make that person in that moment feel like it's the most important thing even though it might be the most trivial damn thing in the world. If you had his attention, you respected that so much that very rarely did you want to go have a conversation with Coach. You knew he was there for you. You could be the cashier at the training table, one of us, or one of his assistants; it didn't matter. He would listen so intently that it better be important. At least that's how I viewed it. It was "Hi, Coach, how are you?" You could stand around and BS with him. But he took everything so dadgum seriously. You felt like he was all-knowing.

We were at the first Big 12 championship game down in San Antonio in 1996. I was there with Jake Young, my dad and my brother. We went down on the field and Coach walked up. I hadn't seen him in, gosh, in probably five, six, seven years. He walked right past me and kind of winked, saw my dad and my brother, who he hadn't seen since the 1990 Fiesta Bowl, and he goes, "Rocky, Guy…" He knew their names, even though he hadn't seen them in several years. "I can't believe you're still running around with such a goofball like this kid over here," referring to me. It just made them feel like a million bucks. That was Coach Osborne. How he could remember everybody's name, I guess, just speaks to what a sincere, good person he is. It just blew me away, and it blew my dad away. He still talks about it. "He remembered my name," my dad will say. Coach Osborne is just a wonderful, wonderful man.

Doug Glaser (1987-89)

Nebraska went head-to-head with Oklahoma in recruiting Doug Glaser. His senior year in high school, the big offensive tackle from Balch Springs, Texas, was in Norman, Oklahoma, to watch the Sooners defeat Nebraska 27-7. The Cornhuskers would have been shut out if defensive tackle Chris Spachman hadn't returned a fumble 76 yards for a touchdown with 26 seconds remaining. Even so, Glaser wasn't dissuaded from accepting Nebraska's scholarship offer. The image of Osborne on the sideline stayed with him and made victories against Oklahoma in his final two seasons as a Cornhusker even more gratifying. Glaser started both of those seasons, earning All-America recognition as a senior co-captain in a line that included two other starters from Texas, center Jake Young and guard Bill Bobbora. Young was a two-time All-American.

For me, it came down to Nebraska, Oklahoma, and Texas in recruiting. I just felt like Coach Osborne was the only one who was honest and truthful with me. He said, "Hey, if you can contribute for two years, you've been a success. And we're going to work hard on trying to get you a degree. I can't promise you any playing time." That wasn't the way the other recruiters were. I remember going to Oklahoma on a recruiting trip and Barry Switzer telling me I'd be starting at right guard the next year.

Coach Switzer and Coach Osborne were total opposites. Just being around Coach Osborne, you could see who he was, the integrity. I felt he was honest. Really, the two things about it were I trusted him; I felt like he was the only one shooting straight with me. And I wanted to go somewhere with a winning tradition, which Nebraska had.

Coach Osborne came to my high school the first time I met him. I was running late. I couldn't believe he was there. Actually, he wasn't supposed to stop by the school. He was going to see my wife's father, who was like a father figure to me. Coach Osborne and Coach Gene Huey were going to go visit him that morning. But they ended up stopping by the school first. That was a big deal at school. It was a very big deal. You can just imagine the coach of a nationally ranked school, not one of the Texas schools.

It wasn't a big deal for me not going to a Texas school. But it was for everybody else. Everybody, including my mom, wanted me to stay close or in the state. She wanted me to go to the University of Texas. My mom loved the Longhorns' coach, Fred Akers. But it just felt right going to Nebraska. I remember Coach Osborne called me—it was a Super Bowl Sunday when I committed to Nebraska—and he was the same as he always was. He said he was happy I was coming, and all he asked was for me to stay with my commitment. He was just steady and expected me to be.

I didn't redshirt. I thought I'd come in my first year and play with the freshmen, redshirt my second year and hopefully contribute something my third year. I never thought I'd be playing my second year. I thought for sure I'd redshirt. It was a surprise when I reported for camp my sophomore year. Right when I got there Milt Tenopir pulled me aside and said, "Hey, there's a possibility you'll play; it kind of depends on what you guys do in fall camp." It was kind of obvious that Jake Young wasn't going to redshirt. Jake was from Texas, too— Midland. And Coach Tenopir was shuffling tackles around, trying to find a tackle.

I don't think I started to get a good sense of Coach Osborne until my senior year. Being a captain and having had some success, you get to know him a little bit more. I think everybody was just so—not afraid of him—but in awe of him, that they don't loosen up around him. But my senior year, I really got a good feel for Coach Osborne. People think he's so bland and dry. But after you got to know him, he kind of started opening up. He had a sense of humor. Whenever he did say something funny it was such a surprise that it made it even more comical.

As captains he expected us to lead by example. I think he always felt pretty comfortable, at least when I was in there, that he had the right guys leading the team and that he didn't have to say too much. He didn't really have to tell us too much, even though my group was some of the quietest captains we ever had, especially following Broderick Thomas and that group—Broderick, Neil Smith, Lee Jones, and Lawrence Pete. I don't think there were a lot of emotional speeches. And if there were, Jeff Mills took care of those for us. There wasn't any pressure to have to do that.

There was pressure playing Oklahoma, though. I was on a recruiting visit to Oklahoma for the Nebraska game my senior year in high school, and the Sooners just put it on them, like 27-7. Chris Spachman was the only one who scored for Nebraska, intercepting a pass and returning it right at the end. I can remember Coach Osborne looking so sad on the sideline after getting beat that badly, and then again two years later, when we jumped ahead of the Sooners in the rankings the week before the game and they beat us 17-7. I can remember how relieved Coach Osborne was the following year, Coach Switzer's last game against Nebraska, when we beat them to win the Big Eight championship. I think there was a lot of pressure on Coach Osborne when we played Oklahoma, and in a way we played to that pressure. We weren't as loose. I think the pressure got to all of us a little bit.

We tried to be almost so perfect against Oklahoma that sometimes we put too much pressure on ourselves. My junior year we beat the Sooners only 7-3, but there was a big sense of relief. We always thought we were better than they were, all four years I was there. It was never the case that we thought we were going to lose. One, you had some leaders on the team who kept bringing up that winning tradition. And two, Coach Osborne and his staff set the bar high. He always set the goals high and got you to believing that you weren't going to lose. And he tried to keep us on an even keel, not get too high or too low.

I saw him six or seven years after I left Nebraska, and my brother was with me. He remembered my brother's name and asked about my mom, remembered my mom's name, too. How he remembers the names of family like that, after 12 or 13 years, is just amazing.

Coach Osborne was always strong in his values. Looking back, you didn't realize that he was instilling those values in you, not only on the field, but in the way you conducted yourself off the field and the beliefs you had, from spiritual beliefs to relationship beliefs, and what you did in your social life. He always preached to us, "Nothing good happens after midnight." All those things filter down to you, but at that age, you don't really realize what he was doing until later on in your life.

He spoke at one of our stockholders meetings in Omaha, talked to 300 businessmen—some pretty influential businessmen—and told them the same things he used to tell us. The same values he used to talk to us about, he related to the business world. He's never going to change. It was amazing. I could even finish some of his sentences. He was speaking the same way he used to speak to us.

If anybody deserves to be in the Hall of Fame, he does. It doesn't surprise me at all that he's in, not just because of his records but because of the men he produced. I think when you're there and you're young, you don't see how much of coaching is dealing with people.

But once you leave, you realize that's half the challenge. It's 50-50. He was a genius on the field and a genius off the field.

It's passion. I think winning was important to him, but it probably wasn't as important as people believed. Early on I thought it was all about winning—Xs and Os. But you can start putting it together. It's not all about winning. It's about tradition and the type of people who come through there, the kind of leaders we are off the field. You start seeing that. After you leave, it's very apparent.

Mark Hagge (1988-89)

Mark Hagge wasn't big for a major college linebacker at 5-foot-11 and 230 pounds. And he wasn't particularly fast. But he was tough. And he could play, as he proved at Omaha Creighton Prep, earning all-state recognition. He also loved football, so much that he walked on at Nebraska and paid his own way all four years. Though he never had a scholarship, he made a significant contribution, particularly on special teams. He embodied the walk-on tradition under Osborne. "I was grateful for the opportunity to get to play for the Nebraska Cornhuskers," said Hagge. "I was doing what I wanted to do." He is the head football coach at Valentine (Nebraska) High School, after getting his first head-coaching job at Superior, Nebraska, with an endorsement from Osborne.

I can remember as a kid parking across the railroad tracks north of Memorial Stadium, tailgating with my dad and my uncle. We were Cornhuskers. It cannot be overstated: It's every kid's dream in the state of Nebraska to play football for the Cornhuskers. I grew up in an era when not all games were on TV and so we listened to the radio, to Kent Pavelka and Gary Sadlemeyer. I think I might have caught the end of Lyell Bremser's career, too; that was big medicine. That's what we did on Saturday afternoons. If we weren't in Lincoln watching the game, we were listening to it on the radio and then playing backyard football games, pretending we were whatever Husker star there was that day.

Coming out of high school, I was recruited by some smaller schools, but when Cletus Fischer showed up at our home, there was no decision as far as I was concerned. It was an opportunity of a lifetime. Coach Fischer was wearing a red ultra-suede sport coat and a red houndstooth hat with a feather in the band. We followed him in the door, and I remember my dad putting his arm on my shoulder and saying, "Son, we're going to Nebraska." They were asking me to walk on, giving me a chance to play big-time football. That's all you ever want, an opportunity to prove yourself. It was an opportunity I couldn't pass up, playing for the Big Red. I didn't need a scholarship to go to Nebraska, because I was doing what I wanted to do.

I wasn't big for a linebacker, but you know, it's not the size of the dog in the fight. Football, particularly college football, is a game of emotion and momentum, and a lot of the intangibles can carry you a long way. I like to think that's what I brought to the table, some energy and some enthusiasm for the game. Looking back on your career, you always feel like you could do more. But I really feel like I contributed to the success of our football teams from 1986 to 1989.

I lettered twice. I played a lot my sophomore year—my true sophomore year. I didn't have to redshirt, and I believe I appeared in six or seven games on special teams that season. But I didn't letter. They didn't letter me. I don't know why. I didn't make things easy for myself when I was down there with some of the decisions I made, so maybe that played a role, or maybe not. But I've got my letter jacket tucked away. It's a little tight these days, but I throw it on every once in a while just for the fun of it.

Looking back, I may not have said this when I first got out, but I do feel good about my contribution. I wish I would have done more. I wish I would have behaved better, toed the line, worked out more in the weight room—the whole nine yards—but I feel good about it. I just enjoyed playing the game with that edge, a spirit—an unyielding, unbreakable spirit. My attitude was I wanted to impose my will on the opponent both physically and mentally. And I did that during practice because we were competing against each other to be the best every day. For me that competition was a blast.

The lessons Coach Osborne taught me I'm still using today. The thing I really didn't appreciate until the last five or 10 years is that you need to be well rounded physically, intellectually, and spiritually. We had kind of a unique relationship. Lord knows, there were times when I really tested him.

When Tom was running for the Third District congressional seat for the first time, he made a trip to Valentine. My wife and I were in the restaurant where the rally was held. He was surrounded by all these people, but my wife said, "You need to go and say hi to Coach. He'll feel bad if you don't." So I went over and he waved at me to come up. I went and shook his hand and he told me, "Don't go away, Mark. Hold on a second." He came back with his wife and said, "Nancy, I'd like you to meet Mark Hagge." She smiled at me and asked if I had settled down. I said, "Yes, Mrs. Osborne, I have."

I didn't aspire to be a coach. I remember one time when I was a senior, Coach Osborne and I were in the sauna and he asked what I wanted to do, would I be interested in coaching, being a graduate assistant. I said I didn't think so, that I was ready to get out of school and get going. I loved the game. But I never gave much thought to coaching. When I graduated, I thought I was going to light the world on fire.

I was away from football for a year and I missed everything about it. So I did some volunteer coaching at my alma mater, Creighton Prep, and then went to night school to get my teaching certificate. The job at Superior High School opened up in the middle of the summer, so I called and asked Coach Osborne if he would give me a recommendation. He asked when my interview was. I said it was in two days. He said, "Can you be in my office tomorrow at 6 a.m.?" He wanted to ask me about my philosophy, how things were going, how I would approach coaching and teaching, about the responsibilities that go into teaching and coaching. He was beginning to prepare for his upcoming season but he still took the time. We had a great visit. He gave me a great recommendation, and they offered me the job.

Coach Osborne found time for everybody. He knew everybody's first and last name. Without question, everybody was important to him. He made that extra effort. Over the course of time, there were opportunities to get to know him, particularly by the time you were a junior and senior. He was my mentor. He and I had a great relationship. I know he often wondered what made me tick because some decisions I made, choices I made, weren't always the best, and he was always there keeping track of me.

Every game was important to Coach Osborne, every snap was important. That's how he prepared. I use that in my coaching over the course of a game. Some people had a feeling he was kind of cold, that he didn't have any emotion. But he had plenty of emotion. Being a leader, you have to have that, particularly in games. That's one of the reasons he was so successful. He wanted to win. I appreciate that now. To a certain degree, I was worried about him when he stepped aside from coaching. I was worried about what he would do, how he would fill that void. He's a driven man. I could understand where he was coming from when he went into politics. He had a new challenge.

What's funny about it is, when I was in high school, a priest at Creighton Prep asked me what I was going to do with my life and, at that time, I thought I would be going into business with my father. The priest said, "No, you're going to be a teacher. That's what you're going to be." I just kind of sloughed him off, didn't think much of it. Then there was the Coach Osborne example, and a few years later, I find myself deciding that is, in fact, what I wanted to do. That was the main reason I decided to be a teacher, so I could coach. But as I've progressed in my career, I've really enjoyed the classroom. It's neat to get these kids motivated and excited about learning. It really is.

Without question, coaching provides an outlet for my competitiveness. It provides the camaraderie you get when a group of men have a common goal and work to achieve it. I like the ability to work with young men and get them to believe in something bigger than themselves, a goal that's worthy of their greatest efforts. That's a lot of fun. I've been in coaching now for 12, 13 years, and we've had some teams that have been really close to being state-championship caliber. But in the big games, we just haven't been able to make enough plays to win. But we keep grinding. It certainly is an outlet. I'm not getting rich, but we've helped develop a lot of young men, and I like to think I'm making a difference in their lives.

Certainly being a walk-on has helped. Coaching is teaching and it's helped me a lot, not only the football knowledge I acquired at Creighton Prep and at Nebraska under Coach Osborne and Charlie McBride, but also the life lessons. Those lessons, to be quite honest, are more important for these young men that I'm working with on a daily basis than the football knowledge I'm going to pour into them because I've yet to produce an NFL player. So I would just say, certainly the football knowledge that I've acquired helped, but working with Tom Osborne and trying to emulate the type of leader he was for me, that's what helped me more.

When I was at Nebraska, I made some poor decisions I wish I could take back. But we live and we learn. Coach Osborne helped me get through those. He never quit on me. He always kept his faith in me, and we worked through those times. I'm a better man today because of it. That's the key right there. Everybody mattered to Coach Osborne. Everybody had their role to play in making the program a success, and Tom recognized that. He went to great lengths to see to it that everybody felt their worth. One thing I just really want to emphasize: For me, it was the time of my life getting to play football for the University of Nebraska. As far as I'm concerned, there's no better college experience that I could think of from a lot of different angles. I was working with a legend of the game, Coach Osborne, and I was playing for Nebraska. When I travel somewhere, I let everybody know I'm a Nebraska Cornhusker. That's important.

Especially for my generation, Tom Osborne is the face of the program and not only that, but the heart and soul of it. There's not any question about it.

Jim Scott (1990-92)

Jim Scott, a center and senior co-captain, was among three starters in Nebraska's offensive line in 1992 who played eight-man football at small high schools in the state—Lance Lundberg was a tackle and Ken Mehlin was a guard. Lundberg was a scholarship recruit. Mehlin, like Scott, walked on. "We had pretty successful teams with a lot of Nebraska kids on them. That's pretty neat," said Scott, who was from Ansley. "We're not a big state, not a lot of kids."

He began his college career at Kearney State, now Nebraska-Kearney, transferring after his freshman year then sitting out a season. The smallest of the offensive line starters, he was first-team all-conference and first-team academic all-conference as a senior. "I know I was pretty dang lucky to have that chance," he said. "In today's world, I never would have come close. I came in below the radar screen."

Scott is a banker—at a bank he established—in Broken Bow, Nebraska.

Trying to think of something a little different, two things come to mind about Coach Osborne. One was something that I thought took some nerve and for which he could have taken some heat. And the other was an example of his kindness.

My senior year, we were struggling offensively. We had gotten beat at Washington and we were a game or two into the Big Eight season, playing at Missouri. Mike Grant was our starting quarterback, but halfway through the game, Coach Osborne brought Tommie Frazier in. Tommie was a true freshman. I knew there were some true freshmen who had played before that, maybe come in for a series or two, played sporadically throughout their first year. But I think

Tommie was probably one of the first true freshmen at a skill position who came in and played the rest of the season, and started.

Anyway, I thought being in the Big Eight season, where we hadn't lost a game, that it was a big step to go with a true freshman. Mike was a fifth-year senior. Coach Osborne could see we were struggling, and Mike was struggling. But it took a lot of nerve, a lot of guts for him to do that. The players felt it needed to be made. If you had asked some of them, it probably should have been made earlier. But we also understood it was a big step. Coach Osborne went out on a limb that day. But he knew from practice and half the season what Tommie could do, and he trusted Tommie. He made the right move and it kind of changed Nebraska football from then on.

The second thing was in my senior year, after the Orange Bowl game. We had lost to Florida State, I think by 13 points. Afterward, I get on the bus and here comes Coach Osborne. He sits down in front of me. You would think the guy would be down and out. I don't know how many years it had been since he had won a bowl game, and you'd think the pressure would be getting to him. But he turned around and we had a discussion about what I was going to do after football. We didn't talk about the game or his frustration. He was concerned about me, "Okay, Jim, what are you going to do after football?"

He said I should try pro football. He thought I could play in the pros. He got me interested in that. I didn't even think about going on, but he said, "I'm going to make some calls to some teams. I think you need to look at that." That got my fire burning again. I went on to free agency with the Chicago Bears, but once I got to training camp, I was basically tired of football and ready to move on. I just didn't have the drive anymore to play. But I appreciated him doing what he did for me so I could have that experience.

His thoughtfulness, the kind of person he was, showed. He said, "I want to help you out in any way I can." He thanked me for my years of service to Nebraska football. The guy could have been frustrated and not wanted to talk, but he spent the time on the way back to the hotel telling me thanks for the time and the hard work, and that he would do anything to help me in my future.

I can't tell you the first time I met Tom. I had been to one Nebraska football game before I went to college. I wasn't a big Nebraska football fan. I transferred, and the first year at Nebraska I was redshirted. If you're a walk-on, it's hard for the coaches to know you unless it's your position coach. Milt Tenopir was my position coach. I don't think Coach Osborne really knew who I was.

My sophomore year, in the fall, Coach Tenopir would bring me up with the first team, more than anything to give Dave Edeal, the No. 1 center, a rest during practice. It wasn't because I was No. 1 or even No. 2, it was just to give Dave a breather. We usually ran 25 or 30 plays per station. I'd go in every four or five plays just to give him a break. That was probably my first experience with Coach Osborne because he was always watching the first units. He didn't know who I was.

My first time to go in and give Dave a break happened to be some play that was complicated and I messed up. Coach Osborne came into the huddle yelling, "What's going on here?"

I had to say, "I messed up my call."

And he said, "Well, if you don't know it, then get out of here."

That was my first experience. I thought, "My God, what am I doing here?"

Being a walk-on that he didn't recruit, a walk-on that came the second year from another college, I didn't expect him to know me. I kind of came in under the radar, basically.

That spring, I had gone through spring ball and come out tied for No. 1 on the depth chart, so, of course, by that time he knew who I was. It was kind of a rapid relationship. In a year's time, I went from him not knowing who I was and chewing my butt to knowing who I was.

Coach Osborne was a decision-maker and would deal with the consequences later. He knew what he wanted to do. When we played Oklahoma my junior year, we were behind a couple of points in the fourth quarter and there were a couple of minutes left. We were on Oklahoma's 20- or 30-yard line, fourth-and-1. So we called timeout. As we walked to the sideline, I thought, "We're going to spend this whole timeout figuring out what play we're going to run." But there was no question in his mind. He was looking out where the ball was being spotted. He said, "We're going to run a '49 pitch.'" And he basically went through what everybody was going to be doing. We made a first down, and then on the next play we ran it up the middle and scored a touchdown.

I think I was the last center for the guard-around play, the "fumbleroosky." It was the Colorado game, on Halloween night. I think there was kind of a rainstorm, too. We practiced the play for a couple of years and you wonder, "Are we really ever going to run this? Yes, they ran it in the '70s but are we ever going to run it?" We were ahead in the game. We were headed to the north end zone. I think we called a timeout and the play comes in. Finally, your old heart starts beating. "My God, we *are* going to run this."

I don't think people realized the difficulty with it, because you had to snap the ball and then you had to set it back down on the ground. But you had to be going forward. If you weren't, there was going to be someone on defense plowing you over. Your instinct was to hurry and get the ball on the ground. That's why you always practiced it. You had to lay it on the ground. You couldn't let it drop because it would bounce all over the place. It was easier to do it on grass than on turf.

Anyway, the nose guard was offset on me and had good penetration. I got the ball set down, but my foot hit it. It was a play for Will Shields, the guard, to pick up the ball. Because of me kicking it, that thing was bouncing, and luckily it bounced right into Will's hands.

He didn't have to pick it up off the ground. I was pretty fortunate. I think we made a first down and eventually scored. I'm going to say, realistically, that was probably the only play we practiced and wondered if we were ever going to run in a game. We ran everything else.

When you were first at Nebraska, you were like, "Oh, my God, this is Tom Osborne." As you went up the totem pole, you felt he was very approachable, but you still held him in high regard. Once you got to know him and play for him, his door was always open. He was always happy to take the time to talk to you.

4

Finishing Strong

(1993-97)

The journey rather than the destination was the most important thing.
Tom Osborne often pointed that out. "As I said many times, to the chagrin of
many Nebraska fans, I'm not in it to win the national championship," he said
the week before the final regular-season game in 1994.

The Cornhuskers had positioned themselves to play for a national title.
They were undefeated and ranked No. 1 at the time. "Believe me, if we win
the national championship, I'd be pleased," Osborne said. "But I wouldn't feel
any different after that game than when we beat Colorado.

"Trophies and whistles and bells and rings don't excite me that much.
What really excites me is playing as well as you can, getting the most out of
your football team, doing it a certain way. When it comes time for me to go,
it won't be tied to trophies or a specific set of events."

A month and a half later, the Cornhuskers won the national champi-
onship by defeating Miami 24-17 in the Orange Bowl. And when the time
finally came for Osborne to go, they had won two more.

No major college football coach has finished stronger. Nebraska's record in
his final five seasons was 60-3 with the three national championships and
opportunities for two others. If a 45-yard field goal on the final play of the
1994 Orange Bowl against Florida State had sailed through the up-rights

instead of wide left, the Cornhuskers would have won a fourth championship. And if a flu-ridden 1996 team could have avoided an upset in the Big 12 title game, it probably would have played for a fifth.

Osborne's national championship breakthrough was a result of several factors, including the recruitment of quarterback Tommie Frazier from Bradenton, Florida, and a change in defensive alignment, replacing the "50" front Nebraska had used since Bob Devaney was coach with a 4-3 base that allowed the Blackshirts to be more aggressive in dealing with pass-oriented offenses.

Frazier, who became the starter in the sixth game of his freshman season, proved to be a playmaker and the definitive quarterback for Osborne's option offense. When Frazier was sidelined for seven games with a blood-clot problem in 1994, Brook Berringer came off the bench and directed the team to a conference title and a fourth consecutive trip to the Orange Bowl, where he and Frazier divided time.

Frazier ran the offensive show in 1995, on a team regarded among the best in college football history, though Osborne's enjoyment of that journey was diminished by off-field problems involving players, most notably I-back Lawrence Phillips. The national media criticized Osborne for suspending Phillips rather than dismissing him from the team, claiming Osborne's compassion was based on a desire to win.

Nothing could have been further from the truth, however. The 1995 team didn't need Phillips. Osborne believed Phillips needed the team and acted accordingly, despite the ramifications. "One of the real gratifying things about coaching is, you see what players do after they've left here," Osborne said later. "That's one reason I've learned to never give up on anybody. I've seen so many cases."

As it turned out, Phillips continued to let him down after leaving Nebraska. But he had done what he thought was best for the troubled Phillips. He hadn't compromised his principles.

The change in defense was rooted in seven consecutive bowl losses, with Osborne emulating what Miami and Florida State did to utilize speed in a 4-3 "dime" package. Initially, the Cornhuskers substituted personnel in apparent passing situations. But when Osborne and defensive coordinator Charlie McBride realized that the "dime" alignment would hold up against the run, it became the base.

Talk that Osborne's 25th season might be his last faded as it began but resurfaced near the end, fueled by his 250th victory—appropriately enough against Oklahoma by an unlikely 69-7—and a late-night trip to the hospital with an irregular heartbeat following a 77-14 victory against Iowa State two weeks later. Osborne didn't announce his decision to step aside until after the Big 12 championship game, however, less than a month before the Cornhuskers were to play Tennessee in the Orange Bowl.

A 42-17 victory against Peyton Manning's Volunteers and some impassioned pleas from players, among them quarterback Scott Frost, convinced those in the coaches' poll to vote Nebraska a national title, splitting that honor with the Associated Press national champion, Michigan.

The Tennessee game needn't have been Osborne's last. At age 60, he could have continued coaching. Though the irregular heartbeat was under control, other factors had entered into his decision.

Despite rampant speculation that he was retiring, he met with his players first to let them know. He had always encouraged them to take themselves out of games when they didn't think they could perform their best, he said, and that's what he was doing. He hoped they understood.

Later, during the news conference, he said, "The hardest thing was talking to the players, because those are the people I care about a great deal. The thing I enjoy about coaching is the players and the coaches. I will miss them very much." He would miss them even more than the journey.

Tommie Frazier (1992-95)

Just as Johnny Rodgers was the difference-maker on Coach Bob Devaney's national championship teams in 1970 and 1971, Tommie Frazier was the driving force behind Osborne's first two national titles, *despite missing most of the 1994 season because of a blood-clot problem. He was chosen as the most valuable player in both national championship bowl-game victories.*

Frazier, who was recruited out of Bradenton, Florida, became the starting quarterback as a true freshman, a first under Osborne. He earned All-America honors in 1995, finished second to Ohio State's Eddie George in Heisman Trophy voting and won the Johnny Unitas Golden Arm Award.

However, his most significant statistic was 33-3, the Cornhuskers' record in games he started. "To me, it's not about what I did. It's about: Did I help my teammates perform at the highest level by the way I performed? And if I can answer that question 'yes,' then that's all I need to say about it," said Frazier, whom Sport Magazine *included on a list of the century's 10 greatest college football players.*

He is the head football coach at Doane College in Crete, Nebraska.

Coach Osborne is a person you would love to send your kid to learn football, and also to learn how to live your life the way he lives his. He doesn't show favoritism. He treats everyone the same. If you screw up, you're going to be disciplined. I don't care if you're a starting running back or starting quarterback or the third-string defensive tackle. His knowledge of the game, it's unbelievable. It's amazing. But it's the way he treated the players. He truly was a father to a lot of the players, because he cared.

We joked all the time. People don't realize he has a somewhat dry sense of humor, but it grows on you. He jokes quite a bit, but you know when he's serious and wants you to stay focused. Spending four years with him, I kind of helped him open up. Being a doctor of psychology, he tried to play mind games with you. Once a guy like that gets into your head, he can have you do whatever he wants you to do. Well, he never got into my head. I always did something out of the ordinary to make him wonder if I was sane.

One time we took one of the backs off the seats in the team meeting room, the one he always sat in. I knew he would lean back. This particular day, he didn't check the seat. He fell back and his feet were up in the air. And the first person he turned to was me. I didn't say I did it. But I knew who did. I was part of it, put it that way. I'm not saying who it was. I helped plan it, though. It was funny.

That's the way I live my life. I don't like people trying to figure me out, because once a person figures you out, they can pretty much dictate to you what they want you to do. My wife always says, "Gee, what are you doing? I never know how you're going to react or what you're going to do." Well, maybe that's the wrong way to act because she is my wife and I'm going to be with her the rest of my life, but I've always been that way. You're not going to figure me out 100 percent. I'm going to surprise you every now and then. And you're going to say, "I never thought you would do that."

Coach Osborne surprised me, too, when he started telling jokes in meetings, when he sat back there in meetings and he would call somebody out about the way they were dressed or what they were doing on the sideline in a game. I still remember the time we were playing in Japan my freshman year, and Calvin Jones and I, at practice we're in the background dancing like we were Madonna. When he showed the practice film, he sat there and would rewind that play and say, "At least you guys aren't entering a dance contest." I was like, "I can't believe he just did that." Coach Osborne could have fun also.

I hated losing. I hate losing to this day. It kills me to lose at something. I understand I can't win everything. But I hate losing with a passion. And if you have that—if you hate losing as much as I do—there aren't going to be too many times that you're going to lose, because you're going to do whatever you need to do to make sure you win. You're going to go out there and play hard all the time.

That's the way I played, no matter what sport it was. I remember times playing Little League football, when I lost, I cried because it bothered me that much. People said, "Well, you're just a poor sport." But it's not being a poor sport. It's being passionate and wanting to be successful, wanting to be the best. Eventually I got over that. But I still hated losing with a passion. If I lose at something, I'm going back for revenge, right now, to this day. And if I lose again, I'm going back.

Playing video games, if I would lose to one of my buddies, it was like, "Let's sit back down here. We're going to play this again. And we're going to play until I win." That's just the way I've always been. Losing doesn't sit very well with me because I feel I'm always better than the person I'm playing against. I understand things can happen that can change the outcome of a certain event, or game, whatever. But losing doesn't sit well with me.

Coach Osborne, I think, hated losing too. But he put it more in perspective. It wasn't about winning and losing. It was about are you becoming the best player you can be or are you learning anything from losing? I think that's what it was, because Coach Osborne lost big games and it didn't deter him from still going out and trying to be a very successful person. If you approach it that way, eventually you can handle losing. But you don't accept it. When you start seeing people accepting losing, they're not going to maximize their ability. I never accepted losing. I never will accept losing, because losing is not part of my nature, not part of my character. Anything I do I'm going to be successful; I'm going to win. I'm not going to let someone beat me.

For Coach Osborne, it's the journey. At first, it's hard to convince someone of that. But then you start realizing, "Hey, what he was saying was true. It is a journey. Everything is a journey. Life is a journey. Your destination is to make it to heaven. But you have to go through a journey in order for that to happen. The same thing is true in sports; everybody's goal is to win a championship. But there are games. The games are the journey; the workouts, the conditioning, and all that kind of stuff are the journey. The destination is to get to the championship. And if everything falls into place and you do everything you're supposed to do, you're going to reach your destination. That's what Coach Osborne taught.

Trev Alberts (1990-93)

After the Cornhuskers defeated Miami in the 1995 Orange Bowl game, Trev Alberts visited the locker room to congratulate Osborne on his first national championship. Almost apologetic, Osborne said he wished the championship had come the year before so Alberts could be a part of it.

Alberts, an All-American and Nebraska's first Butkus Award winner, was a part anyway. He was a key in the shift to a 4-3 base defense because of his pass-rushing ability, finishing first on the school's tackles-for-lost list and second in quarterback sacks. He was the Big Eight "Defensive Player of the Year" in 1993 and an Academic All-American as well as a three-time academic all-conference honoree. He came from Cedar Falls, Iowa, with the kind of work ethic he admired in athletes from Nebraska, particularly walk-ons. They were the foundation of Osborne's program. "The core of the team was people who came from the state, who understood its values," he said. "I'd take in a heartbeat a guy with a little less talent who is a character guy with a heart. Nebraska had players who would never quit."

I think a lot of people never understood how competitive Coach Osborne was, because they sort of read him as this laid-back, gentle man, which he was. But he had a purpose, and I certainly understood it. I knew how much it meant to him, and I think the players understood. He would be loyal to a fault, but if you betrayed that sense of loyalty, you weren't going to get it back any time soon. He was so different in how he went about his business that a lot of people missed how competitive he was.

Ultimately, most of the success Coach Osborne achieved, and I'm not trying to limit his ability to run an offense and that sort of thing, but I think he achieved an unusual level of loyalty from his players. Every coach would dream of having the sort of loyalty he had. Guys would go to extraordinary levels to try to give back because we were so loyal. Other than my mother, my father and my wife, he's the guy to me. He developed that. And we would play at a different level. We probably overachieved in a lot of areas just because of how much we respected him and wanted to perform for him.

There are two ways to treat a dog. You can either beat the dog until it obeys you or you can love the dog, and it will want to please you. I believe Coach Osborne mastered that sort of motivation. We had such a deep care and respect for him that we wanted to please him. And we wanted to achieve the goals he set out for the team. Because of his background in educational psychology, he understood people better than just about anybody else, and he understood how to push the right buttons.

The respect is instantaneous when you meet him. When he walks into the room, he demands attention. When he walked into my house as the head coach at Nebraska, there was immediate respect for him, based on how he handled himself, how he acted, how he treated people. He had an aura about him. Some people have it. Some people don't. When Coach Osborne came to my house, he demanded respect by not saying a word. He had a presence and it was real. And when I got to Nebraska, he talked about loyalty, about family, that we would stick together; it didn't matter what side of the ball you were on.

He rarely talked about football. Mostly he talked about things outside of football, whether it was your academic life, your social life or your spiritual life. Football was always fourth on the list in terms of importance, because he felt if a student-athlete was well-rounded and had the first three components in order, the fourth thing would take care of itself. He was more interested in developing the whole person. I believe that's probably not something that's talked about at most Division I schools now. In the old days, you'd take a kid, he'd leave Mom and Dad and you would develop him. The real joy the coaches got was seeing the development of kids. Not only did they become better football players, they became better people, intellectually, spiritually…Coach Osborne tried to develop the whole person.

I think that's sort of fallen by the wayside. Now coaches are just interested in whether or not you can play football. Coach Osborne fostered an environment. He didn't allow negativism. He didn't allow assistant coaches who were constantly at our throats. They demanded an awful lot, but I was never cursed at. I was never told how worthless I was. Coach Osborne and his assistants didn't coach out of fear. A lot of assistants coach out of fear. They're worried about their jobs, so they've got to make the head coach think they're really coaching you up. They're screaming and yelling and getting in people's faces. Ultimately, when it comes down to it, third-and-1 and you've got to get off the field, or fourth-and-1 at the end of a game, who are you going to play for, the person you've developed a genuine respect and love for, someone who cares about you and your family, or someone who just screams and yells at you?

Coach Osborne made a real effort—and I believe Bob Devaney had an impact in this regard—to know about your family. To this day, he asks, "How are your mom and dad doing?" He makes an effort to include the rest of your family. You just felt like although you left your immediate family, there was an extension. I felt at home at Nebraska. I knew I could count on those people. We stood up for each other. We backed each other up through thick and thin, unless there was something where you stepped outside the family. He told us, "If you look me in the eye and tell me you didn't do something, I will stand by you." But once you betray that trust, he's done with you.

Even though Coach Osborne had the presence about him, even though he demanded and commanded respect, I never felt uncomfortable walking into his office. I remember as a sophomore, or even as a redshirt freshman, thinking that maybe I didn't have the talent to play there. I didn't want to get stuck behind David White my whole career and have one year to play, and I went to his office to talk to him about it. I was a scholarship player, but I believe if you asked many of the walk-ons, he gave them and showed them the same amount of respect that he showed someone like Broderick Thomas.

You don't get respect unless you give respect. If you were on the elevator screwing around and it stopped on the second floor and Coach Osborne was standing there waiting to get on, everybody stood up, manners changed. I've always thought your team is a reflection of the head coach. He was human. He had faults. But he lived a life that was pretty pure, and when you lead by example like that, people follow. I remember as a young kid, not trembling, but you just had so much to try to live up to. He was what you'd only hope to be. That's why I ended up at Nebraska. My mother and father saw immediately in him that he was what they hoped and dreamed their son would grow up and someday become.

Tom talks about some of his favorite players. Darin Erstad, I think, was one of his favorite players. I think he respected guys who weren't in it for personal adulation, who wanted to be part of a team, enjoyed working and understood where they fit within the concept of team. I think he liked Darin because of the fact that Darin was a baseball player but cared enough to come over to football and help out in punting, help the team win a national championship.

Tom just was not interested in selfish players. Guys he really, really appreciated were like Roger Craig, who would put the team above personal interest. And I think Brook Berringer was a favorite because Brook was sort of brought in with the understanding that the offense was going to change, that he was going to throw the ball. But then you get Tommie Frazier and "We'd better run the option, still." So Brook, because of his hard work, turned himself into a pretty darn good quarterback in the option system, never really complained. Hard-working people with proper morals and ethics, who understood the concept of team, were well-rounded, weren't just football players, tried to become better people, those were Coach Osborne's favorites.

When I was recruited, Coach Osborne just said, "The great news is, we have a great university. You'll get a degree. And you'll get the opportunity to compete for playing time." That was it. That was what was promised to me. He told my mother and father they would take good care of me at Nebraska. They wouldn't practice on Sunday. If my spiritual life was important, I'd be given an opportunity to go to church. They wouldn't demand anything of me then. He promised that they would do everything they could to facilitate my getting a college education. They would treat me well, and in the meantime, we would have some fun because we would win some games. That was the promise I was made.

Nowadays, kids want to be promised playing time immediately and be promised that they will get to the NFL. With him the opposite was true. He brought people in to tell us what the odds were of us ever making it to the NFL. The odds weren't good. He laid it out: If you got a degree, you were ultimately going to make more money. It was just a different focus.

I believe what we did at Nebraska was not done the easy way. The easy way would have been to go out and take anybody with talent. I think Coach Osborne was pretty consistent about how important it was that our team reflected the personality of the state. People embraced our team because we were like those people. We never gave up. We might lose but we fought all the way. We had our share of problems, but ultimately we represented the state, the university, in a way that was in tune with what people expected.

Here's Coach Osborne in a microcosm. I went to the Orange Bowl the year after I finished, when they beat Miami to win the national championship. I went in the locker room to give Coach

Osborne a hug. Here he is, he's been coaching however many years it is and he finally wins his first national championship. He gives me a hug and you can just see his demeanor change. And he says, "Trev, I really feel bad that you didn't get to win one of these." He genuinely cared about the players. It wasn't fake.

I see coaches who try to act that way. But he was real about it. He cared. Coaching, for him, was more about seeing us succeed, almost like having kids. I've got kids now and what gives me joy is when I see them happy, when they accomplish something and I see them revel in it. I believe he viewed us in that manner. When we did something good, he was happy for us. It just wasn't really about him.

I feel like he felt it was a privilege to get to coach the kids. Nowadays it's all about the head coach. Players are sort of an afterthought. I think players were the central theme of everything he did. I watched his retirement when he announced it. I don't think it hurt, having to retire, because he would miss doing press conferences and being known as the head coach. It hurt because he wasn't going to get to be with those kids. He had recruited them. And he probably felt that he was going to let them down.

Ed Stewart (1991-94)

Ed Stewart skipped a practice or two during the preseason of his second year at Nebraska. He had come from Chicago's Mt. Carmel High School expecting to play safety, but in the transition to a 4-3 base defense, he had been moved to linebacker for the Red-White game the previous spring. Preseason practices under linebackers coach Kevin Steele were intense and physically demanding. He weighed less than 200 pounds, and "it was overwhelming," Stewart recalled. "A couple of days I was AWOL. 'Man, I'm out of here. I'm not doing this. I've got to transfer.'" He was dissuaded from that, however, to his benefit as well as the program's. A three-year starter at weak-side linebacker, he was a co-captain, the Big Eight "Defensive Player of the Year," an All-American, and a finalist for the Butkus Award on Osborne's first national championship team. He completed a psychology degree before that senior season and is now an associate athletic director at Missouri.

I truly think Coach Osborne was a father figure to a lot of guys in that program. Just watching him and the way he carried himself was a great example for us all, how to handle success, deceit, criticism, what have you. It's something I do today. You just keep grinding. You just keep doing what it is you're doing, regardless of public opinion—whether it's positive, negative—just do things based on your faith, your values, and your beliefs. Try to do things the right way; at the end of the day that's all you can do.

He developed an environment where you wanted to do the right thing. You didn't want to let the guy down. He was like your parents. The worst thing about getting in trouble at school was, the teacher was going to call your parents. He was like your parents.

My trust of the man began during my true freshman year. Being away from Chicago, I was kind of homesick. I remember it was right around the Oklahoma game. Nebraska and Oklahoma always played on that Thanksgiving weekend, and at that time all of the redshirts and the other guys needed to stay to practice on the day before the game.

So he was walking by and I stopped him and said, "Coach, do you have a minute? Can I talk to you?" This is when I realized he knew my name. He said, "Well, sure Ed." So we went into Coach's office and he said, "What's the problem?" I said, "Coach, I'm really homesick, and I was wondering if there was any way I could go home a day early to be home for Thanksgiving?"

And like he does sometimes, he put his hand on his chin. He gets his thinking face on and he looks at me and says, "Well, sure Ed, that won't be a problem. That would probably be a good thing for you to do." That was just a small thing him saying that, but at that point in time, I was sold. I was willing to do whatever it took for the guy to help the team be successful.

He never made decisions without thinking them through. He was really good as far as reading situations, reading people and trying to make the best decision for the individuals involved as opposed to just having a bunch of arbitrary rules, saying, "This is my way and this is the way we do it." He tried to deal with every individual case as that, an individual case.

The guy was so well-informed. I was a defensive guy and he spent a lot of time with the offense, but I remember at practice one day, he was down at one end of the field with the offense, and all of a sudden, I hear him calling, "Now, Eddie, you need to get a little more width in that drop." I stood there amazed. First of all, you didn't know he was paying attention from where he was standing. And then second of all, he was so in-tune to the preparation that just from his distant view, he knew what defense it should have been and exactly where people should have been in a certain situation. That was impressive.

I'm probably somewhat spoiled, though that probably isn't the right word, but I see things a lot differently now, working in athletics and being able to play a little bit after I left Nebraska, but I've had the opportunity to be around a lot of different coaches, and it has only intensified my belief in how special and how unique Coach Osborne was. A lot of us learned so much from Tom. Maybe you didn't think you were learning it at the time, but as you get away and time passes, you begin to see things differently.

One of the things I continue to be impressed about is how long all of those coaches stayed together and how well they worked together. I'm sure they had their tiffs. They had different personalities and maybe everybody wasn't the best of friends. But you never would have known it, the way they handled themselves and the way they got along. Unity, working together, was so integral to our championship run. And it was evident that message came from the top down, that those guys were practicing what they were preaching. They were telling us to get along, play well together. You're taking all these people from different backgrounds, races and different levels of ability, getting them to buy into one vision and then work in concert to get something done. It was just phenomenal. And it's not easy to do.

I'm talking about egos and different personalities and things of that nature. They had to like working for the man because you don't stick around and work for somebody for multiple years like that if you don't respect and like working for and with the guy. That says a lot about him.

You know what? To be honest—and I could be wrong—but I think winning the national championship meant very little to him. I don't think it meant as much as people probably made it out to be because I really do believe—and this is one thing I learned from Tom and I've tried to practice—it's about controlling what you can control. You can't allow a headline or what other people say about you to determine how you feel about yourself. So I think him winning that championship was nice. But I don't think it changed anything. I think if you ask him, he felt he did a pretty darn good job of coaching, or at least the best job he thought he could do with what he had, all those other years. It just so happened at this time, we won one and then they won two more. But I don't think he was driven by that.

I think he was driven by excellence in general, and the fact that we did well in school, that we were good people, that we came out and practiced hard, that we played hard, and if you do those things, everything else will take care of itself. He believed that.

That's one of the things I carry with me. I try to do that with what I do now. When I talk to my coaches, I don't talk about winning. I talk about the process, because in my mind, if you go by the process, if you do things with the right steps in the right way, work hard, the other will take care of itself. You're going to win more times than you lose if you go out and play hard, with great effort, if you're prepared.

I think I've been really fortunate. I had great coaches at Mt. Carmel High School. I think I had unbelievable coaches when I was at Nebraska. I'll never forget how Kevin Steele, my position coach, got me motivated. I was a sophomore and I was playing okay. He said to me, "You play really well in the big games. But the difference between being a good player and a great player is that it doesn't make a difference who you're playing. You've got to play the same way all the time."

That was a subtle thing. But it was something that really triggered me to motivate myself, to "see gray." We always talked about seeing gray. It didn't make a difference what color the other jersey was, if it was Colorado or Wyoming or Pacific, whoever. It didn't matter. You were establishing a foundation for the way Nebraska was going to do things. You were laying a foundation for the way linebackers would play, how hard they would play, how they would do it all the time. That's what you have to do if you want to be successful over the long haul, be successful consistently.

Coach Osborne was the reason I went to Nebraska. It was between Michigan and Nebraska, but when he visited, it was pretty much hook, line, and sinker. My mother was sold on him after the home visit. She was very impressed. She's a religious lady. He's a religious man. He's got just an amazing presence about him when he walks in a room. I remember that presence and how humble he was, and is.

Working in athletics now, I see the egos all across the room, with football coaches and men's basketball coaches, in particular. It's frustrating for me a lot of times because I compare them to Tom Osborne. I think about all of the wins and all of the accolades that guy had and still how humble he was and how he went about his business. That's a testament to his character and who he is. You look at people who haven't won nearly as much he has, who aren't nearly as accomplished as he is, who are so ego- and self-centered. It's amazing. I have a lot of respect for the man. I consider myself fortunate to have had the opportunity to play for him and play at the University of Nebraska.

Tony Veland (1992-95)

Nebraska envisioned the versatile Tony Veland as a defensive back when it recruited him from Benson High School in Omaha. But he wanted to play quarterback, and Osborne gave him an opportunity to do so. A patellar tendon injury, suffered in the second game of his sophomore season, ended the opportunity, however. He played in only six games at the position. Prior to his junior season, after recovering and with Tommie Frazier and Brook Berringer at quarterback, he was moved to free safety, where he played for two national championship teams and earned second-team all-conference recognition as a senior. He was a co-captain for the 1995 team, one of the many highlights of his career.

Coach Osborne influenced my coming to Nebraska big time. I've lived in Nebraska all my life, but I'm not one of those guys who was 10 years old and said he was going to play football for Nebraska. Actually, when I was in high school, my first couple of years, I wanted to go out of state. I wasn't really thinking about Nebraska. But I went down for a football camp and had a great time, listening to Coach Osborne, listening to some of the other coaches. I kind of got a feel for the atmosphere there.

Then he came to one of my basketball games when I was in high school. Obviously, that was a huge deal. And after the game, he came over to my house. He was standing in the living room and, honestly, he didn't have to say a word. It was like, "I'm there. I'm going to Nebraska." That's the way I felt in my heart. Honestly, I can't tell you what it was exactly. I think it was his presence.

When somebody has done so much good in their life, they just have this presence or this aura of sincerity and honesty. You can kind of feel it. I felt like I was going to be in a situation where this guy was going to lead me on a good path, and he was going to be more worried about me as an individual than about winning games for himself. And that turned out to be right. That was the best choice I could have made. The Nebraska coaching staff was phenomenal, and Coach Osborne led by example.

I had that sense of trust early on. And I'll tell you what solidified it. I never thought negative of T.O., but what really made me respect him probably more than anything else was in the season when Lawrence Phillips was having all those troubles, when Coach Osborne suspended him and then brought him back. Obviously, Coach Osborne knew he was going to take a lot of flak for that. And he did take a lot of flak. But that meant a lot to me because it said, "Okay, consider Lawrence, consider his past and consider his future." If I was in that situation, would I want somebody to give me a chance? Would I want somebody to look after me? Or would I want somebody to close the book on me and write me off, send me back where I came from? When he gave Lawrence a chance, that really proved to me, really showed me, he cared about the individual first. He didn't care what everybody was going to say about him. He was that strong of a Christian. His convictions were strong. And he was looking out for our best interests. After that, I was really glad I made the decision to go to Nebraska.

Coach Osborne doesn't play favorites. He treats everybody the same way. He's always trying to encourage people to do the best they can in life. I think you can only do that once you've come to grips with the fact that's how you're supposed to act with people and you've led your life accordingly. I know there were a couple of players who felt like T.O. didn't give them a fair shot. But when it really comes down to it, he is probably the most unselfish person I know, the most caring, loving person who ever coached the game. That care and love weren't just for his players. It was for everybody.

I sensed some of that while I was playing for him, but you really get a feel for it once you're out, kind of away from the program a little bit. Now you never see coaches at a school for 10, 20 or 30 years. It's more about coaches being out for themselves, trying to go up the coaching ladder. You had five, six, seven assistant coaches who wanted to stay working under Coach Osborne and playing their part for 10 or 20 years. You don't see that anymore, either. Once you're away, you understand how special he was.

He loosened up a little bit while I was there. I think I sensed that when he let us know the confidence he had in us, being really blunt about that confidence. I think that started at the beginning of the 1995 season. I can't remember for sure, but I think it was the Michigan State game or the game after that. In so many words he told us we were going to be national champions. He didn't see anyone really challenging us through the whole year. Those weren't his words exactly, but after he said whatever it was he said, that was the general feeling on the team. In the past, T.O. hadn't done that. It was, "One game at a time, don't get too cocky, too arrogant." Not that the statement he made was arrogant. It just allowed us to relax and feel good about where we were going and feel good about where we were as a team. That was the first time I noticed he had kind of loosened up, telling us, "This is a great team. We're going to be a powerhouse."

He'd get upset, and you knew when "Dadgummit" came out of his mouth, you'd better buckle down and do what you were supposed to do. But that was about it. A swear word never came out of his mouth. He never did anything to disrespect anybody or belittle anyone, even when we weren't doing what we were supposed to do. Because he had that character, once he got mad, people knew it was really time to turn it on. "Dadgummit, run it again" was about the extent of what he would have to say.

Coach Osborne and a lot of other coaches were really helpful in my transition from quarterback to safety. They had wanted me to play defensive back when I came there. But he gave me the opportunity to play quarterback, and I guess I proved myself. But all of a sudden I had injuries left and right.

A couple of times he pulled me aside and told me adversity was something I was going to have to conquer in life. I understood where he was coming from. I had so many injuries it was kind of ridiculous, but just the way he carried himself and the way you could see the attitude he took toward coaching, the attitude he took toward players, was something that kind of rubbed off on me. I think his belief in us and his belief in the fact that, okay, we've been through that stuff in the past but things can change in the future if we work hard enough, that's what inspired us to do the great things we did.

He was doing well. His teams were going 9-2, 10-1 every season. But everybody was on him about not winning the "big game." He had to go through that adversity every year. He kind of hid his problems. He went about things basically the same every day, optimistic about what we were doing, optimistic about where we were going, encouraging us along the way. If we had sensed his frustration, I think that might have prohibited us from achieving our goals. I saw that, and I saw the positive attitude he had and that gave me encouragement going through the injuries. It let me know that if I continued to work hard, continued to push through, good things were going to happen. That had a really big impact on me.

Things changed so much for me. I think about what might have happened without the injuries. But a part of me is so satisfied with what did happen that I don't go there much. I had a lot of respect for Tommie Frazier and Brook Berringer. Maybe I wouldn't have had the ability to lead us to national championships. Maybe I would have affected that whole thing. I think they made better decisions than I probably would have made if I had played quarterback. I don't know. That's just speculation. But I'm happy with the way things turned out. I had my time at quarterback. It didn't work out, and I made the switch.

Everything turned out great. I played for the game's greatest coach. I got two national championships. And I had a chance to play professional football. I can't complain about anything. I also was a captain, a really great honor, just from the fact that you had been with those guys for four or five years and you had built up enough respect with them that they wanted you to lead them. To say I was a captain of a team that arguably was the best in history, it doesn't get much better than that.

If I had to boil it down to one thing that made Coach Osborne a great coach, I really think it was his integrity. I don't think he would compromise his integrity for anything. You could relate that to pretty much every area of his life, whether he was supposed to run a football program a certain way or treat people a certain way. He just carried himself in a manner that was excellent. People gravitated to him. He did the right thing. He worked hard. That's all a part of who he was.

Regardless of whether people agree with all the things he wants to do for our state as governor, if you just look at his past and what he's done, he's always been about the people. If you've always put other people ahead of yourself, I don't think you can ever really go wrong.

Adam Treu (1994-96)

Matt Shaw and Adam Treu were friends. Both went to high school in Lincoln Nebraska. And both walked on at Nebraska. Shaw, a tight end, was a "determined guy," Treu said, describing himself as well. "Those were the types of guys we had on our team, the ones who shoveled the manure and did things every day you needed to do to make up for something you might have lacked in another way."

A multisport athlete at Pius X High School in Lincoln, Treu played defensive line on the Cornhusker scout team as a freshman redshirt before moving to offensive tackle. He didn't become a regular until his junior season, when he was the line's sixth man, and he didn't become a starter until his senior season, when he also handled the long-snapping. That skill earned him a shot in the NFL. And he is still playing.

Growing up in Lincoln and getting to meet Coach Osborne was quite an amazing thing. I received a letter from him asking me to walk on my first year and telling me they would give me a scholarship the next three or four years, depending on whether I redshirted. My dad made photocopies of the letter and carried it around in his wallet to show everybody. That's how excited we were.

I wasn't big enough as far as weight. That was one of the reasons they didn't offer me a scholarship right away. They mentioned getting in the weight room and eating at the training table, being able to bulk up. I had gotten more interest from some smaller in-state schools to play basketball. But I knew if Nebraska was going to give me a chance to play football that was the route I was going to take. A 6-foot-5 guy who can't really jump or dribble is not going to do much in basketball.

I grew up with Nebraska football. My dad was a carpenter in the university maintenance department. He was great friends with Bill Shepard, the grounds keeper, and on game days all the maintenance department guys would go to Shep's office at the stadium, tell jokes and have coffee and rolls at seven o'clock in the morning and then go set up chairs in the box seats. At the time, the box seats used to have folding chairs. They would also put up the flags on the pressbox, put up the goal post pads, all those things.

When I was old enough, my dad would take me down there with him. I would get to watch games from up in the southwest corner, where the flag was. I would sit up there, and a policeman would be standing up above me, hanging onto the flagpole, or sitting on what looked like those big stairs in the east and west stands, camping out up there. After the games, of course, I'd go around and collect empty cups and those little plastic deals that held camera film. They were all over the place. Then I'd run around the field and pretend I was Turner Gill or Mike Rozier. It was great.

Shep had a grandson who was a year or two older than I and he'd be down there, too. We'd sit on the Big Red four-wheeler and pretend we were driving it, and we'd go in the north fieldhouse and razz the other team when they were coming in through the garage doors to head up to the visitors' locker room. So I thought I was real lucky to get to go to Nebraska and play.

I don't know that I was treated differently, being a walk-on. Maybe, personally, I felt different. Maybe that was just a hang-up of mine. Maybe being in the locker room at the north end the first two years made me feel different. But I don't believe the coaches treated me any differently.

Moving out of the north locker room was a big deal. You didn't have to leave an hour and a half before the game to walk across the field with your pads and pants on. And then afterward, you didn't have to trudge back to the north fieldhouse while there were still some people on the field or fans in the stands. I didn't really care, though, because I was able to dress out for games.

Playing for Nebraska was a big deal in my family. My dad had since retired, but when we won the national championship, the box that my championship ring came in, plastic covered with some felt, he carried that thing around in his pocket he was so proud. The felt wore off a couple of the corners because he had it with him all the time. Photo Day was another huge deal every year. My parents would come down, cousins. I have a fairly big extended family, and they would all come down to the stadium, take pictures with their kids and things like that. I remember going to Photo Day as a kid.

I don't think I knew Coach Osborne all that well when I played. But I understood him and I knew what he wanted. I also knew he would respect me. I didn't deal with him on a daily basis; I was with Milt Tenopir and Dan Young, the offensive line coaches. Coach

Osborne would give me a "dadgummit" or something like that if I messed up in practice. That was about it.

Coach Osborne was a people person, though; that's safe to say. His door was always open. As a younger player, maybe you're a little intimidated to take advantage of that, but as you got older you would. He would always try to point out things in daily life or obstacles you were going to have to deal with off the field and when you were done playing. A few times he brought in former players who were living a normal life and have them talk about how good we had it to make us understand and to see that we were very fortunate in living a lot of people's dreams to be playing at Nebraska. A few times former players would give us pep talks, talk about never losing a game to Kansas or Kansas State or something like that, because the former players kept up to speed with the program and understood what was about to take place. I think 10 years ago that was something guys responded to, maybe not now.

At halftime of games, it was real businesslike. We'd split up into groups and get together right before we had to leave the locker room, and Coach Osborne would tell us we were going to win, we were going to do the things we needed to do. I don't like to use that word "businesslike," but the coaches would be there and they'd have the grease board full of formations and defenses. It seemed like it was fairly rushed because there was a lot of information to maybe get across. But Coach would summarize at the end. If we were ahead by a lot, and we often were, he would tell us not to get complacent, not to ease off.

We had very few plays, but we could run them with little variances and take advantage of a defense. As a kid, if a game was on TV, my dad, I remember, was a typical Nebraska fan, wanting a touchdown every play. Every time Nebraska would run the option to the short side of the field, it would just drive him crazy. I remember him cussing at the TV when they would do that. When I got down there as a player, I explained it to him. "Dad, every play we run can go either way, okay? When you see Tommie Frazier tap his helmet that means it's going the other way because of the alignment of the nose tackle or a linebacker or a defensive end. As a fan, you're not in tune with that; you don't know what's happening." I never heard him complain after that. But I remember he would always get upset when Gerry Gdowski or whoever the quarterback was would get strung out to the short end of the field and then pitch the ball to the running back, who would get a yard and then run out of bounds.

My dad—he died in 1998—was diagnosed with prostate cancer while I was at Nebraska, and I asked Coach to give him a call one time because his spirits were kind of down. Sure enough, the next day, my dad told me Coach Osborne had called and talked to him. That was a pretty big thing in my mind. Then the spring before my senior year, I had a meniscus tear and had knee surgery, and I remember when I was leaving the hospital, going by the desk, Coach Osborne called and I talked to him there at the nurses' station. Those things meant a lot to me.

I remember I called him after I had gotten drafted by the Raiders and thanked him, told him how much I respected him and appreciated him giving me a chance to play. He in no way celebrated with me or anything like that. He just thanked me for my service and wished me luck. He didn't say, "Well, you've got it made now, buddy." He just kind of left it at that. Maybe he knew through dealing with the NFL and some of the coaches and stuff that the NFL wasn't the ultimate goal. That's just the way he was.

Eric Stokes (1993-96)

Even though he grew up in Lincoln, Eric Stokes considered going to a school other than Nebraska. He made an oral commitment to Iowa, in fact. But he changed his mind and played four seasons in the Cornhusker secondary, at both safety and cornerback, starting every game as a senior and earning all-conference honorable mention. He also earned a sociology degree, graduating in three and a half years. "The odds of making it to the next level are pretty slim unless you really are a unique player," said Stokes, who played briefly in the NFL and now scouts for the Seattle Seahawks. "So I think it's important that the guys do have an understanding that there comes a time when you need to be realistic about what you're doing. Graduating, getting your degree is very important."

Coach Osborne, as you went through the program, that's how you got to know Coach. When you were a freshman, you were just so awestruck by the man. At least that's how I felt. I would say maybe 99 percent of the guys, the first year or two, were pretty awestruck by Coach Osborne and probably didn't say a whole lot to him. But by the time I was a sophomore, I remember feeling very comfortable in terms of talking with Coach Osborne. I felt like he knew me and kind of knew what I was about. Coach Osborne literally knew everybody's name on the team. He knew everything about them. He knew where they went to high school. He knew their parents, and not just of the starters and the big-time players.

Coach Osborne knew the last guy on the roster, who might have been a walk-on from who knows where? He was very, very thorough and knowledgeable from that standpoint. The man knew every little detail about every player. He knew the heartbeat of the team. He knew what was going on with everybody, like I said, from the biggest problem to the smallest problem. Regardless of who the player was, he was aware and conscious of it. That's just the type of individual he was.

I never saw Coach Osborne get mad. He raised his voice in his own way, but on a scale of 1 to 10 it was probably about a 4. As a matter of fact, I never saw him get rattled. He always kept his composure. That's why our team played the way it did.

The only time I ever saw Coach Osborne get riled up, believe it or not, was the Florida game in the Fiesta Bowl for the national championship. He made a speech at halftime and the point of his speech was, "Hey, let's not be content with what we're doing. Let's go out there and make a statement." The way he said it, he had conviction in his voice. I remember we were so fired up. The atmosphere in that locker room…probably sent chills through everybody because you could tell in his voice, his demeanor, there was a passion. He wanted it. We were going to make a statement that night. Florida had done all the talking that week. We never said anything, as usual. The game was pretty much over at halftime, but he said, "Let's pour it on 'em. Let's turn it up and make a statement." Those words stick out vividly in my mind. And he kind of pumped his fist, which he never really did, because he wasn't a man of gestures or anything. We were fired up heading out for the third quarter. Florida was in serious trouble. There was nothing that was going to stop us from winning big-time after his speech. I think the score really showed that.

I'm from Lincoln, and I remember when Nebraska lost to Miami in the 1984 Orange Bowl. Coach Osborne was so stoic, and he handled it with so much class. I know it had to eat at him, though I don't know if he would ever admit it. But the man is ultra-competitive and it comes out in the way we prepared from week to week. We were leaving no stones unturned in terms of preparation for games. He was very competitive. Maybe some of the offensive guys could see that more in dealing with him on a day-to-day basis. Being on defense, I never really saw Coach Osborne much in practice. He always let his assistants coach and kind of took it from there.

I can't really say he loosened up. I don't know how he was before. I only saw it with our group, our class. But I thought Coach Osborne was very loose. I didn't sense tension, stress, that he was trying to press. I didn't sense any of that. When I look back and reflect, I thought that was probably a pretty relaxed time. There was some off-the-field stuff with Lawrence Phillips and all of that. But putting that aside—I'm talking about on the field—I thought Coach was as relaxed as anybody I've ever been around.

I wasn't surprised when he stepped aside. To be quite honest, if we would have won the national championship in 1996, I wouldn't have been shocked if he had retired then. We were certainly good enough to win it in 1996, and the irony is, I knew they were going to win the national championship in 1997, because I knew how good they were. They had lost a few pieces of the puzzle but not very many. Scott Frost was just figuring out the offense. He got better and better and better. You could just tell he was going to be a really, really good quarterback, and they were going to be really strong.

If we had won it in 1996, Coach Osborne might have retired then. But I think he knew what kind of talent he had coming back. And I think, honestly, he knew they could win another national championship. I have no doubt in the back of his mind he felt like they'd be right there, one of the two or three top teams in the country at the end of the season, and sure enough, they were.

You're talking about four national championships in a row if we could have won in 1996. We should have had a chance to play for it. I have no doubt that if we had gone to the championship game we would have won it. And in 1993, we came close, too. So you're talking about one heck of a string that could have happened. Of course, you have three of five, so I'm being kind of greedy. But really, the 1996 season, my senior year, is the only kind of asterisk in my career. It left a sour taste in my mouth because we were good enough to win the national championship. We just came up short in a big game. But winning in 1997 allowed Coach Osborne to go out on a good note.

When I got there, I don't think winning the national championship was talked about, with Coach Osborne being so humble. But no doubt about it, inside he wanted it. He's as competitive as anybody. I think the focus changed about that time. Just winning Big Eight championships wasn't going to be enough. It was time to take it to another level. And that was what was so unique about the recruiting class I was a part of—the 1992 class with Tommie Frazier. We had enough guys who were so confident, who had so much swagger, who didn't know any better, that our focus was about winning the national championship. It wasn't about just winning the Big Eight championship. It was about really doing something big.

We played that Orange Bowl game against Florida State in 1993 and barely lost. And from that point on there was never a time while I was there where the focus wasn't winning the national championship. I go to all these college campuses now as a scout and it's amazing what the focus is. Sometimes, the focus is just getting to a bowl. Some teams can't look at the big picture. They set their goals on a marginal scale, whereas Nebraska, to me, while I was there, was all about winning championships.

That was what was so disappointing about my senior year in 1996, not winning a national championship when it was right there for the taking. Obviously, we had a great season. We were a good football team. We went on and won the Orange Bowl, but I just remember having an empty feeling about winning the Orange Bowl against Virginia Tech. It just wasn't the same.

It really wasn't that big of a deal. There wasn't a lot of excitement. I remember after the game it wasn't like we had done anything great. We handled Virginia Tech pretty easily. I just remember thinking, "Hey, it's too bad we didn't have a chance to play in the big one again."

Believe it or not, at one point I gave an oral commitment to go to the University of Iowa. In a way, I didn't really want to be the hometown guy for a while there. Other guys from Lincoln had gone to Nebraska and hadn't had a lot of success, hadn't really panned out.

So at first I was hesitant. I kind of wanted to make my own way in the world, so to speak.

But the turning point was my junior year in high school. I went to the Nebraska football camp. After the camp, Coach Osborne offered me a scholarship. I went up to his office and the thing that kind of put the icing on the cake was, he said no matter what happened my junior year, if I got hurt, if I had a bad season, whatever the circumstances might be, he would guarantee me a scholarship.

You know Coach Osborne's word is as good as anybody's. So I told my dad that, and it was just a no-brainer to go to Nebraska. No one else was willing to guarantee me that.

But Coach Osborne and his integrity…it was just a no-brainer then.

Grant Wistrom (1994-97)

No Cornhusker defensive player has been more decorated than Grant Wistrom, who epitomized the Blackshirts. He contributed to all three of Osborne's national championships, playing in the regular rotation as a true freshman, at a high level almost from the first time he stepped on the field. He started his final three seasons, was a two-time All-American and the Lombardi Award winner as a senior. He also was a two-time, first-team Academic All-American—Dave Rimington is the only other Cornhusker football player to earn both All-America and Academic All-America recognition twice—and an NCAA Top Eight Award winner, as well as the Big 12 "Male Athlete of the Year."

He considered declaring for the NFL draft after his junior season but returned, and along with tackle Jason Peter, provided the 1997 team with determined leadership as a co-captain. Wistrom came from Webb City, Missouri, and grew up an Oklahoma fan. But he became passionate about Cornhusker football. "No matter where I go, where I end up, this place is always going to be home to me," he said following his final game. "If I could do it all over again, I wouldn't be wearing any other colors but red and white." A first-round draft pick, he is among the best at his position in the NFL.

I remember the first time I met Coach Osborne. I didn't realize how tall he was, and to this day, I still remember thinking, "Golly, he's tall." It's part of his presence. Was he a big part of my decision to go to Nebraska? He was and he wasn't. Obviously, getting a chance to play for Tom Osborne was an amazing thing. But he wasn't the main reason I went there. It was mainly just when I went there on a recruiting visit that I liked the group of guys who were already in place. I knew if I could go there, live there for four years and be around those guys for four years, I was going to have a good time. I knew I was going to enjoy the people I would be around at Nebraska.

There was talk of being able to play as a freshman, but definitely no promises. That's the way Coach Osborne is. He isn't going to tell you what you want to hear just to get your name on the dotted line. He's just an honest man, and he's going to tell you exactly the way it is. He told me there was a chance I could play. But they wouldn't make any promises.

Coach Osborne was very much hands-on. He was always around practice, always coaching. You could definitely feel his presence. But he was more of an offensive coach than a defensive coach. So he kind of left the defense to Charlie McBride. About the only time I heard from Coach Osborne at practice was when I got into a fight with someone and had to leave practice for the day. I saw him get angry out there, with us fighting, messing up plays, just little things like that. I always felt as a player it was important to go out there and mix it up a little bit at practice. But he saw things differently. And there was some frustration because he had put a lot of time into every game plan to make sure we were going to be successful. So he would get angry. But I never heard him curse.

He could remember names. It didn't matter if you started for three years or were a walk-on and you only saw the field in mop-up situations, he knew your name. He knew players' names, and he also knew their mothers' and fathers' names, their brothers' and sisters' names. That still impresses me to this day. Whenever I get back and happen to get a chance to run into him, he always asks how my parents and brothers are. "How are Ron and Kathy? How are Chance and Tracey?" It's just an amazing ability of his.

Remembering names doesn't make him a great person. But all of the things like that about him do. His integrity, you never questioned that. His loyalty to his players, it was evident during the few years I was there that he was never going to hang a player out to dry. He was going to do everything he possibly could to help a guy out, to make sure that even if you might never play football again for the university, he was going to do everything he could to make sure you had every chance in life to become a good, successful human being, a good person. You can't say enough about his character. Put all of those things in there and it's no wonder why guys went out and played their butts off for the man. He put as much into that program as we did, and he cared as much about us as he ever did about winning a football game. A person like that who's running the show, you're going to play hard for him on Saturday.

I was pretty close to leaving for the NFL after my junior year. But the information I had gotten as far as the draft was concerned, the things I heard about me coming out in the draft, weren't exactly what I wanted to hear. I'm lucky enough to have a good family. My parents were a part of the decision and they were going to support me either way that I went. But at the same time, they were going to give me their opinions on the situation. I value my father's opinion more than anybody's, and he was there every step of the way, trying to help me make the decision.

We kind of went with the feeling that I wasn't going to be a top 10 pick, so it was probably in my best interests to stick around school.

Plus, I really hadn't accomplished everything I wanted to accomplish at the University of Nebraska. Coach Osborne didn't try to sway me one way or the other. He didn't say, "Grant, you shouldn't go," or "Grant, I want you to stay." He just tried to present the facts to me as best he could, base on the information we had, and let me make my own decision.

Coach Osborne really cared about his players. You know, a lot of coaches pay lip service, but very few of them actually care like he did. A lot of them talk the talk but very few of them walk the walk. I always believed that Coach Osborne had my best interests in mind, not just winning football games but always wanting what was best for Grant Wistrom and every other player who walked through those doors. I sensed that right away.

I think I had a good relationship with Coach Osborne. The main reason was, he knew how much that program meant to us and how badly we wanted to go out there and win. I think he appreciated that about us because he felt the same way about it. I grew up an Oklahoma fan, so it wasn't really that I loved Nebraska growing up and I dreamed of playing for Nebraska. But I went there and I invested four years of my life in that program and did everything I possibly could to make it the best program in the country, one of the best runs by a college football team of all time. I have a lot of sweat equity in that program, and I still care for it a great deal. I still want them to do great things.

I don't know that I felt like I got to know Coach Osborne real well while I was at Nebraska, but I definitely got to know him a lot better as the years went on. As you went along, your junior year and then your senior year, and you were kind of looked at more as a team leader, you had more conversations with him. He started to realize what motivated you and what would help you, and at that point, I think you get to know him a little bit better. But I don't think I knew him extremely well. I'm sure there were guys who knew him a lot better than I did. But at the same time, I still consider him a very good friend.

I wouldn't change anything about my experience at Nebraska, not at all. It was a great four years. Other than the pain now, I would go back to the University of Nebraska in a heartbeat and play football there for as long as I could.

Jon Hesse (1994-96)

In-state athletes were crucial to Osborne's 1995 national champi-onship team. "We had a good nucleus of Nebraska kids who understood what it meant to the state, and I think we got that across to the rest of the team," said the introspective Jon Hesse, the Nebraska prep football player of the year as a senior at Lincoln Southeast High School. "That team was extremely tight—black, white, young, old—all good friends. And boy, there were a lot of good coaches." He backed up Phil Ellis and Doug Colman in 1995, then started at middle linebacker in 1996, earning first-team All-Big 12 and second-team Academic All-America recogni-tion. He played his final season as a graduate student, earning a psy-chology degree in three and a half years. He spent three years in the NFL, mostly on practice squads, and has a Super Bowl ring. He is an invest-ment advisor in Lincoln.

Coach Osborne was very talented at keeping everybody feeling like they were important, from the strength coaches to the trainers to the last guy on the practice squad. That says a lot. People can talk how-ever they want and try to lead by talking, but Coach Osborne has always led by action, whether it's his spirituality, his coaching or just getting things done. It's always been about action. He's not a big believer in talking about it. His players would do anything for him. And here's an example of why.

One day we were on the elevator, me and a couple of older guys. I remember Vershan Jackson was one of them because he was wearing a couple of really thick gold chains, and when Coach Osborne got on the elevator, he asked Vershan if he had enough gold on. Everybody laughed.

People don't understand, but Coach Osborne didn't like the media. I think he was burned by the media quite a few times, so he was very rigid with the media. He was in control of it and he didn't let people in on what a funny person he is. But he has a real dry sense of humor. And he had a real good relationship with his players. He loved his players, and his players loved him. He wouldn't mess around with a freshman or a sophomore, but once he got to know you, he'd give it to you pretty good. Nothing dirty—"Gosh darn" is about as dirty as Coach Osborne would get. But something like that, where he asked Vershan if he had enough gold on…all of us had a good laugh.

Anyway, he just kind of said hi to all of the older guys. And there was one kid on the elevator, a freshman. It was probably four or five weeks into the season, maybe a little bit later, but the high school football season was still going on. This kid, he wasn't going to be there in a year or two, most likely. He was a walk-on wide receiver, I think, or a defensive back. I had no idea who he was because there were like 150 guys on the team. But Coach Osborne looked at this kid and said, "Hi, Jimmy," or whatever it was, calls him by his first name. I didn't know this kid's name, but Coach Osborne did and then he said, "Hey, how ya doing?" The kid was from some small town in Nebraska, and Coach Osborne said he saw where Jimmy's high school team had beaten its big rival. He gave that kid respect, made him feel important, not only acknowledged him and said his name, but also acknowledged his high school team had won a big game. The kid was right out of high school and that was still important to him.

Coach Osborne made the kid feel like a million bucks. The elevator opened and everybody walked out, and I just stood there and thought, "That's why he's the man." People can talk all they want to about being this or that, but that's having everything under control in action. Coach Osborne was good about making everybody feel like they were a part of team.

Another thing I'll really give Coach Osborne, we had a great coaching staff in the mid-'90s and a lot of different personalities, saints to sinners. But for the most part, everybody respected each other. And Coach Osborne gave everyone their own little place. I wanted to change positions when I was younger. I had another coach who said, "I won't make any promises, but come on over. We're ready." But the linebackers coach wouldn't let me go even though I was going to be on the bench until I was a senior. Coach Osborne let him make the call. I remember saying to Coach Osborne, "I'm just insurance until I'm a senior." He said, "You guys are both head-strong individuals. I'll make sure it works out." I think that's another reason he was so successful and the reason assistant coaches stayed a long time. He let them rule their little position fiefdoms as long as they weren't out of bounds and did a good job.

To be a great leader, you can't control everything. You've got to outsource some of your coaching. His assistants could be themselves as long as they were getting their work done. And sometimes I think Coach Osborne could still make up for some guys who weren't maybe as good as some other guys. But all in all, I think our staff was excellent in the mid-'90s.

There are reasons Coach Osborne won so many games and people who played for him loved him like a father. You've got to walk the walk. He's just a solid individual. Like I said, he didn't talk a whole lot, he just got things handled. He made everyone feel important. And that is an important skill. If you get every single person pulling on the rope in the same direction, that's a lot of force. Each person you lose, who pulls in a different direction, not only subtracts what they were pulling but takes another person away because they're pulling in the opposite direction. Coach Osborne understood that.

He taught us a lot if we were listening. You don't win a game on Saturday. You win it in the off-season and preparing during the week. It's not the will to win that's important. It's the will to prepare. You can get pumped up for about the first couple of plays of a game, but it's the team that's best prepared that wins. He maximized what he had. But you can't maximize anything more than you can maximize it. And so, in the mid- to late '80s, his teams were just outmatched. I think those mid-'90s championship teams were a perfect blend of national talent and great kids from Nebraska who understood what Nebraska football meant to the state. I think we got that across to the out-of-state guys. I just think it was the right mixture. I remember Coach Osborne talked about it the year before we beat Miami in the Orange Bowl for his first national championship. He talked about it a lot going into camp, and if my memory serves me right, before we went down to the bowl game. It was just about maximizing.

That's a hard conversation to have with 18- to 24-year-old kids. He talked about how we weren't Miami or Florida State. He told us we were good athletes, but we weren't the best athletes, man for man. I think he might have been a little bit more gentle than that. But basically the gist of the conversation was, if they're at 95-percent talent and they're lazy and they don't work hard, if they're not on the same page and they drop down to about the mid-80s, 85 to 88 percent, and we start at 85 percent, just below them and if we function as a team, if we work harder and we're better conditioned and we know our stuff better, that can get us up to the 90-, 92-percent area, maybe 95-percent efficiency, and we can beat them.

You put Coach Osborne somewhere like Notre Dame, Miami, or Florida State, where he would have had the best talent, and he wouldn't have lost a game. It would have been sick what he would have done. I would see people at bowl games from around the nation say, "We really respect Nebraska because you guys play with heart. It's not just talent. We can tell you guys love to play football, you like to punch people in the face, nothing illegal but just physical football."

Coach Osborne is a deeply religious man, but football is about leaning on somebody until they quit. And that's how he did it both on offense and defense. He coached physical football. There was nothing dirty about it. It was just football. If you play that way, at some point, the other team is going to quit. Whatever it is, it all starts with the chief.

As with anybody who functions at the highest level, I like to beat people. I want to win. I'll go the extra step. I'll go the extra mile that somebody who doesn't care as much won't go. I can handle losing. I think athletics has taught me that. And I think Coach Osborne taught a lot of people that. It's not about winning. It's about doing something as well as you can and continuing to strive for perfection, understanding that you're not going to be perfect, understanding that you can do everything under your control and you can still lose. But you do everything you can, you prepare.

Honest to God, I don't think it bothered him as much as it bothered other people that he didn't win a national championship until his last four years. I think it made him feel good that he finally got that monkey off his back. It made him feel justified, but I don't think it was as big of a deal for him. I don't think it would have bothered him playing with his grandkids if he had never won a national championship.

We're a tiny, tiny state. We have no business competing on a national level in anything, except maybe farming. It means something to people because this is our source of state pride on a national level. It meant a lot to me that there were people out there listening on the radio. And if we lost, it meant something. They were bummed out for a couple of days. I think those teams understood how important it was to the state.

Recruiting wise, Coach Osborne was pretty intuitive. He offered me a scholarship during my senior year in high school, the summer before my senior year, actually, and I remember Charlie McBride, his defensive coordinator, was the one who talked to me about it first. Charlie told me, "You're going to play here, but you're not going to play safety."

I said, "Oh please, I'm playing safety."

Charlie said, "I like the way you hit, Jon, but you ain't playing safety."

And I said, "We'll see."

Coach Osborne told me, "We'd like to offer you a scholarship, Jon, and I know you're a smart guy and you're going to want to look around. I just want you to know that this scholarship is here for you. When you make up your mind, it's here."

I really appreciated that. I think that's the best way to let people make decisions. I think cornering them makes them wonder if it's going to be a good decision or not. Coach Osborne said this is here for you. Now go find out if it's the place for you. I remember I asked him about his lack of winning the "big one." That was kind of a stupid high-school-senior question. I didn't have a dad growing up, and I probably shouldn't have asked that. I can't remember exactly what he said, but he took it head-on.

He kept working towards winning it. That's what it's all about, winning a championship. His answer, whatever it was, was satisfactory. I just felt that after I really looked into every other place that Coach Osborne was due. And I wanted to be a part of winning championships at Nebraska.

I really felt like that when I went down there. I didn't have the easiest time of it my first couple of years. But I think being around Coach Osborne made me a better person. Those mid-'90s years, there were a lot of guys who were going to be successful after football because they were listening. We saw how Coach Osborne handled his business. He wasn't lucky. He took care of everything and paid attention to detail, didn't step on people, was respectful to people, and like I said, got everybody moving in the same direction. You're going to see a lot of people being extremely successful coming out of that because they had their eyes and ears open listening to what he had to say.

Coach Osborne created this culture where the coaches didn't have to mess with the team much. The older guys pretty much punked out the younger guys and got them in line. There was a very clear line between the adults and the kids. It was just like a good marriage. You don't fight around the kids. The kids can't pawn us off against each other. You can't go to the strength staff and say, "This hurts," and have them say, "Okay, you don't need to practice," and then go to the training staff and them say, "No, you're practicing." That's not acceptable. How Coach Osborne did it was, the adults could talk among themselves and disagree, but when they came back to that kid, he was either practicing or not. There were no gaps in the wall. Once again, that was just Coach Osborne. He was in control of everything.

Great leaders pay attention to details. They do not sweep things under the rug. They attack problems when problems come up. And everybody's on the same page.

Coach Osborne got it. He had a good way of not browbeating people. One time a year, during two-a-days, he would talk about his faith. He would say, "You guys are at an age where you're making a lot of decisions that are going to affect the rest of your life. Life is hard sometimes, and what has got me through it is my faith in God." And that's it. He's a strong Christian. But he's not a browbeater.

"I live my life. I don't need to tell anybody I'm a Christian. If they ask, I will talk to them about why I'm successful and why I feel good about things." But it was just that one time he would talk about it because I think he believes that God gave us all free will. "You've got to make your own decisions. As long as you're not making terrible decisions, I'm not going to get in your business."

There aren't a whole lot of people like Coach Osborne walking the face of the earth. He's an exceptional person. He's not perfect. But he is an exceptional person. He's a great example of, if you're the man, you don't have to tell anybody. That's another thing about Coach Osborne. He won't take credit for anything. It's always, "*We* got lucky," or "*We've* got a lot of good players, a lot of good coaches." But at the end of the day, he's the man.

I take what he taught into my daily life now: It's about the journey. Championships, who cares? You want them, but they don't make you feel any different. So you'd better enjoy getting there and just doing things with excellence. If you're going to do it, let's do it as well as we can and at as high of a level as we can. I've got another championship ring. Who cares? If you don't enjoy that journey, you're screwed.

It's about winning until you figure out it's not about winning. It's about doing your best and being more prepared and working on things you're not good at, just preparing better than anybody else.

Three national championships in his last four years, that's just beautiful, after really going through a long, dark night for 20 years before that, even having recruits asking him why he couldn't win the "big one." How much crap is that? I think that's how Coach Osborne looks at his life. What's the lesson I'm supposed to take here? Let's just keep trudging along and make the most out of this.

Matt Hoskinson (1995-97)

Nebraska's success under Osborne depended on a winning attitude. "Right or wrong, it might have been cocky, but we knew we were going to win," said Matt Hoskinson, who walked on from Battle Creek High School in Nebraska with a promise of a scholarship after his first year. He was accustomed to winning, playing in only four losing games in junior high and high school and then only three at Nebraska. Hoskinson had been a linebacker but he wasn't fast enough for the position at Nebraska, so he played in the offensive line. He never started, but he was regarded as a starter, alternating at guard and center. He was second on the team to two-time All-American and Outland Trophy winner Aaron Taylor in knockdown blocks in 1997. Line coach Milt Tenopir called him the best sixth man in college football.

Coach Osborne loved football. He loved the nuances of what we did every day. He loved practice. He would get excited about things. You could tell. And it got us pumped up to see him get excited. When he'd put in new plays for a specific team and we'd run them to perfection, you could see him get excited, have that confident look, knowing we understood them and could run them well.

He was an extremely prepared guy, and he wouldn't accept us not being prepared. If we didn't run a play perfectly, he'd have us run it again. If we fumbled the ball, he'd say, "Dadgummit." And he'd have us run it again. If he said "dadgummit," you'd done something wrong. That was his cuss word.

If he said "dadgummit," and his face got even one shade more red than it already was, he was fired up. In practice, he wanted us to run with a tempo. He ingrained that so much into the culture of the team that we used to get on each other about not running up to the ball in practice.

Our goal was to run as many plays as we possibly could in the time allotted, see how quickly we could run them. The 1997 team, our goal was to get a snap off with 15 seconds left on the play clock. We used to get on Coach Osborne because sometimes he wouldn't get the play in fast enough.

We wanted to get the defense tired. We wanted to wear them out. We wanted to run plays quickly because we were in shape. We ran and we ran and we ran some more. We ran gassers at the end of every practice. That was always a challenge for fat guys like me. Linemen didn't like doing that, but I can honestly say there wasn't one fourth quarter where I was dragging, ever. That was his mantra: "Wear 'em out, and in the fourth quarter we'll be exactly where we need to be." He would tell us that every single week.

Situational coaching was definitely his strength. He knew our offense so well he didn't need to look down at a script of plays. He knew what we needed to run when we were second-and-2, when we were third-and-7. He was very good about having the play right away in his head. You often see coaches spend too much time thinking about it, and that's where you see timeouts wasted. People look to the quarterback or the team, but sometimes it's the coach's fault. We never got into that situation. Coach Osborne knew what would work in every situation. He could play them out in his mind a thousand times.

Another of his strengths, he would find something that worked and run it and run it and run it. He would continue to run it until the defense found a way to stop it. He was a good game manager. And because he was a good game manager, he always provided us with a certain calm. The example I think of was the Missouri game in 1997, Matt Davison's catch. It would have been easy for a coach to get frazzled in that situation, where we had to pass the ball and we weren't a passing team. But he was very calm about it. Standing in the huddle before we went on the field, he looked at us and said, "All right, guys, we're going to get this done. This is what we're going to do."

This goes back to my previous point. We ran the same play, I believe, eight times in a row. It was called a "roll pass." We pulled a guard out and we'd run a little pass to the flat or hit the tight end, kept it on the sideline. We ran the play left. We ran it right. We ran it left. We ran it right. It got us all the way down the field in no time flat.

Another thing that impressed me was, he would always concede to us. If we wanted to run a play we thought would work, he would let us run it. If we disagreed with a play call, and we had a better one and we all agreed on it, he'd let us run it. If we wanted to run a counter-sweep and we felt it would work because the end was collapsing, he would say, "Okay, let's give it a try." He would always listen to us.

The Tennessee game in the Orange Bowl my senior year, we came in at halftime and I was all fired up. It was my senior year and I told Coach Tenopir, "Coach, run the ball right at them. We can just kill this defensive line." He said, "Well, don't tell me; go tell the redhead."

That's what he said. So I went to Coach Osborne, thinking, "What the heck, it's my senior year." I said, "Hey, Coach, run the ball right at them. We're just killing this defensive line." He looked at me and said, "I see. That's what we're going to do in the third quarter." Those at Nebraska know what happened. We just ran all over them. He listened to us. I'm not sure some coaches do that. Some of their egos are too big.

The maddest Coach Osborne got was probably in practice. On game days whether we were playing good or bad, he and the other coaches were pretty calm because they wanted to give the impression, "We're okay." But he was very intolerant of sloppiness in practice. One of the biggest frustrations for him was jumping off-sides. He wasn't tolerant of penalties at all. If we jumped, you could see his face turn about three shades of red. He was not afraid to get on you. "Dadgummit, Matt, we've been working on this for three days. What's going on here? Run the play again." And he was very intolerant of fumbles. You didn't fumble the ball at any point during any practice, whether it was a walk-through or in pads. You didn't put the ball on the ground. Turnovers are the key to any game, especially when you're running a ground-game, ball-control offense.

Thursdays were probably the time when we saw him the most angry because he expected by Thursday we would have everything in place. We'd be able to run well. We'd be able to get our blocks. And if we weren't able to do that against the scout team without pads, he wouldn't be confident that we could run it in the game. So he would get pretty fired up. The other thing he would get angry about was being late. If you were late to practice, first of all, you would take your "dadgummit" chewing and then he'd send you running up the south stadium steps. And that was never fun before practice. Your legs would be a bit buttery by the time you got down to practice.

The day he announced he was stepping aside was very emotional. Chris Anderson, the sports information director, came into the locker room, looking for the captains and some of the guys who had spoken to the media before. She asked me if I would say something. I was like, "Uh, okay." None of us expected it. Usually things like that get leaked. But we were blindsided. And on top of that, I was going to speak. I thought, "I want to, but I don't want to." It all happened very quickly.

When Coach was talking at the press conference, I'm not going to lie, I was crying. I wasn't sobbing, but before I knew it, tears were running down my face. There were certain guys who had a connection to the program that other guys didn't. And that's no offense to guys from other states because they're equally important to our program, but I'm a Nebraska kid, born and raised my whole life, sitting in front of the TV, watching Coach Osborne on the sideline. He WAS Nebraska football.

Coach Devaney was before my time. I just knew him as a former Nebraska coach. So Coach Osborne was Nebraska football for me and always will be. It was really difficult for me to grasp, a guy I thought was in his prime stepping away. It was more selfish than anything. I didn't want to see him go. He meant too much to the state of Nebraska and the football program. I just felt that was his calling and he needed to be there. When he was talking, I started to realize a little bit what he had missed, what he had given up, some of his kids' functions. He was very happy that he had such a good wife in Nancy. He spent a lot of time at the office.

When it came time to talk, all I wanted to convey was what he meant to me as a person, what I thought he meant to the people of Nebraska, personally and as a football coach, just to let him know he would be missed. Despite the fact that Coach Osborne always came across as a very distant person, he's an emotional guy. He was very emotional that day. You could see he was choked up.

I was trying to keep it together and say what a guy like that had meant to me. The father-figure term gets thrown around pretty liberally, but I've got to be honest, it held true for me. This is a guy who served as a father figure at a place where we didn't have family. He directed us. He taught us how to be men. He taught us about football. He taught us how to be good citizens. He was everything you expect a father figure to be. He cared about what we did away from football. That's a hard thing to let go of.

You can imagine the emotions after we played Tennessee in the Orange Bowl, too, knowing it would be his last game as head coach. There wasn't a dry eye. We had played our hearts out. We had earned a split national championship. Coach Osborne retiring may have played a part in us getting the split. I think we deserved it, but some of the coaches who voted maybe had a soft spot for that being Coach's last game. But what better way to send out a legend like Tom Osborne than an undefeated national championship. I'm very proud of the way we sent him out.

It was a long, emotional speech he left us with, telling us how proud he was of us as men. He would always tell us that. I think he spoke from the heart when he said it.

Matt Davison (1997-2000)

Matt Davison played only one season for Osborne, the coach's last. But his dramatic pass reception for a touchdown on the final play in regulation at Missouri made that one season memorable, and enabled Osborne to finish a Hall of Fame career with a third national championship.

Nebraska trailed Missouri 38-31 with 1:02 remaining and no timeouts. Quarterback Scott Frost directed the Cornhuskers 67 yards on 10 plays, the last a pass that deflected off the leg of Shevin Wiggins and into Davison's hands, setting up a tie and allowing Nebraska to win in overtime, 45-38.

Davison, an all-class, all-state wide receiver from Class C Tecumseh High School in Nebraska, was among six true freshmen who played in 1997. He finished his Cornhusker career with 93 receptions, second only to Johnny Rodgers. None was bigger than the one in Columbia, Missouri.

Coach Osborne, he was always "the coach." Some coaches are really players' coaches and you become kind of friends, chummy with them. Coach Osborne really wasn't that way. He was more of a figurehead to the program, a guy who, you always had his respect. And he had yours. I can't say I got to know him extremely well. But I think I had a good relationship with him as player and coach. Because I was recruited pretty early on, I committed after my junior year of high school, so I had my whole senior year where I would see him when I'd come up to watch practices or come to games in the fall, and then all summer when I moved up here to prepare for my freshman season.

I'll tell you what kind of guy he is. Obviously, he's a great guy—hard to figure out sometimes, but he has a great sense of humor that I don't think everyone gets to see. Every so often when he's speaking to a group or it's one on one, you'll see that side of him come out, that personality that really isn't the coach. It's more that he's kind of a playful guy. He has a great sense of humor. I was fortunate to see that. It's kind of dry humor, but it's very interesting. He's not a guy who will laugh at his own jokes but he comes up with some good ones. He's so smart. Shoot, he was always on his toes around the media. Even if it was a sarcastic question, he wasn't going to give a sarcastic answer because he was afraid it might be taken out of context. So he was always on guard over what he said, though I don't think he had to try too hard because that was just his personality. That's the way he always dealt with things.

He rarely got too upset. He dropped a "dadgummit" or a "golly Moses" once in a while. "Golly Moses, fellas, let's pick it up." And that's about all it would take in practice.

He was just so great at preparation. He was such a student of the game, even after so many years of coaching. He was always thinking ahead, always keeping everybody working toward the same goal. We had so many plays. The playbook was so big, and yet every week we'd pick 50 plays or 25, whatever it was, that we knew we were going to run and we worked on those that week. If a play was going to work against a certain defense, he knew it and we would practice the play that week. But we never forgot about the ones that maybe we hadn't run for a month.

The pass play we ran for the tying touchdown against Missouri we hadn't run all season. It was going to be an option to the left or a pass, either a "39 sprint" or a "99 double-slant." Some guys wanted to run "39 sprint." But he said, "Let's go with '99 double-slant.'" That was a little bit surprising because we had never run "99 double-slant" in a game. To call it in that situation…and maybe it didn't happen just as it was drawn up, but the things he called and made decisions on always seemed to work out.

After we scored, I went off to the sideline and it was mayhem. Everyone was elated, so I didn't see Coach Osborne except when I was taking in another play in overtime. He never really had a chance to say anything to me about the touchdown. And quite frankly, it didn't matter at that point because we still had a game to win. There wasn't any reason to celebrate.

After we won, everyone was going nuts again in the locker room, so I never had a one on one with Coach Osborne there, either. All the players were hugging and in a really good mood. I did a million interviews. Cameras were everywhere. So the first time I really saw Coach Osborne was walking onto the bus. I was one of the last guys on because I had to do so many interviews. Coach Osborne was sitting in the front right seat, as he always sat in the bus. I walked up the steps, looked to my left and there he was. He looked up, saw me and said, "Nice catch, Matt." I said, "Thanks, Coach," and walked to the back of the bus. That was all he said.

I don't know how many times after that play he would say that to me again, "Nice catch, Matt." One time he did tell me, "You know, with this many years of coaching you don't remember all the plays that happened. But that's one I'll never forget." I guess that means a lot to me, coming from a guy who's coached in so many big games and had a lot of great things happen to him. For him to say it's something he'll never forget means a lot to me.

What the normal fan didn't get out of watching Tom coach was, every time he ran a play, no matter what the play was, a pass, a run, an option, whatever it was, it was always setting something else up or seeing how the defense lined up against that formation. He was always at least three plays ahead of everybody, knowing what he wanted to call later, for a certain down and distance.

He had the vision of what he wanted to do down the line in each drive, and not only on that drive but in the next drive and even what he might want to call down the stretch in the fourth quarter. He always had that planned out. And I'll say this, and I know I've talked about this with other players, too, he could see more from the sideline on what the defense was doing and what might work offensively than any coach in the press box. It was amazing. If we were in a certain play and the defense was lined up a certain way, he could see from the sideline what block needed to be made for a play to be successful.

He could tell right at the beginning of a play if it was going to work, and you would see his reaction. He knew what the key blocks were at the point of attack on each play he called. Every block is important, but he knew which ones were critical to get the play started. And he could see if those blocks were being made. So he pretty much knew and would look down at the play card for what he wanted to run next.

More than anything, he was always on the same level emotionally. One thing he said that I'll never forget, "Don't ever let your highs get too high or your lows get too low, just try to stay on an even keel." If you did that, it would keep your work ethic, your discipline and all the time you had put into being great, on the right path. Like his reaction after that play at Missouri—you wouldn't have known if I caught it or not by the way he reacted. "Well, okay, there's another play. First of all, we have to kick the extra point. Then we have to win in overtime."

The first time I met Coach Osborne might have been at football camp after my junior season in high school. Then he came to a basketball game in Tecumseh my senior year. That was a spectacle. It was quite a deal. I told people he was coming. He sat with my parents, and I think they kind of protected him a little bit from the autograph seekers. He had no reason to come to Tecumseh, really. I had already committed. He knew I was going to sign. But he came to a game because he wanted to show his support. It was plain and simple. I had a pretty good game. I can't remember how many points I had, 20-some.

I missed some free throws in the fourth quarter. I couldn't tell you exactly how many I missed. But we won the game. Afterward I went to meet him. The first thing he said, and it was so typical of Coach Osborne, "Matt, I guess we need to work on those free throws, don't we?" It didn't have anything to do with anything else I did in the game. It was just the part of the game I could improve on. Of course, I was probably nervous shooting free throws with him there anyway. But it was just like Coach Osborne to say that, not grill you on it, but just say that was the part of the game you needed to work on.

His leadership was unbelievable. He had the ability to get everybody to see the goal, and everything you did, every single day, all year long, not just during the season, the preparation, was directed at that goal. He made everybody believe they were a part of this great thing. That's what made the Big Red machine so successful for so many years. He had the ability to get the most out of everybody.

It's like his mentoring program. Mentors tell kids from tough backgrounds that they can do something. If you hear it enough and you have the support to do it, pretty soon you find yourself doing things you didn't know you could do. That's the way he coached. He made everybody believe they could do things they didn't know they could do. That was probably his best characteristic.

I was in the room the day Coach Osborne announced he was stepping down. It was a room full of big, strong, supposedly tough, football players, and you saw the tears and the emotion. It wasn't only because of the games and his coaching; it was because every day we got to have this person in front of us in meetings and on the field and everywhere. His door was always open to you. You had the luxury of getting to hear him talk. I always found myself really listening to everything he said, because even in a normal conversation or speaking in front of a group, you never knew when he was going to say something that you were never going to forget, something that might impact your life until the day you died.

So I was really tuned into everything he said. That's what was going through my mind that day. "I don't get to enjoy his company. I don't get to see him live life the way it's supposed to be lived, doing things the right way, treating people the right way."

He was the ultimate mentor. You think about all the people he has mentored, not even knowing it. He doesn't know the effect he has had on people. That's what makes him special, too. He's so humble. He's had this effect, literally, on thousands of athletes, just on the player-coach side of things, not to mention the thousands of other people he's come in contact with in his life. That's what was making me sad, not so much that he wasn't going to be telling me the play to take in the next season, just that I was going to miss his company.

I remember after that meeting, we went upstairs and had a team meeting and after the meeting, he talked to Bobby Newcombe and me, guys who had just come into the program, and said that was something he felt bad about because he felt like in some ways he had let us down, that he had committed to our parents and to us that he was going to be our coach, and he was letting us down by stepping aside. Obviously, we understood. But he felt a sense of obligation to all of the underclassmen to stay until we were done playing. So that was tough to deal with, too.

5

Assistant Coaches

One year after his announcement that he would be stepping aside as head coach, Tom Osborne was inducted into the College Football Hall of Fame. The Hall's three-year waiting period was waived for only the second time. Grambling's Eddie Robinson was the other coach who didn't have to wait.

Osborne's accomplishments warranted immediate inclusion. His record was 255-49-3 (.836). His teams won nine or more games in each of his 25 seasons, and they won at least 10 games 15 times, with 11 or more in each of his final five seasons. They earned bowl bids every season. They won or shared 13 conference championships. And they were voted national champions three times.

His Cornhuskers won 26 consecutive games from the 1994 opener in the Kickoff Classic until an upset at Arizona State in the second game of the 1996 season. Their undefeated and untied back-to-back national championship teams were major college football's first since 1955-56.

Nebraska enjoyed the national respect earned under his predecessor Bob Devaney throughout Osborne's tenure as coach. The Cornhuskers were included in the Associated Press rankings all but three weeks during 25 seasons. Beginning in mid-October of 1981, they would earn a place in the rankings for 348 consecutive weeks, a streak that wouldn't end until after Osborne had stepped aside.

Many factors contributed to that success, among them assistant coaches whose faces became familiar on the sideline while he was coach. He considered staff stability essential to success and did what he could to retain trusted assistants, dividing money from shoe contracts and summer camps among them. He even consulted his staff when he looked into the Colorado job following the 1978 season.

"There's no question that most of whatever has been accomplished here that's been good has been because we've had a great bunch of assistants," Osborne said prior to the 1997 season.

Concern for assistants also figured into his decision to step aside. The timing was significant, he said during the news conference to announce his decision in early December of that year.

He was referring not only to players but also to assistant coaches when he said, "I think it's better that it happen this way, now, than it happened at some point [where] they may end up with a guy coming in from the outside who treats them differently than they've been treated. All of a sudden, everything they've had that's familiar is taken away from them. So continuity has been critical."

By leaving when he did, he could ensure that Frank Solich, to whom he had given the title of assistant head coach in 1991, would succeed him, and that all of the assistants who wanted to stay could.

"One guy is moving out, but in terms of the overall program, in terms of stability, our ability to get the job done, not much is going to change. It all fits together," he said. "It hasn't been a one-man operation. The one thing that the people of Nebraska can't afford to lose is the coaching staff. You can lose me, and not much is going to change. But to lose all the assistants—then a whole lot would change.

"It has to do with consistency, and I want that to continue."

Frank Solich (1979-03)

Frank Solich was a member of Devaney's first recruiting class, arriving in 1962, the same as Osborne, who taught an educational psychology class in which Solich was a student. Despite his size—5-foot-8 and 158 pounds—he played fullback in addition to returning kicks, on teams that were a combined 29-4 and won three Big Eight championships. He was a co-captain as a senior in 1965.

He was a head football coach his first year out of college, at Omaha Holy Name High School, and after three years there, he moved to Lincoln (Nebraska) Southeast High, where he spent 11 seasons and coached two teams to the Class A state championship. Osborne hired him as head freshman coach in 1979, and he became the running backs coach in 1983, following Mike Corgan's retirement. Corgan, nicknamed "Iron Mike," came with Devaney from Wyoming and had been Solich's position coach.

Osborne named Solich assistant head coach after Wisconsin coach Barry Alvarez, a Cornhusker teammate, tried to hire him as offensive coordinator in 1991.

Solich, whose record as Nebraska's head coach was 58-19, is the head coach at Ohio.

I think Tom is an extremely organized person and really able to move through things in a timely fashion, so meetings and time spent together as a staff were always productive. He could make quick decisions but he took in the views and thoughts of his assistants, was open to ideas. He would measure those ideas very quickly and process them in a manner that enabled him to move forward.

He was time-efficient. He knew the game extremely well. But above and beyond knowing the game, he knew people extremely well, and he was able to get his staff and his players on track all the time, and for an extended period of time, not just one game or two games or preseason, but all the way through a season and into the bowl game, one year after another.

He was, and is, a man of his word. When he told you something, that was the way it was. You didn't have to worry about it, debate it. You knew his word was good. For a long time at Nebraska we didn't work with contracts. But no one felt uncomfortable about that.

I don't know that he ever had a team that didn't believe in him, that didn't believe in the system and what we were doing. Sometimes a few fans, maybe, didn't believe in the system, and maybe even a few writers didn't believe in it. Tom kind of went against the grain a little bit with the option game, as heavy as we were into it. But everybody understood that he felt this was the best way to go.

His sincerity came across to his coaches and to his players, and he was so even-keeled, even when something wasn't going right, he didn't fly off the handle. He would show his emotions at times. It would be under control, but you knew when he was upset, when he didn't feel you were playing to your ability. It came across. It didn't come across in a berating manner. It wasn't a screaming Tom Osborne you would get. But his feelings and emotions would show when things weren't going well.

I think Bob Devaney was probably just a little bit more explosive than Tom. And I very much enjoyed playing for Bob, as I enjoyed coaching under Tom. Bob was a fun guy to do anything under. He was a tremendous competitor. That's what both of them had, that tremendous competitiveness within themselves, in their own styles, making it work and not accepting anything that wasn't the best.

In some ways their personalities were different, but what they were all about and what they wanted to accomplish was the same. Competitiveness is a key because your competitive nature is going to show to your staff and it's going to show to your players. And if you're not a great competitor, it'll show. Your staff and your players are a reflection of you. Tom took a business approach to everything, and his players followed suit. You always knew how Coach Osborne was going to show up in terms of what he was about. He wasn't on a rollercoaster to where you never were real sure what you were going to get.

He had a sense of humor. It would show in staff meetings, but didn't necessarily show in public. Maybe the media didn't see him as a guy with necessarily a sense of humor. But I think if you worked with Tom on a daily basis and you coached for him or played for him, you'd say he had a sense of humor. Now, that sense of humor only went so far. He took a business approach to football and preparing, leaving no stone unturned. But he also understood that he was dealing with young men and it was a tough game, so I think he was lighthearted at times to a point where it was fun; it was enjoyable.

Everything he asked you to do, he was doing the same thing. He was so intense in his preparation and his on-field coaching that he let nothing distract him, whether it was opponents, fans, his own team. He was zeroed in. I think that's what enabled him to be a head coach and offensive coordinator at the same time.

There was some give and take, but he would get on a roll calling plays, and when he was on a roll, you just let him go. But he was open to suggestions and would use those suggestions or store them away and you'd see them later in the game. He would take things and process them and use them when they needed to be used. He was great at not only the basics of an offense and defense but also plays that were special for a given game or given moment in a game. His timing on those kinds of things was excellent. That helped him be the great coach he was. He also was great at being able to make adjustments and understanding that, hey, you've got to give the other guy some credit, too. They're going to be pulling some things out of the hat. They're going to do some things they haven't shown.

Maybe as he coached and continued to have success, he understood we were going to get everybody's best shot and that everybody had athletes, and if you didn't play well and they did, you were going to be in trouble. So he prepared his teams that way. He never went into a game overconfident or allowed that from his staff or his players.

It wasn't surprising when Tom went for two in the 1984 Orange Bowl game. He had thought it through. We had talked it through, and he made that decision, basically, prior to the game. We were in that thing to win it. And if the opportunity was there to win it, we were going to go for the win. I think probably no one on the sideline was surprised—none of the coaches, and I doubt the players were surprised. They always saw Tom as someone who accepted nothing but his best.

I was still up in the booth at the time. The play was close to working. I really thought it had a chance. You could have called three or four different things and had a chance because of the great players we had. The pass was an excellent call, and really an inch, no more than two, from being completed.

After the national championships it was the same Tom Osborne. He felt especially good for the program, especially good for the players. And I think he felt good for himself, but Tom was never one where that showed. He was the same Tom Osborne who went into those games. Winning one national championship and then two and then three didn't change him one bit. I do think it was a relief to get that first one after so many opportunities where he was close. Not being able to get it done was frustrating for everybody. But he handled that extremely well. As much as you want to feel good about yourself in those situations, I don't think there was a player or coach in the system who didn't feel great about Tom, because he deserved to win those championships, and probably a few more.

There's no doubt he's one of the best ever to have coached the game at the college level. I think his 25 years and his record show that. But I think there are a lot of other things that show it, too. I think Tom would be successful in anything. He's bright. He's got a great work ethic. And he's able to adjust. So if you've got those things going for you, you could jump into about anything and have a chance.

When Tom contacted me, I was comfortable with what I was doing. I really liked high school coaching and had been at Southeast for 11 years, with really good success. I knew there were some tough things about college coaching. You might have to move your family numerous times. But that really didn't happen to me. I was really fortunate in my career. I had no reservations about going to Nebraska other than the fact that I really enjoyed working with high school kids. I liked it at Southeast, great administration, great people. But the chance to coach with Tom was a deciding factor. He was already a special coach.

Guy Ingles (1976-78)

As an assistant, Osborne coached Guy Ingles, a small but tough split end from Omaha Westside High School who finished his playing career in 1970 as Nebraska's all-time leading receiver. He was the first player in Cornhusker history to amass 1,000 receiving yards. He held the top spot on the list for only one season, however. Johnny Rodgers, to whom he was second in receptions and receiving yards on Devaney's first national championship team, surpassed him in 1971.

Ingles was a graduate assistant under Osborne and became the full-time freshman head coach in 1976. He coached with former Nebraska assistants Jerry Moore at Texas Tech and Monte Kiffin at North Carolina State before returning to Omaha, where he is an investment advisor.

This is 1995; Nebraska is a couple of practices from going to Phoenix to prepare for Florida in the Fiesta Bowl. My daughter Bailey—who would have been 11 or 12—looks up to me at the dinner table and says, "I want to meet Tom Osborne." And I go, "Well, you know what, we'll just figure something out." I don't know what day it was, but there was a practice outside, on the grass fields. We walk in the back door by the old fieldhouse and here comes Tom down the stairs. Everybody is walking out to the field.

I go, "Hi, Coach."

He says, "Hi, Guy."

And I go, "My daughter wanted to come to practice today and meet you."

He leans down and shakes hands with her. "Come on in."

So we go watch practice, and I'm like everybody else, thinking, "I hope we can beat Florida. Are we really as good as we think we are, or hope we are? Florida has got to be so fast; how are we going to stop them?" At that time, I think they had the most prolific passing attack in college football history.

The first thing Nebraska did was break up into group work. So I watch that for a few minutes. I've got Bailey by the hand. These guys are banging around pretty good, and she's almost timid. I say, "We're okay right here." Then they break into one-on-one drills. My impression is, "Well, Florida is going to have to be real good, because these guys can just flat-out play."

Pretty soon, they're going to teamwork. You had two offensive teamwork stations and a defensive teamwork station, all kinds of players running around—150 guys on the field, redshirts and scout teams. The scout teams are pretty accomplished because by that time in the season, they know what they're doing. And so I go over to the offensive station. They've got the first two offenses going against bags.

It's not live. They're not taking the back to the ground or anything like that. But it's a nice-paced practice. I'm there for 40 minutes and they run play after play after play, and I swear they ran no more than one play over in those 40 minutes. Milt Tenopir said something like, "Oh, that's not right." Well, maybe one other time Tom said to run a play over. But that was it. There wasn't so much as a guy twitching on the line of scrimmage. There were no fumbles. There were no bad option pitches. Nobody was raising their voice. It was absolutely a perfect football practice from an offensive standpoint.

I've got Bailey by the hand. We're right behind the huddle. And I know what plays are being called. Turner Gill is talking to Tommie Frazier, and one time Tom goes to Frazier and says, "When they're in that and you've got this called, you've got to go to this play or that play." Frazier is just nodding. He knows what he's doing. He audibles 10 or 15 times during the practice and never misses a beat. Nobody jumps offside. No receivers are in motion. No dropped passes or dropped pitches.

We go over and watch the defense, and it's the same thing. Nobody's raising their voice. Grant Wistrom is coaching people. He's the leader. There's no question about that. It was the same thing with Frazier and the offense. There was no question who the boss was.

Wistrom is exhorting people to hustle, and I'm thinking, "This guy is a rush end and he knows what everybody on the defense is doing." They're not going full-speed but they're rushing the passer pretty good. Bailey thinks we're a little too close, that we'd better back up. "Honey, we're fine."

Her eyes are as big as silver dollars. These guys are big, and they're moving around; they can run. I'm trying to explain things to her, but I'm basically just there with my mouth open for two hours.

Later, I told my wife, "Florida has got to be the best thing you've ever seen or we're going to kill them, because this is the best football team I've ever laid eyes on, in 30 years of watching Nebraska football." They just looked poised and confident, on top of their game. And I swear, nobody yelled the whole two hours. Nobody made a mistake. I'm going, "Oh, man. This is the perfect coach with the perfect offense and the perfect quarterback."

I remember having lunch with Bob Devaney, in 1993 or 1994, and I asked him, "When did you really know that Tom was the guy?" I was expecting him to say 1969 or 1970, 1971. He said, "1965." It can hurt people's feelings, but Tom had been there for three or four years as a grad assistant and part-time assistant, and Bob knew seven years before the fact that it was going to happen, if he could name his own guy.

When I was a graduate assistant in 1971, I remember standing behind Tom in the press box, listening to him call the plays. He called every one of them, from 1969 on, every single play, for all practical purposes. Bob was on the sidelines pushing people out there. Bob never had the headphones on. Carl Selmer, the offensive line coach, had the headphones and was talking directly to Tom. I'm not saying Carl didn't get something called he wanted called. But the offensive coordinator was Tom Osborne. By the time I was a senior, it was apparent. He went from being the receivers coach when I was a sophomore to being the offensive coordinator, without the title, by the time I was a senior in 1970.

The preparation, the playlist, that's what Tom did every morning. They sat there in those offensive staff meetings and he figured out the playlist, which plays were going to be audibles and which plays weren't going to be. He took input from Cletus Fischer and Carl Selmer and everybody else. If they had a problem with a play, a blocking assignment, an audible or any of that stuff, he brought it up. If Milt said, "We need to do this differently," they did that. But the guy who ran the show, there wasn't any question who had the brainpower. Everything fit together. Tom was a genius at knowing what somebody was going to try to do to you.

I've never forgotten this; the very first staff meeting as a head coach, not the second, not the fourth, the first thing out of his mouth was: "The walk-ons are going to be the difference, guys. We have got to recruit walk-ons." That was in 1973. I remember distinctly. He said, "They'll be the difference with scholarships declining. They'll be the thing that keeps us in the ball game, our difference-maker."

Say what you want about walk-ons; they were great. But you don't need them at Ohio State or Michigan or Penn State. Everybody is lucky Tom wasn't at Notre Dame or Ohio State, because he would have run the tables. He was perfect for Nebraska. He is a Nebraskan. He's from Hastings. Nebraska is what he cared about. I think if you had asked Barry Switzer if he could have won with Nebraska's players, he would have said no. But Tom could have won with Oklahoma's players. That's why, in the long run, Tom is going to be thought of as a better coach. He lasted longer and did it with less talent, at a clip that nobody's ever going to equal.

Tom finally got the players. And then it wasn't fair. Recruiting was difficult. Tom was just relentless in recruiting; when I think of the people that almost came to Nebraska in the 1970s and 1980s, guys that made All-Pro and All-America....As good as he was, it took 20 years to get there, 20 years of knock-down, drag-out struggle. But he got the talent level to the point where they could beat everybody. I wasn't surprised it finally came to that. I think everybody was a little bit lucky he didn't win six or seven national championships. He probably would have won at least one more if not for Switzer.

It's never going to happen again—25 years with at least nine wins. I don't care if the next Vince Lombardi's out there somewhere; it's never going to happen.

Jerry Moore (1973-78)

Jerry Moore, a native of Bonham, Texas, and graduate of Baylor, came to Nebraska from Southern Methodist University, where he was an assistant to Hayden Fry for eight years. He was the first of three assistants Osborne hired after succeeding Devaney. The other assistants were carryovers from Devaney's final staff. Moore replaced Osborne as the receivers and quarterbacks coach. He left Nebraska to become the head coach at North Texas in 1979. After two years in Denton, he went to Texas Tech, where he was head coach for five years. He was out of coaching for two years, then returned as an assistant to Ken Hatfield at Arkansas for one season.

Moore coached Appalachian State to the NCAA Division I-AA championship in 2005, his 17th season in Boone, North Carolina, and is the winningest football coach in school history. After the championship, he received a congratulatory phone call from Congressman Osborne in Washington, D.C.

I was the first outsider Tom hired. I had met him at Estes Park at Fellowship of Christian Athletes conferences three or four years prior to that. The last conference we went to at Estes Park, he asked if I would be interested in coming to Nebraska. I'd never given it any thought, to tell you the truth. I was a Texas guy, born and bred, Southwest Conference. I was coaching at SMU. But when he asked me, I said, sure I'd be interested in doing something like that. He said, "Well, I'm probably fixin' to be named head coach up there."

Back then I don't think everybody was as aware of things as they are now, like people in the South probably didn't realize Tom was going to follow Coach Devaney. When the FCA conference was over, instead of driving straight back to Texas, we drove through western Nebraska, to Lincoln, to Omaha, and then went back down to Texas through Kansas. We got a look at the university and the state of Nebraska. We didn't tell Tom we were going there. We spent a day in Lincoln just driving around and looking. We went on back, and he called and made kind of an offer to come up there. About that time, Bob decided to stay another year. Tom said, "Can you stay at SMU another year?" So I went in with my hat in my hand and begged Hayden Fry. Well, I didn't really have to beg. I said, "Coach, Coach Devaney decided to stay another year; can I stay here?" He said, "Go put yourself back in the office." Hayden was a fun guy for me to coach for because I had played for him at Baylor and coached for him there at SMU.

The next year we moved to Nebraska. Tom called after everything was set and said he would like for me to come to the Orange Bowl with the team, to watch them practice. This is what made him such a successful coach. Obviously, it was fun for us to go to the Orange Bowl. But he knew we were going to open up the next season against

UCLA on national TV. So he said, "I'd like you to come watch practice, sit beside me in the press box on game night and see how we do things."

I saw how they did things, and whether that was the reason or not, there was a comfort zone coming into Nebraska. I've never forgotten the fact that he was looking ahead to the UCLA game as far as I was concerned. He wasn't looking past Notre Dame. But he wanted me to see how they did stuff. I've never forgotten the organizational or thinking-ahead process he did. Every meeting we dissected plays, stuff that most people would think was so simple. He wouldn't take it for granted. He went over things time and time and time again. He was so meticulous with things, so detailed.

Tom never really divorced himself from the offense. After a while, he asked if I would ever be interested in being a head coach. I said, "I haven't given it any thought." He said, "If you need to have a title, you can always tell people you're an offensive coordinator." That was about the time Monte Kiffin became the defensive coordinator. They had never had coordinators at Nebraska, which I think it is a great idea. But I'm the only guy on our staff who thinks it. All of our guys want to be coordinators. The thing I think it did was, it made everybody work.

If I learned anything from Tom—and I think I learned a lot—the number-one thing I learned from him was handling people, dealing with people, dealing with coaches, dealing with players. I hadn't been there long, and there was kind of an outburst and a misunderstanding in the offensive staff room. It involved a long-time coach there. And Tom dealt with it. He dealt with it like you're supposed to. It was a tough deal for 24 hours. But I'll always remember he handled it the only way you could handle it.

I say the only way, because he could have been a jerk and handled it a different way. But he handled it and made everybody feel good about themselves. I think that's one of the things that creates success. You make players feel good about themselves, you make coaches feel good about themselves and feel confident about themselves, and they're going to do a better job of coaching, a better job of playing.

Tom was magic at that. I used to spend a lot of time with John Melton. And John said Bob Devaney was that way, too. Bob would walk around the players during the week, just get them one on one, maybe in the hallway or on the field. John and Bob were together at Wyoming, of course, and John said Bob was magic about handling players, putting a burr under a guy. I think Tom was that way, too. But never once did I hear him raise his voice, not once. I don't know if it's because of that, but I seldom raise my voice. I don't know if it's because of being around Tom, but I seldom do.

Everybody had great respect for him. They had great trust in him and great respect for him. Well, what else do you want? You trust somebody. You respect them. What else is left?

The first time I ever met him, I didn't know who he was. He was just another guy at the FCA conference. Those guys out there referred to him as "Dr. Tom." I didn't know. "Well, he's the quarterbacks coach at Nebraska." That didn't mean anything to me. I'd been around pretty good coaches in the Southwest Conference. Who's Tom Osborne? That's that isolation in the South. If you had asked me who Emory Bellard was, or somebody like that, a guy at Texas or a guy at Arkansas—Johnny Majors—I knew those guys. But I didn't know who Tom Osborne was.

But I'll tell you what, I heard him speak at the FCA conference. This was to a group of coaches; it wasn't kids. And you said, "That guy's different. There's something different about him." Then I found out who he was. I'm talking about inside out. My first deal was great respect for him. "Well, I'd like to end up being that kind of man," is what it amounts to.

Tom's success didn't surprise me, not at all. He was a great football coach. He's smart and a tireless worker. He never showed being tired. I think that's one of the things I've tried to pick up on myself here. I used to run with him at lunch. I hadn't even thought about it until now, but I like for those players to see me working out. I like them to see me run and work, get sweaty and all that stuff. Tom didn't do it for that. And I don't do it for that, either. But players would make comments about him working out, and I think there's a certain amount that they buy into. They see you working. They see you doing things similar to what they do. And I think that's important. There's a certain amount that those players lock onto. They sit around that locker room, they sit around the training table, and they talk about, "Hey, Coach is out there running the stands. Coach is out there doing this." It's one of those respect things.

We used to play basketball against the players at noon sometimes. And I remember we played in a charity game once. All of the rest of us would just rebound for Tom. I remember Guy Ingles and I, we'd just get the ball to him. He was a great competitor. Those fish in Lake McConaghy hated to know when he was on his way out there. They were in trouble. He was going to win. He would be tough at anything he does.

We drove back up there when they dedicated the field at Memorial Stadium to him. We left Boone about three o'clock in the afternoon and got into Kansas City, gosh it had to be one in the morning, spent the night there, drove on into Lincoln to be there when they named the field after him. You wouldn't have done that if it weren't for him being the kind of guy he is. I could have said, "Well, we couldn't make things work." But you've got great respect for him.

I enjoyed every second of being at Nebraska. It didn't even seem like work. Tom was so much fun. And he's so smart. Every day you were learning things.

John Melton (1973-88)

John Melton was among the assistants who came with Devaney from Wyoming. The others were Mike Corgan, Carl Selmer, and Jim Ross, who served four years as head freshman coach for Osborne. Selmer left following the 1972 season and became the head coach at Miami.

Melton was as loyal to Osborne as he had been to Devaney. Osborne adjusted the staff after taking over. Melton had coached linebackers for six seasons, but Osborne assigned him tight ends and wingbacks and hired Rick Duval from Colorado to work with linebackers and coordinate recruiting. Two seasons later, with Duval focusing on recruiting, Melton was back on defense, coaching the linebackers. His dry wit made him a favorite of reporters.

I didn't see a dramatic change in Tom when he became the head coach. Tom is Tom. He's very well organized and he's very patient. The two things that really made him a good head coach, besides being smart, he's patient and he's organized. A lot of times one of us would get on a kid pretty good and he'd say, "Now wait a minute, he's going to be all right. Maybe his high school coaching wasn't as good as the coaching at other high schools." Tom was very, very patient with kids.

What Tom would do was, after you visited with a guy, he might stop by and say, "Well, this coach gets a little excited once in a while." He always made the kid feel like we were on him because we wanted him to improve, and maybe sometimes we got a little impatient.

One of the things that made Tom a great head coach, he stuck up for his ballplayers. And they knew it. As long as they gave him 100 percent, Tom was going to stick up for them. They respected Tom and they liked Tom, and they knew he was behind them all the time. He'd never forget you.

And there were some ballplayers on the team I'd just as soon forget.

Tom was very, very easy to work for because he let you do your thing. You explained to him why you were doing it in meetings and he'd leave you alone. But sometimes he'd drive the defensive coaches crazy. A player would make a mistake and Tom would say, "John, why did he do that?"

"I don't know, Tom, why he did that." Then he'd say, "Charlie, why did he do that?"

Tom used to say that a lot: "Why did he do that?" How did we know?

Was Tom similar to Bob? Well, Bob approached it as probably a little more fun than Tom did. Tom was right on that watch. If it was a 15-minute deal in practice, we went 15 minutes. If Bob had a 15-minute deal and it wasn't going good, it could turn into a 20-minute deal. Bob could always put his watch back where it ran right on time. Tom's practices were very organized.

Both of them spent a lot of time around the offense. Very seldom did you see them around the defensive units. Offense was Tom's forte. Now don't misunderstand me; he knew what was going on with the defense, because the first meeting of the day, in the morning, was with the defensive coaches. He sat in there with us and we looked at the defensive film, went over our mistakes and what we were going to do the next week. If we did something, we would have to clear it with Tom. You look at the defensive coaches, we've had some honeys, who had some brilliant ideas. Sometimes the brilliant ideas didn't work out real good.

Tom was very, very loyal to Bob. And as time went along you could see Tom taking over maybe a little bit of the offensive thinking. Then we went a little to the passing game. Remember how, at the one time we went to that unbalanced line and just ran it and ran it and ran it? Then we got out of that. We got Dave Humm and Vince Ferragamo and went to a little more of a passing deal. Then he got another kind of quarterback and we went into another offense. Tom did a lot of fitting his offense to the type of quarterback he had. Those were his babies, the quarterbacks. He enjoyed that. He knew them.

Sometimes he'd get a little excited. Bob would change something on offense during the game and not tell Tom or anybody. He might change a pattern or something on the sideline and sort of keep it a secret until we ran it. Tom would think the quarterback made a mistake. "No, Coach Devaney said run a different kind of pattern." Tom and I were up in the press box. That was always interesting.

Tom had everything written out in front of him. He was always two plays ahead. That's the way he was, very intense up there in the press box. He had a good idea of what was going on. He really did. Tom was just a great football coach. That's the only thing you can say: Tom was a great coach.

There were no problems in the transition from Bob to Tom that I know of. We knew it was coming. Everybody knew a year before Bob made the announcement.

Tom has a great sense of humor and he doesn't mind being joked about. He didn't mind telling stories about me, or any of us. When he had the heart bypass, he said he knew he had a bad heart because when he was running one day George Darlington passed him up. I think the minute he got out of surgery he was on the phone with us, wanting to know how things were going with the team. It didn't take long. I'll bet the day after he had the operation, he was on the phone wanting to know how recruiting was going.

You knew Tom was mad when he said "dadgummit." He got mad sometimes. Then he'd say, "Dadgummit." And that was it. Then you knew Tom was really about at the end. Or if he'd punch his fist in his hand and say "Dadgummit," that was really it. But that didn't happen very often.

Tom could not put up with mistakes, especially if he went over it with you once, like, say, you made a mistake and he got a little perturbed and went over it with you—you were blocking the wrong man or something like that—and then you made the mistake again; he'd let you know. He really would. He'd get in your face once in a while, "Dadgummit" and punch his hand.

Am I surprised that Tom's in the Hall of Fame? Take a look at his record. How many coaches have won three national championships? You figure it out.

Nothing Tom does surprises me. He's a guy who wants to do something for the state. And that's the whole thing. He just wants to do something to pay back. He's always paying back for what the state did for him.

Gene Huey (1977-86)

Gene Huey's cousin, Ben (Bennett) Gregory, was a Cornhusker co-captain in 1967. They both were from Uniontown, Pennsylvania. Huey played against Nebraska in 1969, as a defensive back and wide receiver at Wyoming—he was the only player in Western Athletic Conference history to earn all-conference recognition on both offense and defense. So he was familiar with the program when Osborne offered him a job coaching wingbacks and tight ends. He had been an assistant at New Mexico for three seasons, after coaching the freshman team at Wyoming. After 10 years at Nebraska, he coached one season at Arizona State then went with head coach John Cooper to Ohio State, where he spent three years before moving on to the NFL. He has worked with the Indianapolis Colts' running backs for 14 seasons, the longest continuous tenure for an assistant coach in the organization's history.

We all grow. We all learn, no matter what we're doing, what we're pursuing. But what makes Tom a great leader is his consistency, not only with the Xs and Os on the football side of it but also the way he carries himself, his faith, his family, his courage, his discipline. Those are special people. I have been very fortunate to have gone, five or six years into my coaching career, to Nebraska and to have maintained a relationship and friendship with him ever since. And now, I'm working—where I hope I'm able to finish my career—for the same type of person in Tony Dungy. It's been awesome.

Those are men who have always been steady and confident, with a sense of purpose. They don't waver, through their faith, how they are in various situations. You see how people make compromises and cut corners and maybe have some success. But it's an up-and-down success and becomes more related to a wins-and-losses kind of a thing. With guys like Tom and Tony you're always winning, even though you may have a setback on the field occasionally, because of the way they carry themselves.

When you see the calmness that's always there with them—the direction, the discipline, the leadership, the support—it provides a sense of calmness. "Hey, things are going to work out all right. Just keep chopping wood." You always felt you were okay when you were working with Tom, no matter what the situation may have been. "Whether we win, lose, or draw, it'll be okay. We'll bounce back, keep going." That's the confidence he gave to you as a coach, as a player. It trickled down from his leadership.

I had a conversation with Tom when he called me after my mother's death to offer his condolences; I was so touched. But that's Tom. While we're talking, he says, "I don't know Tony. I remember playing against Tony when he was at Minnesota as a quarterback. But I've never met him." I said, "Coach, every day you get up and look at yourself in the mirror when you're shaving, you're looking at Tony Dungy, because you guys are the same kind of people." And that's what they are.

It's a privilege to have worked on both ends of my career for people like them. They are cut from the same cloth. I've had a great career in coaching, given the people I've been able to work for and with.

I used to play tennis against Tom. He's a competitive person. Some people are more animated. But that doesn't make them any more competitive. Guys like Tom are always thinking steps ahead of things that are about to occur. And in order to be able see that and know what their reaction is going to be, they have that sense of calmness. They may be two steps or three steps ahead, looking at something that hasn't presented itself to most people. Tom stands at that daggone net and brings it right back at you. We were both fair players. It was a nice competitive exercise.

We went on a fishing trip in Canada, Tom and some of the other coaches. We flew from Lincoln to International Falls, Minnesota, and then took a seaplane up to a fishing lodge in Canada. Boy, it was beautiful. But there was a storm brewing, lightning. I thought, "Well, we'll get to our cabins and just go on to bed." It was twilight, but Tom wants to go fishing. So we're out in these aluminum boats, on that daggone water. I was thinking, "I know this guy's got a strong faith. The Lord's with him. I just hope that the Lord includes all of us, even though we might not be as strong as he is." The lightning is jumping all over the lake. There again, he had that calmness about him; he was going to go fishing....So he went out there and caught a few fish.

George Darlington and I were probably the two poorest fishermen on the trip because we slept when we got out in the boat. We had guides who basically baited the hooks and took the fish off the hook, so we slept until we had a hit. Then we'd wake up. I had never fished before. We might have been there a week. Everybody else wasn't catching a lot of fish, but George and I were catching salmon. They were practically jumping in the boat. We had a "shore lunch" the last afternoon and ended up feeding that whole crew with the fish George and I caught.

Some of Tom's calmness, never getting mad, goes back to his upbringing, maybe the house was like that. I used to watch Tom's father come up to the office, never knew his first name, just always called him "Mr. Osborne." He'd come up there and quietly wait, sit patiently until Tom would finish whatever he was doing. He'd just sit there calmly, like "When it's time, I'll get a chance to see him for a few moments." Just watching his dad, the way he carried himself, there was a lot of similarity. So I'm sure that calmness was a learned response.

We would be sitting there in a meeting toward the end of the season, and invariably, Tom would get a phone call from Barry Switzer. The week before we played Oklahoma. "Well, Tom, we need to get together to try to make some decisions on where the loser is going to go to a bowl game." The winner was headed to the Orange Bowl. Tom would take that call right to the side of the conference room. He wasn't trying to hide anything. Everybody was privy to it. He was just talking in his calm tone of voice, "Yes, Barry."

I kind of looked at it like Luke Skywalker and Darth Vader. It was funny. You loved Barry Switzer and the theater we were all in because of those games. They were great games, so much drama. I think they both started at the same time as head coaches, and Barry was always made out to be the free-wheeling, shoot-from-the-hip guy, just out there, having a great time. Barry was a good football coach. Anyway, Tom would talk to him in such a nice, calm tone—so respectful. And you just wished one time, right before he hung up, there would be a pause and Tom would say, "Hey Barry, when you come to Lincoln, we're going to kick the heck out of you."

Tom and Nancy his wife are a great match. They make a great couple. They're always doing something to better humankind. And they always do it as a team. It's nothing pretentious. It's just that true Midwestern spirit of giving and helping and sharing. And those are the things that are dear to me about Nebraska.

I went out there in the spring a couple of years ago. I flew out to Minneapolis and took a small jet into Lincoln. And as I was coming in over the farmland and down through the clouds, I felt like, "Boy, I'm home." It felt like it. A lot of it had to do with my cousin Bennett playing there and my opportunity to coach there for 10 years. Bennett's son, Morgan, played there, but I didn't get a chance to coach Morgan because I had left by then. I thought about Brian Hiemer and his death, other guys I had coached, Brook Berringer, all those things start hitting you, all that connection to Nebraska, the good times. There is no place like Nebraska, the people who live in that state and support that program. There really isn't. And Tom embodied what people of the state think they are, the way they should act and be.

I was surprised when he announced he was stepping aside, shocked. It's like, no, you don't want him to leave because with Tom at the helm that is Nebraska—the place to live and be, go to school, to play football, sports, and to be good people. I'm not trying to make it sound like it's a fairyland. It's just a feeling when you're there, living there, growing up there. And I felt like I did all of those things.

The first time I came back to Nebraska and saw Tom after he had stepped aside, I lost it because I started thinking about Mike Corgan and Cletus Fischer and Bob Devaney being gone—guys who have passed on, all of that. And it was like, "Now who's going to take care of this? You've got to stay. Get Barry Switzer up here; let's get going again." That's what I was thinking. But the thing about Tom is how principled he is, the principles he lives by. When he tells somebody he's going to do something, he's going to do it. So when he told Frank Solich, "Hey, I'm going to step down," he was going to do it. If he told you something, you didn't have to write it down, have it signed and notarized. He meant it when he said, "I'm going to do it."

I remember how excited I was—it's trivial, really—but Tom had a helmet in his office, one of those plaques with a football helmet cut in half on it. It was my first year, and I saw it in his office. I said, "Hey, Coach, what are you going to do with that?" He said, "Oh, it's nothing. Do you want it?" I remember how excited I was that he gave me that plaque. I thought, "I've got a Nebraska helmet plaque." I put it in my home, boy, because it took me back to when Bennett would come home and how excited he was about being at Nebraska, playing, being a part of that program. They all tie in. I read some stories that I keep in my desk, about Bennett coming to Nebraska for the first time and some lady at the car counter at the airport. Bennett needed a ride into town. Whoever was supposed to pick him up hadn't picked him up. So the lady closed the counter and said, "I'll take you into campus." Another thing Bennett once told me, when he was coaching at Colorado—and this is what gets me—he said he came out of the roped area and one of the Nebraska fans said, "Hey, Ben, you will always be a Husker." Boy, that touched him so much.

When I was in grade school in Uniontown, I'd go down to the library in that little town, get back in the stacks and read football stories. I read about those heroes, the coaches in those books, and then I got to work for a guy right out of those books, Tom Osborne. Here you are an adult, and you're working for a guy who takes you back to those stories. Then not having seen people of color in those positions all those years as head coaches and now I'm able to work with Tony Dungy.

Tom was so well prepared and kept his teams prepared. He had the ability to dissect things and see, as he used to say, "the big picture." Some people could see pieces of the puzzle, but he already had the whole puzzle put together in his mind, a lot sooner than others.

As somebody who worked for him, and certainly with a lot of respect for him, I would not use "genius." He was one of the best to come down the road in doing what he did as a football coach and offensive coordinator. Some people become geniuses and gurus. But I think those terms are too loosely thrown around. Tom was a motivator. He was disciplined. He was a leader. He knew what things went on with the defense. He certainly knew the offense. He had an overall view and picture of everything that was vital to the success of his program, athletically and academically. He had it all put together.

Tom's election to go for the two points against Miami in the 1984 Orange Bowl, raised eyebrows. But when your leader says, "We're going for two points," and you've been with him that long, you're going for two. Everybody's on the same page.

We hadn't been defeated, so Miami would have to beat us to win. He wanted to make sure it was won outright. You instill in your people, "Hey, we're going to win this thing all out."

He won three national championships. To me, if there had been a situation when he won those three, any of them, as to whether to go for a tie or win it outright, he would have done the same thing, and his players would have understood, "They did this thing in 1983, so let's buckle up and go get it." It comes around, and if you're going to be the leader, those who are following have to work hard and diligently to continue that success and believe in the leader. And we believed in our leader.

I was in that press box when we went for two. You sit there and watch all that bedlam afterward, people all excited. I think even some of the Orange Bowl Committee people were excited that Miami won it because you could tell who they were for. You understood it was basically a home game for Miami. No problem, you go play where you have to play. That competitive grit about Tom is always going to be, "We're not settling for ties. We're going for wins." Anything you do in life is not about settling for a tie. So those are life lessons. They don't just stop with football.

Tom got it done, like the guy on the farm. On the farm, you've got to be everything. You've got to be a mechanic, be this and be that. The farmer has to do it all because he can't drive 50 miles or a hundred miles to get it done. So he's got to take what he has right then and there and make it work. Tom made it work, year in and year out.

Kevin Steele (1989-94)

Kevin Steele played an important role in Osborne's first two national championships, even though he was an NFL assistant for the Carolina Panthers, when the Cornhuskers won the second in 1995, because in addition to coaching the linebackers, Steele was an outstanding recruiter.

He was responsible for Florida and helped persuade quarterback Tommie Frazier, a prep All-American at Palmetto High in Bradenton, to accept Nebraska's scholarship offer over offers from Clemson, Notre Dame and Colorado.

Osborne hired Steele from Tennessee, his alma mater, after John Melton retired. He also had been an assistant at New Mexico State and Oklahoma State before coming to Nebraska. After four seasons with the Panthers, he was the head coach at Baylor—with Frazier coaching the running backs—for four seasons. He is now executive head coach and linebackers coach for Bobby Bowden at Florida State.

It's ironic, when I came to Florida State to work with Coach Bowden…when you start talking about the great ones, certainly in the last 50 years of college football, Bobby Bowden and Tom Osborne, without argument, are there. And it's amazing how similar they are. It's uncanny. I found myself thinking, "Wait a minute, I've been through this; I've been here before."

I think the biggest thing about Coach Osborne is, first and foremost, his faith is lived and carried out every day by the way he works and walks and treats others. And not with a speech, not with a sermon, it's the way he carries himself every day. That's the first thing that, I think, makes him great, and Coach Bowden, too. They're so well-grounded. Their foundation is so strong that the ripples and the earthquakes and the storms of college football, college athletics, don't rattle them.

Then you've got his personality; Coach Osborne had an uncanny ability to make you feel like you were the most important person in the program. He did that with everybody. And you knew. You knew he made everybody feel that way. When you talked to the players, the first thing was, "Coach Osborne cares about me." That was so real to everybody who worked there and played there that it made them want to excel even beyond their own personal goals, and even beyond the team goals. It made them want to excel for him. They didn't want to let Coach down, which is pretty strong.

I'm sure there are a lot of programs out there where the players want to excel for their own personal goals. And there are a lot of teams out there—or several—that want to excel for their team goals as well as their personal goals. But there are very few places where anybody goes to work, where those things are true, and on top of that, they don't want to disappoint or let down their boss.

That was Tom's personality. He had a calming effect on everybody because of his faith and because of the fact that you knew he cared about you. It was the same way on the coaching staff, whether you were Frank Solich, who was the assistant head coach, or Charlie McBride, who was the defensive coordinator, or the new guy who was the linebackers coach. To this day, and I talk to Coach Osborne pretty frequently—there aren't too many weeks that go by that we don't talk—he still has that effect on people.

And it's not self-serving. It's sincere. I can tell you this: The greatest pain in losing at Nebraska was seeing Coach Osborne's face. That was the greatest pain for me personally. It didn't happen much, but in coaching you've always got the pain of consoling the player, the disappointment of the fans, your own personal goals and competitiveness. All those things you've got. And I've had them every place I've been. But never has it been where you look at his face and it just kills you.

Really, he was a man of few words. I'll never forget my first game at Nebraska because one of my dreams was to coach for Coach Osborne. I wanted to coach at Nebraska, for Coach Osborne. I grew up around Bear Bryant and Alabama football when my dad was a high school coach. I grew up around Auburn football and Tennessee football. I'd heard Johnny Majors' pregame speeches.

So the first game we were going to play at Nebraska, I made it a point to go hear Coach Osborne's talk to the team in the locker room beforehand. Sometimes as assistant coaches you're doing other things in between warmup and last-minute details before you go back out to play. But I made it a point to listen. The talk was not about the game. I stood there and thought, "Wow, okay, this is not about winning and losing. This is about being the best you can be." That's all he asked you to do, to understand there were going to be mistakes, understand there were going to be frustrations, and you weren't going to be perfect. That was okay. Just be the best you could be that day.

It wasn't, "We've got to go out there and score this many points on offense, and on defense, we've got to do this, and you guys have got to go out there and execute to where those guys can't make a yard. You've got to win this game." It wasn't any of that. It wasn't, "We fully expect you to win this game. Now you've got to go win it," the traditional stuff. It was: "Hey guys, go do the best you can do. This is not about winning and losing. It's about doing your best."

Coach Bowden is like that, too, very much so. They are so similar it's unbelievable. It would be amazing to write a book of the similarities of the day-to-day operations, teaching styles, handling of players, handling of discipline, handling of practice, the expectations of the team, those kinds of things, the Friday night talks, the Saturday pregame talks, the postgame talks. Sometimes, it's like I close my eyes and whoa, I'm in a time warp. They have the same foundation and the same ability to relate and make people feel important, whether it be the last-team walk-on player or the starting quarterback.

I don't think there's any doubt that anybody who knows Coach Osborne quickly figures out that he's a very, very intelligent person, not just Xs and Os but in a lot of ways. He had an uncanny ability not only to plan but to alter his plan in the course of action. He had extreme ability in that area. He could make halftime adjustments with ease, and they always seemed to be right because he was so intelligent.

And then the other thing about him that I think just set him apart from most human beings I know, not coaches but human beings, is that he had an unbelievable, extreme competitiveness. But he was always in total control. Most people who get that competitive, lose control. They become emotional. He was extremely competitive extremely so, as much as anybody I've ever been around. He wanted to win more than anybody. But he never lost control. His emotions never took over.

There were probably only two or three times where you thought, "Oops." In fact, I've got a picture hanging on the wall of my basement where he's on his knees pounding the turf with both hands, beside Charlie McBride and myself. It was taken at an Oklahoma game. It's so not him.

George Darlington (1973-02)

George Darlington was the only assistant with Osborne from beginning to end. The two met at the national coaches convention. Osborne needed a defensive ends coach to replace Jim Walden. And Darlington needed a job after San Jose State fired the coaching staff of which he had been a part.

An All-America lacrosse player as well as a football player at Rutgers, he coached the defensive ends until 1986, when he replaced former Cornhusker defensive back Bob Thornton (1972-73) as secondary coach. While still an assistant, Osborne had recruited Thornton out of junior college.

Darlington's interest in coaching was shaped at an early age. "I never outgrew a childhood desire," he once said. He continues to coach defensive backs at Louisiana Tech, after three seasons at Marshall, where he was the recruiting coordinator and coached outside linebackers and safeties.

Consistency is one of the characteristics Tom had that is just amazing. He's the most consistent person I've ever been around, ever. He was very, very focused that way. And, of course, losing so few assistant coaches during a long period of time, I think he would agree that his attitude about that was a result of the consistency, wanting the kids to see the same coaches every week and every year.

If there were adjustments that needed to be made on the staff, for growth or whatever, then that would be Tom's approach rather than waiting until something went wrong and then firing a coach so it would make him look good in the newspapers. He was very much that way. And he was that way with everybody—the coaches, the secretarial staff, everybody. We had one secretary, I won't name, who was terrible. Not being malicious about it, but she just wasn't very good. But he kind of nurtured her as to what needed to be done and she became a tremendous secretary.

After we won the national championship in 1994, I'm sure he was real excited like all of us, but he certainly didn't show emotions like the rest of us did. We got it done. He was excited. But I didn't notice anything particularly different, to be honest. Again, it was his consistency.

I've never been around a person as consistent. We prepared for the University of Pacific the same way we prepared for Oklahoma. That's probably his biggest legacy success-wise. During the whole period he was coach, we only lost to one team that finished the season with a losing record, and that was Iowa State in 1992. We had some kids hurt that day, and we went over there and got beat.

That's unheard of, being so successful against everybody. And the reason was, we approached every game the same. Some coaches will see an opponent that won't look very good so they'll spend part of their time in practice getting ready for the next opponent. We didn't do that. Occasionally, we would maybe spend 10 minutes or 20 minutes during a week on another opponent. I know we did that for Oklahoma for the whole season a couple of years because we were going to have to do something defensively we hadn't done. So we practiced that a little bit. But it wasn't a deal where we were taking another team lightly. We were up front with the kids. The last game of the year was always Oklahoma. "They run the wishbone, so we've got to get a little extra work every week." We would work 10 minutes a week against Oklahoma. But that was a specific thing. And there was nothing taken away from the fact that, "Hey, we're preparing for this upcoming team, and we're doing everything we can to be ready for them."

Tom's native intelligence is such that it's something to be admired and kind of hold in awe. He was a tremendous play-caller and coached extremely well on game day. There have been some very good coaches who have been basket cases on Saturday. They might as well not even get involved. And some of them haven't. But Tom called all the offensive plays and had a great instinct for what he wanted to call. He had studied and determined what he wanted to call in certain situations, which, you know, everybody does. But he just was so prepared every game.

His tremendous work ethic obviously still serves him well. In coaching, he just literally outworked so many people and didn't make a big show of it. Some guys in this business like to brag about how many hours they put in, what they do and don't do. He wasn't like that.

He has tremendous compassion for kids. A little, if ever, reported example of that was, we had a walk-on from Tennessee, I think it was. I forget his name. It was a time when just about anybody could walk on—there wasn't much scrutiny of walk-ons—and this kid was a very average player. But he got a serious illness while at Nebraska, and instead of not claiming any responsibility, which, in truth, we had none, Tom made sure that kid went to the correct specialists in different parts of the country. He just really cared about kids, and people. That was a big draw, especially as years went on, in recruiting because there would be people who would try to razz-matazz you in recruiting. But Tom would be a consistent person, and a lot of people responded positively to that. There are other places where it would have been easier to have the kind of record he had because of the issues in regards to recruiting, weather, distance and so forth.

Another thing about Tom is his great sense of humor. People don't realize that. One time, I had to ask permission to leave a day or two early in June to go on a fishing trip. And I think I must have brought it up in a meeting. "I'd like to have a couple of days more because I have this trip planned." He was writing on the board, and he looked around at me and said, "Well, you going fishing is like taking a cheese sandwich to a banquet."

Tom's a very serious fisherman. In fact, some of the coaches and their families went skiing in Colorado a couple of years, and one year he went skiing one day and then fishing in the snow and ice the next day. I guess you could refer to it as being competitive because he was definitely serious about trying to catch fish. It wasn't a deal where he was just going and goofing around.

He really was a brilliant football coach, which everybody knows. He is one of the all-time greats, and I'm not throwing the word "great" around. His record indicates that.

I don't have any doubts about him being successful politically for the simple reason that he approaches everything to do the best job he can. He really is a guy who's trying to serve his constituents instead of having some other ulterior motives. He doesn't act like he knows it all. He'll listen to people. He has strong beliefs about what he wants done. And yet he's not inflexible.

He was that way in football. Even though he was brilliant, he wanted input from the staff. And maybe only 20 percent of that input was better than his thoughts. But he would embrace that 20 percent. In other words, he wasn't on an ego trip. Tom was very good. We were really blessed. We really were.

Milt Tenopir (1974-02)

When Osborne became head coach, Milt Tenopir, the athletic director and head football coach at McCook High School in Nebraska, called to inquire about an assistant's job. He had been coaching at the high school level, beginning with an eight-man program in tiny Jennings, Kansas, since 1962 and wanted to move up. Osborne told Tenopir he had no openings on his staff. However, a year later, Osborne called Tenopir and offered him a job as a graduate assistant. Tenopir accepted. He would become one of college football's most respected offensive line coaches. He worked with five linemen who earned six Outland Trophies between them and was instrumental in developing lines that enabled Nebraska to lead the nation in rushing 11 times during Osborne's final 18 seasons. Tenopir was from Harvard, Nebraska, not far from Hastings, where Osborne grew up and was the state high school athlete of the year and, later, the state college athlete of the year.

Tom was a couple of years ahead of me in high school, but I ran the hurdles against him a couple of times. I stayed even with him…through the first hurdle. Tom tried to recruit me out of high school. They used their athletes to recruit at Hastings College, and he came to my house a couple of times trying to convince me Hastings was the place to go. I told him it was too close to home. So I was his first reject.

Tom's dad used to come to high school track meets even when Tom wasn't involved. So there was a relationship, nothing buddy-buddy, but we certainly knew each other. I hadn't seen Tom for 10, 12, 14 years after I left high school and went to college, then coached out of state. But the first time I went up to the football office he greeted me, called me by name, which was pretty impressive. He had a great recall, remembered you. It was amazing. He very seldom forgot anybody.

I was coaching out at McCook when I contacted him and asked if he would consider hiring somebody off a high school staff. He said he had nothing available. He had absorbed Bob Devaney's whole staff. That was one of the conditions of him getting the job. But he told me he'd possibly have a graduate assistant's position open a year from then. He called me back almost a year to the day later. I was fortunate on that end of it. I took the job for one reason: I figured if I was going to get into college coaching that was the way to go, that if I was at Nebraska for a year, there would be all kinds of doors open. That isn't quite how it worked out. There's a fraternity in the coaching profession, and each takes care of his own. But with a little patience and after time, Tom had faith that I could handle the job and he retained me. I couldn't have imagined when I first came there that I would end up with Tom for that long.

There wasn't any question the man, from an early age, was a brilliant coach. Coach Devaney saw that. That's why he put Tom in charge instead of one of the older guys. I know they were over my head when I came in from high school ball. One time I told Monte Kiffin, Tom's defensive coordinator, "I don't even know what's going on in these meetings." He told me, "Just sit and listen for a year. It'll soak in." So I did.

I worked with the defense the first year I was there, with the linebackers on the freshman team under Monte. That was the spot open. Then my first spring I got moved to the offensive line. I wanted to coach the line. I was a high school coach, head coach, for 12 years, but I coached the line too, mainly because you had a hard time finding anybody to coach the line in high school. I worked with the freshman offensive line at Nebraska for two or three years. Then I worked with Cletus Fischer with the line. There weren't any egos involved as far as Clete and I were concerned. We split it up where I had all the running game and Clete had all the pass protections. It worked out that way. We had a great relationship over the years.

We were pretty fortunate in our success. We had a lot of good players. Everything happened to fall right for us in a couple of situations, but we had a tremendous run of kids through that stretch. Also a lot of it had to do with doing it right and getting the right kids to do what you wanted to do. We were just fortunate enough to be able to do that. I think we got a lot out of the kids we had. We ran an offense that was a kind of line-up-and-knock-the-crap-out-of-you system. A lot of kids bought into that. And we played pretty sound on defense. It was a combination of things. There are a lot of good coaches in college football, but I think we got as much out of the kids we had as probably anybody would have. We played against people who, if you looked at them physically, looked like better players than we were. They were bigger and taller. But they didn't play with the heart our kids did. No question about it, there was a burning desire for our kids to compete. It wasn't a thing that happened just one year. There were so many examples set by players throughout the years that the entire program was built that way and kids bought into the fact that, "Hey, we can compete. All we've got to do is give more effort." And they did.

I think Tom's method of motivation was having kids know they were completely prepared for anything they would face. The biggest thing was preparing. We never went to practice without having a game plan in mind, not knowing exactly what we were going to do. Tom was a master at knowing what needed to be done. Nobody will ever match him at that. By Monday night we knew exactly how we were going to attack somebody. Tom had a tremendous mind in that way. He knew how to take advantage of people who might not be right schematically, and I think kids went into every ball game with confidence, knowing they had prepared the best they could. We didn't win every time, but there was never any doubt when we went into a game. We never went in fat-headed. But we always went in with the attitude we were as good as they were, and most of the time better.

Tom ran the show, but at the same time allowed everybody's input. It wasn't, "We're going to do it this way." He let us be a part of it. He had the ultimate say. But he wouldn't close his ears to suggestions from us, whether it was offense or defense. He was the offensive coordinator. Everybody knew that. But he still allowed you to have your input. If you saw fit to change something during practice because your kids weren't able to do it, he would question why but would understand. He'd let you do your thing. And it seemed to work out.

In coaching you have to earn respect. You can't coach it. I've never bought into the adage you can't be a coach and also their friend. I had great friendships developed with kids I coached and the parents of kids that I coached. I never felt there was a separation between friendship and being the guy who ran the show. Tom had that quality, too. Even though there was never a question of who was in charge, who was the boss, who made the ultimate decisions, there was never a kid who shied away from going in and talking to him. I've been around coaches when kids didn't know where they stood. That's not right.

As I said, Tom motivated players through preparation probably more than anything. He wasn't a rant-and-raver. He could get into your face in a halftime speech if he wanted to, but that didn't happen very often. One time it did we were playing North Carolina in the Liberty Bowl. At halftime my job was always to write out the fronts we saw in the first half on the board before we went back out, and Tom would make adjustments off that. We had played terribly in the first half, and Tom started making a correction. Then he threw his clipboard down and jumped up on a bench and walked side to side, ranting and raving. He said "dadgummit" several times. He was ripping the defense first, and I remember Clete and I were hiding in the shower, because we knew he was going to rip the offense later. Bob Prokop was a university regent, and he thought it was his job to tell us when there was five minutes to go before the second half. So he stuck his head in the door and said something to that effect, and Coach said, "I ain't ready to go out there yet, dadgummit, just leave." He got wound up pretty good that game. But after that we came back and won the ball game, and those same kids he scolded were in there hugging and crying with him afterward.

The biggest thing was, Tom let you coach. He had a great leadership style that you knew he was the boss, but at the same time, he let you do your thing. He was a great people person. He was a guy who could manage eight or nine egos and still make it work. Also, Coach treated players fairly, treated them equally. He did an extremely good job of making everybody feel a part of something. He had a tremendous way of having young men realize their roles, whether they were the stars or the back-ups, spot players. Not everybody can be the starter, and yet the approach under Tom was such that every kid knew his niche, knew where he fit in, knew when he was going to get in the ball game, knew what contribution he would make, be it scout team or whatever. He taught kids their value to the organization.

I was with him all but one year, and Tom was Tom. He didn't change at all. He might have mellowed a little bit as he was in the game longer, but as far as the way he treated people, treated players and coaches, he didn't waver. I think that's part of the reason for stability on his staff. There are very few times in life when you have an opportunity to work for a guy of his magnitude. There were people on our staff who had opportunities to go elsewhere. But the bottom line was this: Where were you going to go that would be better than working with Tom? There wasn't any place. Plus, Tom handled us equally, on the field, in meetings, financially, whatever. He made sure we were taken care of in a lot of ways. He was just a heck of a guy to work for. Anybody who hasn't been around him can't quite fathom that whole thing—maybe he seemed too pristine and he wasn't really the way he appeared. Well, he was. There was no front put up on his part. People who got to know him knew that right away. It wasn't something where you had to guess.

The day he announced he was stepping aside was tough for everybody. I was recruiting down in Oklahoma and had to pull off the road and gather my thoughts a little bit. That was pretty emotional.

Celebrate the Heroes of College Football
in These Other NEW Releases from Sports Publishing!

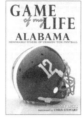

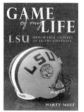
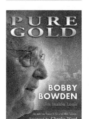